Prisoner of War: The Story of White Boy Rick and the War on Drugs

Vince Wade

Cover design: Kevin Martzolff

Published by Wade Multimedia, LLC

ISBN 978-0-692-99570-9

Introduction

Many of the war stories in this book are based on interviews with individuals with first-hand knowledge. Even so, most of these events happened three decades ago. Memories fade. Key figures passed away or were killed. Records have been purged. Some of the people in this story cannot be located.

A lot of statements of fact are based on documents obtained through federal and state Freedom of Information Acts and on a review of court transcripts, records and media archives.

Numerous battles this country has lost in the War on Drugs are a matter of public record.

Prisoner of War: The Story of White Boy Rick and the War on Drugs proves Mark Twain was right. Sometimes the truth is stranger than fiction.

Table of Contents

Acknowledgements

A book of this scope wouldn't be possible without the help of a lot of people.

Rick Wershe, Jr.'s adventures and misadventures made this book possible. One day he may have a normal life. He deserves it.

Ralph Musilli, Wershe's attorney, and Theresa Mangold, his capable office manager and legal secretary provided endless access to old files with endless patience, answering endless questions.

Patrick McQueeney, Wershe's appellate attorney deserves a nod for taking a drive with me to rummage around in a dusty storage unit for old files he was convinced had been destroyed, only to find the complete transcript of Rick's cocaine possession trial.

Gregg Schwarz, retired FBI agent, gets credit for starting me down the road of the Rick Wershe saga. Schwarz convinced me there was a bigger story to be told. He was right.

Herman Groman and Michael Castro, both retired FBI agents, helped fill in important parts of this tale.

Dan Harris provided great help as a beta reader.

My gratitude is extended to the many individuals who were willing to go on the record and tell it like it is regarding the Wershe story and the War on Drugs.

Finally, my wife Cindy gets big thanks for putting up with this adventure.

Chapter 1—Happy Days and not so Happy Days

"You dirty yellow-bellied rat"
—James Cagney in "Taxi" 1932

At the worldly age of 14, Richard John Wershe, Jr., a street-savvy kid who didn't sell or use dope, was recruited by FBI agents to become America's youngest soldier in the War on Drugs. His secret paid mission was to go behind enemy lines to gather intelligence. He wasn't an ordinary teen and he wasn't an ordinary snitch. Wershe was "arguably the most productive drug informant of the Detroit FBI during that era," according to John Anthony who was the legal adviser-agent of that office at the time.

By the time he was 17, Wershe, who is white, had been consorting with Detroit's biggest drug dealers and baddest hitmen, jetting to Las Vegas and Miami, sleeping with the mayor's hot, married, 20-something niece and telling the FBI about top-level police corruption. His reward, in a strange episode of law enforcement intrigue, was to be abandoned by the federal government. He became Rick Who? Wershe, who was eventually labeled by the media as White Boy Rick, was now a broke school dropout from a dysfunctional family. He turned to the only trade he knew—the one the narcs had taught him. He tried to become a wholesale-level drug dealer, got caught, and was sentenced by local authorities to life in prison without parole. Wershe became a Prisoner of War—the War on Drugs.

Vince Wade

During his life in prison Wershe came to know
Salvatore "Sammy the Bull" Gravano, an admitted Mafia
killer who helped the government put Mob boss John Gotti
in prison for life. He met a world-class drug smuggler
named Steve Kalish who lavishly bribed Panama leader
Manuel Noriega. On numerous occasions, Wershe
discussed the finances of illegal drugs with Carlos Lehder,
one of the founders of the notorious Medellín cocaine
cartel.

Wershe (pronounced Wur-shee) joined the national
battle against the never-ending flow of illegal drugs in
June, 1984. That same month, 13 years earlier, President
Richard M. Nixon declared the United States of America
had to go to battle against the nation's drug habit.

"America's public enemy number one in the United
States is drug abuse," President Nixon told reporters after
sending a message to Congress on the issue. "In order to
fight and defeat this enemy, it is necessary to wage a new,
all-out offensive."

Over a decade later, when the federal government
pressed a young Detroit kid in to service in the War on
Drugs, the country was losing the struggle. In truth, it
never started winning. The story of Richard J. Wershe, Jr is
a down-in-the-trenches view of why the War on Drugs is a
trillion-dollar failure and will never be won.

Whatever Wershe's dreams and fantasies may have
been as a lower middle-class white boy growing up on
Detroit's east side, becoming an FBI snitch, a rat, a fink, a
canary, a stool pigeon and eventually spending his life in
prison was certainly not his life's ambition.

Wershe, known to his family and friends and on the
streets as Ricky or Rick, became a paid Confidential

Informant for the FBI, apparently the youngest in the agency's history, without any real say in the matter or time to think it over.

It wasn't a recruitment, really. It was more like being drafted. The FBI, for its part, was willing to pay and pay regularly for what the kid could find out. For the boy's fast-buck, business-hustler father, the FBI's informant cash was the motivation to agree to this dangerous scheme. The stress of sustained undercover deception on an adolescent mind and the very real physical danger inherent in informing on men who regard murder as a cost of doing business don't seem to have troubled Wershe's father or the FBI agents.

On the other hand, working as an FBI informant didn't seem to have any negative effect on some famous Americans from Wershe's childhood. Growing up, Rick Wershe, Jr. watched Walt Disney movies not knowing that Uncle Walt had been an FBI stool pigeon for over a quarter of a century, keeping the Bureau informed about suspected Communist agitators and Leftist subversives in Hollywood. Most of Walt Disney's informing involved labor unions. He didn't like them.

At the time Rick Wershe was lured in to working as an FBI informant, the man occupying the White House had been a long-time snitch for the Bureau. President Ronald W. Reagan was known as FBI Informant T-10 during the Communist-hunting Red Scare that profoundly impacted the Hollywood film community in the early days of the Cold War.

But Walt Disney and Ronald Reagan were adults when they became police informers. Rick Wershe was a juvenile and a young one at that. To understand how he got in this situation, it is important to examine his childhood and the changing city where he grew up.

❖

Rick Wershe, Jr. was a rambunctious, mischievous kid prone to stunts like shooting at rats in alleys and setting off illegal firecrackers. In his early teens he participated in a few home break-ins as a way to raise easy cash. He was tutored in the art of burglary by a small-time black criminal who was dating his older sister, Dawn. Drugs were plentiful but Rick Wershe was not a drug user.

Dawn had tumbled down the rabbit hole of drug addiction. She has fought her drug habit all of her life. Rick's Aunt Carolyn, his father's sister, was also a drug addict who turned to prostitution to support her habit. Young Rick saw what drugs were doing to his family and he chose not to use them. He was, however, impressed by the lavish, free-spending lifestyle of the city's rapidly growing cadre of drug-dealing entrepreneurs. Over the course of three years, federal agents and local police narcs from a drug task force taught the young boy the ways of the drug underworld. They had a willing student. What thrill-seeking, hormone-fueled teenage boy wouldn't relish the chance to go undercover for-real in a sleazy and dangerous world awash in fast cars, fast women, "bling" and so much cash that machines were needed to count it?

By the time guys his age were prepping for their SAT exams, Rick Wershe had been shot once and targeted for a hit murder another time. When other boys his age were learning to drive, Rick Wershe had been jet-setting to Las Vegas prize fights, flying to Miami to meet cocaine importers, hobnobbing at nightclubs favored by black gangsters and buying himself jet skis, hot cars and flashy jewelry. He also began to give the FBI insights regarding drug-related police bribery.

Yet, by the time he reached his 17th birthday, the feds had abandoned their star snitch. He wasn't just another criminal working off a beef by turning informant against his friends. Rick Wershe had been recruited by government agents.

Suddenly, he was too hot. Too many people knew or had guessed what he was doing. As we shall see, his informant work caused crisis meetings at the very top levels of the Justice Department. He was in danger of being exposed as an under-age FBI informant in the War on Drugs. What's more, FBI investigative files had been falsified to make it appear the information was coming from his father. Falsifying federal files is a felony.

Over time, city officials in positions of power became deeply afraid of what the kid might know about public corruption and what he might expose about them. The feds, having committed file falsification crimes in order to use him as an informant, feared what he might expose about them.

Young Wershe was suddenly adrift. He had worked night after night in his paid role as a Confidential Informant. Now it was over. The cash had dried up. The only trade he knew was the dark art of slinging dope. With all the immaturity and bad judgment he could muster, Rick Wershe set out to become a "weight" man, a wholesaler of cocaine. His adventure as a drug dealer lasted less than a year. He was busted and sentenced to prison for life.

Before all of this, there was a discipline-free and largely love-free childhood that was starved for the right-from-wrong rules that accompany true parental concern for a child.

The skunks were doomed, unaware that death was waiting in the dark. Each night the skunks would leave their colony in the woods next to the Van Dyke Sports

Center, a fun park at the edge of Warren, one of Detroit's northeast suburbs. The critters went on food patrol, wandering the grounds of the entertainment complex. The skunks had an annoying habit of leaving malodorous calling cards after their nightly visits. It was bad for business.

The amusement park owner mentioned the skunks to Richard Wershe, Sr., who quickly came up with an idea. He would eliminate the skunk problem if the amusement park owner would pay a bounty per head. Wershe told the park owner he would get rid of the skunks after hours. He didn't elaborate.

That night, Wershe drove his son, Ricky, and his son's buddy, Dave Majkowski, to the amusement park. The boys were about 10 years old. The senior Wershe, a licensed gun dealer, had taught the boys how to shoot and use firearms. He handed each of them a .22 rifle loaded with .22 short ammo. The boys would be given a share of the per-head bounty.

As the skunks emerged from the woods, Ricky and Dave picked them off. They cut off the tails as bounty evidence and put the skunk carcasses in a pile for the unhappy cleaning crew to handle.

The trio went to a Denny's restaurant to celebrate the successful skunk hunt. The customers and restaurant staff did not share the joy.

"Was shooting those skunks near a neighborhood a bit reckless and irresponsible?" Majkowski asks rhetorically. "Yeah. Probably. But it sure as hell was a lot of fun."

For the senior Wershe, it was his idea of being a "fun" dad—while making a quick buck.

6

It was an adventure the boys would always remember.
They were best friends but destined to travel very different
paths in life. Majkowski and his family moved to the
suburbs. Ricky Wershe became a child of the streets. The
streets of Detroit.

Richard John Wershe, Senior was called Rick. Richard
John Wershe, Junior was known to his friends and
neighbors as Ricky. Rick and Ricky. The fact they shared
the same name differentiated only by Senior and Junior
was significant for the FBI.

The elder Wershe, now deceased, once described
himself as a business hustler. "He was always looking for a
better mousetrap," longtime friend Fred Elias recalls. Elias
says the elder Wershe always seemed to be starting a new
business venture, anything that might turn a quick buck.
Elias remembers Richard Wershe, Sr. as whip-smart about
guns and electronics. Attorney Ralph Musilli knew Richard
Wershe, Sr. for close to 20 years. Musilli says Wershe
never looked beyond making money that week. Musilli
says prospective business partners found Wershe
aggravating, self-serving and uninterested in the basics of
building a thriving, long-term enterprise. Physically trim,
Wershe was a fast talker with a faint lisp.

Those who knew Richard J. Wershe, Sr. as a neighbor
and family member paint a harsh, unflattering picture.
They say he was a jerk. They recall he was an arrogant,
insufferable and controlling know-it-all with a violent
temper; a chronically abusive husband and negligent father
who was obsessed with the next business hustle. He never
held a real job for long. Richard Wershe, Sr. was
convinced he was destined to become a successful self-
made millionaire based on some scheme-of-the-week. He
had two children; Ricky and Dawn. By all accounts both

children had difficult childhoods made more so by their largely absentee father.

When Richard Wershe Sr. *was* around, which was seldom, he wasn't a responsible parent, according to someone well-acquainted with the father and the son.

Wayne LeCouffe is Rick Wershe, Jr.'s cousin by marriage. He's two years younger than Rick and in some ways as street-savvy as his cousin. But he took a different path in life, a path that led to business success and a family. He has clear memories of his Wershe cousins in their youth.

"Rick's father was never home for Dawn or Rick," LeCouffe states flatly. "He was never there. Rick and Dawn grew up without parents."

Rick Wershe, Jr. agrees with his cousin's assessment. "I was basically raising myself," he told state officials in 2003.

LeCouffe tells the story of the time Wershe decided to take some kids—Ricky, Wayne and Wayne's two young brothers—up on a garage roof to shoot at rats in the alley. The elder Wershe gave one of Wayne's brothers a loaded .45 caliber pistol and told him to climb the ladder. As the boy climbed the ladder, he lost his footing. The gun went off. The shot hit the ground inches from one of his brothers. Instead of taking responsibility for his own negligence in giving a loaded pistol to a youngster on a ladder, Wershe smacked the kid who had accidentally fired the shot.

Even as a child, LeCouffe had Richard Wershe, Sr's number. "He was always up to something, trying to make a fast buck," LeCouffe remembers. "When cable TV first came out, you had the illegal cable TV boxes. He was in on that immediately. When cell phones were the size of a cinder block, he was in on that, getting chips for the phones. He was getting the chips so you could use the phone until whoever found out and shut it off. There was nothin' there that was legitimate. Nothin'."

In business Richard Wershe, Sr. tried anything and everything, typically walking along the edge that separates legal from illegal. He prowled estate sales of the recently departed looking for clothing he could sell at second-hand outlets. He owned a military surplus store for a time. He was a bit of a health nut so he tried his hand at selling vitamin supplements. He was well-versed in firearms, having worked in a gun shop.

The elder Wershe eventually got busted by the Bureau of Alcohol, Tobacco and Firearms (BATF) for possessing unreported parts for suppressors or silencers. A box of silencer parts was found in a raid on his mother's home. An appeals court ruled the government had proved the senior Wershe had "constructive possession" of the silencer parts.

At Richard Wershe Sr.'s 1988 federal weapons trial, his elderly mother, Vera, made a sad effort to take responsibility for the silencers. At age 77 and in poor health, she had to use a walker to make her way to the witness stand. She tried to claim the silencers were in a box to be thrown out, but she saw them and hauled the box back to her basement thinking they must be valuable. She admitted she didn't know what they were. The jury didn't buy her story.

Richard Wershe, Sr., his mother and his trial attorney are deceased so we will never know if Wershe talked her in to testifying at his trial. But it's highly unlikely that an elderly, ailing, always-follow-the-rules Polish woman would dream up such a preposterous story on her own and repeat it in front of a jury. What's more likely is, it's an indication of how Richard J. Wershe, Sr. was willing to put

Vince Wade

his own mother in a precarious legal situation to save his neck.

Wershe was convicted and sentenced to seven and a half years in federal prison.

As LeCouffe noted, the senior Wershe had a knack for consumer electronics. He was the first in his neighborhood to have a backyard satellite dish for TV reception. Soon, he was selling them to homeowners. Wershe had enough skill with electronics that he installed several home theaters for wealthy customers. No matter what the endeavor, he wasn't interested in working for someone else in a 9-to-5 office job or in doing shift work in a factory. He relished the idea of becoming a successful entrepreneur. He never made it. Richard Wershe, Sr. died of brain cancer in 2014.

Like many white ethnic families in Detroit, two generations of Wershes lived just a few doors apart. When Richard Wershe, Sr. got married, he and his wife bought a house in the same block as his parents.

Beverly "Bev" Srbich was a neighbor. She was known as "Aunt Bev" to Ricky and his sister, Dawn. Over a period of years Bev Srbich watched the disintegration of the Wershe families—and the neighborhood.

"Richard thought the world revolved around Richard and what Richard wanted," Srbich remembers. "His kids didn't matter. Nothing mattered." Her voice begins to quiver. "You have no idea of the hate I have in my heart for this man."

Prisoner of War:
The Story of White Boy Rick and The War on Drugs

The story of the Wershe family and the neighborhood around Hampshire St. on Detroit's northeast side is a window on the profound changes that swept the city itself. What happened there happened in neighborhoods throughout Detroit.

Hampshire was like hundreds of other tree-lined neighborhood streets in Detroit's working-class neighborhoods. The homes were compact two-story brick bungalows with parlors and kitchens on the first floor and bedrooms on the second. Many had driveways that led to a detached garage.

Trees were plentiful until Dutch Elm disease arrived and began to ravage the shade canopy of block after block. It's estimated half a million trees were lost. It was a harbinger of the blight to come.

The 1967 riots changed Detroit forever. The five-day rampage left 43 dead, over 1,100 injured, more than 7,000 arrested and in excess of 2,000 buildings destroyed. The carnage and destruction started "white flight"—whites abandoning the city for the safer suburbs. Blacks began to move in to previously all-white neighborhoods. Whites would say the neighborhood was "changing." Change did not escape the little neighborhood around Hampshire Street.

"I think right around '78 it started to change," says Bev Srbich, the Wershe neighbor, who remembers when one neighborhood white family sold to a black family. "I'm not saying it's that one family, but then, it's like, when you cut down one tree and it hits and breaks another tree...they seen one black family and they all started to run."

Srbich says when blacks became the majority, the once safe, comfy area changed even more. "It started by theft in

11

the neighborhood," Srbich says. "Some break-ins. They were developing gangs. You were afraid to walk down the street." Srbich says the last straw was when her daughter got beat up when she tried to stop a group of blacks from throwing rocks through the stained-glass windows of their church. The Srbich family moved out in 1980.

"We sold for a fraction of what we paid for it," says Srbich, who is now a widow. "We sold it to a broker. My old house isn't even standing there anymore."

Those leaving the neighborhood included Ricky's friend Dave Majkowski. His family moved to Southfield, a suburb north of Detroit. Majkowski is certain Ricky's life would have been far different if his family had moved out of Detroit, too.

The Wershes remained on Hampshire Street amid all the "change" and Bev Srbich gets choked up when she thinks about it.

"Ricky is like a son to me," Srbich says, her voice quivering. "He was a good boy. Him and Dawn would come over to the house and sit on the porch. I hated to leave because of Rick and Dawn. That gave me a lot of guilt, 'cause they could always run to me." Aunt Bev breaks down crying.

As the complexion of Hampshire Street was changing, the city's nickname changed, too. The Motor City became known as the Murder City. Hundreds died every year, mostly in drug-related killings. It was the town that involuntarily hosted what was known as Devil's Night, the night before Halloween, when vandals and arsonists would go on a rampage settings hundreds of houses and businesses ablaze in an orgy of lawlessness. Each year the police and fire departments knew it was coming. Yet they seemed helpless to stop it. Television news crews from around the world came to town to get footage of the flames and destruction. Some inner-city cynics, noting Detroit's ever-increasing number of abandoned houses and buildings, called it instant urban renewal. For Ricky Wershe, it was home, the city where he grew up.

"It was nice while I was there," recalls Darlene McCormick, Richard Wershe's ex-wife and the mother of Ricky and Dawn. "We had good neighbors. We'd help each other out when we needed help."

"The neighbors were wonderful," agrees her longtime friend, Bev Srbich. "We did things for each other. We had small neighborhood groceries where you could run up to and get a couple of things."

I interviewed the women together at Darlene's insistence. She's a passive woman not given to chatting easily. Her friend Bev did most of the talking.

The Wershes were known as working-class whites. These are people with a modest education but a strong blue-collar work ethic and, usually, a strong sense of right and wrong. Many of the people of the neighborhood were the time clock-punching factory rats of the Detroit auto industry. Roman Wershe, Ricky's grandfather, was a factory worker, but his son Richard knew working on an assembly line was not the road to riches. He was determined to become a self-made millionaire through some scheme. He just had to find it.

Roman and Vera Wershe came from a Polish background and they were steeped in the post-war American work ethic. Darlene McCormick says when

Roman ("Ray") and Vera Wershe were young marrieds they got in an argument that ended tragically. They lived in an upstairs apartment and Ray Wershe pushed his wife down a flight of stairs. She was pregnant and lost the baby. Thereafter, the relationship changed and Ray became very passive and deferential to Vera. She was the boss. She was in charge. They had two children; a boy and a girl, Richard and Carolyn.

Darlene says she observed her husband Richard chafe at the Mom's-the-boss relationship between Roman and Vera. Richard didn't like his father's passivity. He also resented the favoritism shown to his sister, Carolyn. Richard believed the man should be the head of the house, the person in charge, the one who wears the pants.

Richard Wershe's enduring anger over his parents' relationship colored his own marriage to Darlene. He was a bully in his own house.

"Way back then you couldn't do anything about abusive marriages," Darlene says. "I called the police I don't know how many times." Darlene often ran to the home of Bev, her nearby neighbor and friend, for shelter and safety.

"He threw me out of the house one time in the middle of the winter and all I had on was a nightgown," Darlene recalls. "No slippers. Nothing. Thank God it was early in the morning and she (Bev Srbich) opened her door and let me in because I was walking through the snow in bare feet. He locked me out and wouldn't let me in. And like I said, the police wouldn't do anything."

Carolyn Wershe, Richard's sister, was of no help. She was an alcoholic, a drug addict and a prostitute. When she wasn't working the streets or in a bar or a drug house, she stayed at her parents' home and her mere presence and demeanor intimidated her young nephew and niece.

"The kids (Ricky and Dawn) would get scared when she was over there," Srbich recalls. "They would say they're afraid of Carolyn."

Wayne LeCouffe, Ricky's cousin, remembers Carolyn Wershe well.

"They (Ricky and Dawn) would throw her out of Granny's house," LeCouffe remembers. "Literally. They would open the door and push her out on the porch. Because she would come over there and steal to support her drug habit." When Ricky and Dawn would force her out of the house, Carolyn would cry loudly to her mother that her grandkids had no right to force her out of her family home. Vera Wershe would stick up for Carolyn and another family fight was on. Richard Wershe, Sr. didn't intercede in these battles because he wasn't there.

LeCouffe continued his recollection of Carolyn Wershe: "Every time she would go over there (to her parents' house) she would steal. She would steal money from her own mother and she would blame it on Dawn and Ricky."

Sometimes Carolyn would show up battered and bruised from a beating by her pimp. "She'd be out of commission for a couple of days and that's when she'd start to steal in order to get money to support her habit," LeCouffe recalls.

The confrontations and conflicts between Richard Wershe's kids and his sister ended one day when Ricky was fifteen. He entered his grandmother's house and found her trying to get Carolyn to "wake up." Aunt Carolyn was on the sofa. She was dead from a drug overdose.

❖

Dave Majkowski describes his friend Ricky as smart, clever and mischievous. Ricky was a good baseball player and a smart student when he put his mind to it, which wasn't often. He preferred shooting rats in Detroit's alleys to spending time with his school books. His parents went through a bitter divorce. Richard Wershe wound up with the two children, Ricky and Dawn, but he was seldom home. Mostly, he was out chasing another pot of gold at the end of a rainbow.

"I wanted to take the kids, but I kept thinking, all their friends are here and their school and everything," Darlene claims. Money was a consideration, too. "I knew I wouldn't get anything (child support) from him so I left the kids there so they could be in their environment that they were used to." The only choices Darlene had were bad.

Young Wershe almost escaped the clutches of the streets of Detroit. While his father was mostly missing in action, when he was around he was often abusive. Richard Wershe Sr.'s violent temper triggered beatings so bad and so frequent that young Rick begged his mother to let him come live with her. In addition to the beatings, Rick was unhappy about having to raise himself. He moved in with his mother and her new husband in a northeast suburb. "I had nothing but compliments from the teachers over at Fraser High School about how good he was and everything," Darlene recalls. It didn't last. Ricky did not like his mother's new husband. They didn't get along. He moved back home with his father on Hampshire Street in Detroit.

Ricky's older sister and only other sibling, Dawn, remained in Detroit, never moving to her mother's home. Dawn Wershe frequently disappeared in to the perpetual twilight world of drugs.

As he entered early adolescence Ricky came and went
as he pleased. He did whatever he wanted to do whenever
he wanted to do it with no parental supervision, no one to
say 'no.' If he was told no, he ignored it.

Ricky, adapted, as kids often do. He mingled easily
with the black kids who were moving in. He soon picked
up their mannerisms, their gestures and their street slang.
Before long Ricky *sounded* black. White kids like Rick
Wershe, Jr. were disparaged as wiggers—white teens who
walk, talk and act black. Neighborhood blacks were
amused and bemused by the white kid who talked their talk
and assimilated in to the black culture. Ricky's ability to
move easily among blacks and whites would prove to be a
two-edged sword.

The parents of Wayne LeCouffe, Ricky's cousin,
divorced and the kids moved with their mother to St. Clair
Shores, a nice suburb adjacent to Detroit's east side,
bounded on one side by Lake St. Clair, a large water
connector between the Great Lakes.

Wayne's mother didn't want him hanging around his
cousin Ricky. She didn't approve of Ricky's behavior. The
young cousins, however, enjoyed each other's company.
Wayne says he would lie and tell his mother he was going
to a neighborhood buddy's house, then go around the
corner and wait for Ricky or Dawn or Wershe, Sr. to pick
him up and take him back to the old neighborhood.
Sometimes Ricky would drive even though he was too
young to have a driver's license. ""He had a white Z 28. It
was my favorite car," LeCouffe recalls.

Like any adolescent, Wayne LeCouffe had school
friends and a few rivals. He recalls he and a kid named
Greg Biernacki didn't get along.

One day a man showed up at LeCouffe's home. Ricky Wershe happened to be there. The man was Gerard "Mick" Biernacki, a Detroit police officer and the father of Greg Biernacki. Officer Biernacki and his wife were divorced and their kids lived with their mother in St. Clair Shores.

There was a neighborhood rumor that Wayne LeCouffe had stolen Greg Biernacki's bike. LeCouffe says it wasn't true. But Gerard Biernacki showed up at the LeCouffe house, flashing his Detroit police badge and demanding his son's bike be returned.

Ricky Wershe stepped in. LeCouffe says Ricky, displaying his best bad-ass street attitude, stood face to face with Officer Biernacki and said, "That badge doesn't mean anything here. Get the fuck out of here." Biernacki turned and left.

Wayne LeCouffe remembers the confrontation vividly.

Officer Biernacki, a narc, had to be furious that a punk white kid from Detroit, his city, was talking to him this way. But he knew the boy was right. His Detroit police badge didn't mean anything in St. Clair Shores.

Richard J. Wershe, Jr and Officer Gerard "Mick" Biernacki would meet again a few years later. Biernacki would get revenge, and then some.

When Rick Wershe joined the War on Drugs, he stepped in to a national conflict that had been underway since the founding of the nation. Teetotalers, prohibitionists and temperance movements had been at "war" over the use of mind-altering substances in one form or another and to a greater or lesser degree since the days of the American Revolution.

Prisoner of War:
The Story of White Boy Rick and The War on Drugs

Martin Luther King, Jr.. said, "We are not makers of history. We are made by history."

To understand how Richard J. Wershe, Jr came to be a prisoner of the War on Drugs, it is useful to explore the national history of that war and the battles in the city where he grew up.

Chapter 2 – Yellow Brown and Black: The Colors of the War on Drugs

"This problem with illegal immigration is nothing new. In fact, the Indians had a special name for it. They called it 'white people.'"
—Jay Leno

What happened? How did Richard Wershe, Jr. go from being another white kid in a big industrial city, to one of the FBI's most productive paid informants in the deadly underworld of drug trafficking, to being sent to prison for life as a powerful drug lord and "public enemy" by the age of 18?

Astronomer-astrophysicist Carl Sagan, said, "You have to know the past to understand the present."

To understand the story of Richard J. Wershe, Jr., it is important to know what preceded his involvement in the nation's War on Drugs.

Many people assume what we call the War on Drugs began in 1971 during the Nixon Administration. Some believe "the War" began during Prohibition due to the relentless efforts of a racist and moralist federal agent named Harry Anslinger.

In fact, America's War on Drugs began over a century ago. From its beginning in the mid-1800s through modern times the true drivers of the nation's War on Drugs have been racism, bigotry, prejudice, discrimination and a tendency during tough economic times to blame substance-using immigrants for taking jobs from white people. In many ways, the War on Drugs is the struggle between whites and non-whites.

America's first battle in the War on Drug was directed toward Chinese immigrants. Thousands of Chinese flocked to the United States in the mid-1800s to take jobs working in the gold mines of the "49ers" of the California Gold Rush.

China was going through a period of deep instability, so jobs and life in the United States looked attractive to many Chinese. When they arrived on American shores, Chinese immigrants were not socially accepted by the white majority, but they were valued for their willingness to put in long hours doing hard work for low wages. They soon found low-paying jobs outside the gold mines, helping build the trans-continental railroad.

The Chinese were shunned by whites as inferior people. They were "different." Their skin looked yellow, they spoke an incomprehensible language—and some of them relaxed by smoking opium, a habit they brought with them from China. Some adventuresome whites tried smoking opium and soon they were frequenting the opium dens of "Chinatowns" in San Francisco and other cities. It became a cause for alarm when white women started venturing in to the Chinese opium dens, too. The Chinese immigrant horde was labeled the Yellow Peril.

The Chinese did not introduce opium to the United States. Years before the Chinese arrived opium was being imported from Turkey. Opium was used in cough syrups and other medications of the era.

Prof. Gregory Yee Mark of the Department of Ethnic Studies at Cal State-Sacramento has researched the early history of the Chinese in America. He notes the United

Vince Wade

States tried to grow poppies on its own for opium in the 19th century. Poppies are the base for opium. Americans wanted to reduce dependence on Turkish imports. Mark says newspaper accounts of the time indicated poppy cultivation was tried in California and six other states. The United States climate was not hospitable to poppy crops, so imports from Turkey continued.

Most writers who recount this period, focus on widespread racial discrimination against the Chinese. Often overlooked is white dislike of the Chinese for economic reasons. Modern fear of jobs being lost to China mirrors anxiety that first surfaced in the late 1800s. A newspaper political cartoon of the era showed a giant wall around the United States with a long ladder labeled "Emigration" being pushed away by white Americans as Chinese immigrants stood helplessly outside the wall. The caption read "Throwing down the ladder by which they rose." Like the Latino immigrants of today (and the workforce of modern-day China), the U.S. Chinese immigrants of that era were seen as a threat to economic security for white people even though they took jobs doing hard, menial low-wage work that most whites did not want to do. Still, as the nation struggled economically after the Civil War, Chinese immigrant labor was perceived as a threat to white economic opportunity.

Newspapers of the era did their part to solidify the perception among whites that the Chinese were evil and had depraved drug habits. A defunct newspaper known as the *San Francisco Call* (Mark Twain worked there one year) featured numerous stories about opium den raids.

In 1885 the San Francisco Board of Supervisors commissioned a detailed, multi-color map of Chinatown identifying places where evil-doers could gamble, smoke opium and consort with prostitutes.

The *San Francisco Examiner*, a newspaper that has been published since 1865, once did a story on itself recalling its own shameful participation in smearing Chinese immigrants. The paper noted the discrimination against the Chinese grew worse when the U.S. economy careened into a depression. "Civic leaders blamed the estimated 41,000 Chinese people in California for stealing white people's jobs," the *Examiner* article noted. "The *Examiner* was an eager cheerleader of this sentiment..." In the 1880s the paper published articles about "the Chinese Evil" and "the Asiatic Curse." It called opium "the Asiatic Vice" and "the Opium Curse."

Political cartoons of the time (television hadn't been invented yet) reflected fear and loathing toward the Chinese. Often, they depicted a Chinese man with his hair in a long single braid and a symbolic wash tub in the background because many of them found work doing laundry. White men in these cartoons typically held the Chinese character by the hair braid while they beat him. These political illustrations reflected what was happening in real life. One cartoon featured Uncle Sam vigorously kicking a Chinaman in his behind as he and other Chinese fled toward the Pacific Ocean shore. Another cartoon depicted an octopus with a mean-looking Chinese man's head. The creature's arms have names like Cheap Labor. The illustration shows a forlorn unemployed white man with a young child clinging to him. Another octopus arm is labeled Bribery and shows a policeman clutching a bag of money while another arm labeled Opium shows a white man sitting at a table smoking dope. An octopus arm named Immorality features a pair of white prostitutes presumably in the clutches of Chinese pimps.

As economic hard times hit the nation, racial discrimination against the Chinese turned violent. Panic prevailed in 1873 as the economy spiraled in to a depression. Jobs became scarce and racism and discrimination toward the Chinese spread rapidly. An illustrator named Thomas Nast gained fame for skewering the rich, fat-cat Robber Barons of that era, but one of his drawings entitled The Martyrdom of St. Crispin showed the patron saint of cobblers sitting at his work bench while two evil-looking Chinese men held massive swords above him. The clear implication was that Chinese shoemakers were beheading the American workers in the shoe industry through lower wages.

In 1882, the Chinese Exclusion Act became the nation's first law barring immigration by a specific ethnic group. Just below the surface were worries about maintaining "ethnic purity." It remained in effect under several names until 1943.

As Susan Schulten observed in the *New Republic*: "There was of course nothing unique or even new about anti-immigrant sentiment in America in the 1880s: The Chinese were only the latest victims of an economy that alternately devours and then scapegoats cheap labor."

Chinese opium den raids shared newspaper space with reports of lynchings of Chinese immigrants by angry white mobs. One of the worst incidents occurred in Los Angeles. It came to be known as the Chinese Massacre of 1871. *LA Weekly* quoted extensively from a researcher's investigation of the episode.

Two rival Chinese criminals got in to a shootout in LA's Chinatown. When a policeman and a white civilian tried to intervene, the civilian was shot and killed. Word spread quickly. An angry white mob went on a rampage in Chinatown. The mob lynched Chinese men and boys that night, 17 in total. The racist massacre made headlines around the world. The killers escaped serious prison time.

Taking the lives of Chinese immigrants wasn't a California phenomenon. In Texas, the notorious judge Roy Bean, who described himself as "The Law West of the Pecos" (river) was once confronted with a case where an Irish railroad worker murdered a Chinese immigrant. The Irishman's friends showed up at court and made it clear there would be hell to pay if their friend wasn't released. Judge Bean consulted his law book and said the law prohibits killing a human being but not a Chinaman. The Irishman was released.

With the turn of the century came a new immigrant menace and a new drug to fight. The Mexican Revolution, beginning in 1910, prompted thousands of Mexicans to flee to the United States. Like the Chinese before them, they took menial, low-paying jobs. And like the Chinese they brought with them a smokable substance for relaxation. Whereas the Chinese immigrants smoked opium, the Mexicans smoked cannabis.

Throughout history the sturdy cannabis plant was used to make hemp rope. In the 1600s, the American colonists were encouraged to grow hemp for sails and ropes for British ocean vessels. George Washington was among the hemp growers of his day. In the 1800s, the medicinal value of cannabis was discovered and accepted. Medicines with cannabis were sold in pharmacies. But when people started using it for relaxation and enjoyment, the moral majority of the day decided it was evil. It was labeled a poison in the early 1900s.

Some say the term *marihuana* entered the lexicon through the Mexicans who fled their country's revolution. A National Public Radio (NPR) report states anti-cannabis activists in the early part of the 20th Century popularized the name marihuana "because anti-cannabis factions wanted to underscore the drug's 'Mexican-ness.' It was meant to play off of anti-immigrant sentiments."

Dr. Ernest Abel, a doctor and professor at Detroit's Wayne State University, wrote in his book, *Marijuana: The First Twelve Thousand Years*: "The Mexican was the Negro of the southwestern United States. While not a slave or a sharecropper, he was a peasant. The stereotype of the Mexican was that of a thief, an untamed savage, hot-blooded, quick to anger yet inherently lazy and irresponsible."

While most people associate lynchings with blacks in the South, historic photographs and evidence suggest Mexican immigrants were lynched, particularly in the West and Southwest parts of the United States during the same period, although these racist atrocities are less well known. The *Harvard Civil Rights-Civil Liberties Law Review* published a piece on Latino lynchings based on research by Richard Delgado. The reasons were remarkably similar to those given for black lynchings; "acting uppity, taking jobs away from Anglos, making advances toward Anglo women, cheating at cards, practicing 'witchcraft,' and refusing to leave land that Whites coveted."

The Harvard report states Mexicans were lynched for acting "too Mexican"—speaking Spanish too loudly or reminding Anglos too defiantly of their Mexican-ness. Even Mexican women, often belonging to lower economic classes, were lynched, frequently for sexual offenses such as resisting an Anglo's advances too forcefully.

Prisoner of War:
The Story of White Boy Rick and The War on Drugs

In sheer numbers, the Latino lynchings paled in comparison with black lynchings; about 600 Mexicans were lynched versus an estimated 3,400 to 5,000 blacks.

Once again, the news media played a role in whipping up anti-immigrant hysteria with scare stories about the use of marijuana. The headline of a February, 1925 *New York Times* story read, *"KILLS SIX IN HOSPITAL.; Mexican Crazed by Marihuana, Runs Amuck With Butcher Knife."*

Like many news organizations over the years, the *New York Times* has had a long history of swallowing whole the anti-marijuana line parroted by people in authority. A 1927 *Times* story featured the following headline: *"MEXICAN FAMILY GO INSANE; Five Said to Have Been Stricken by Eating Marijuana."* The article cited doctors *"who say that there is no hope of saving the children's lives and that the mother will be insane for the rest of her life."*

The *Times*, which fancies itself the nation's "newspaper of record" also ran a blatantly racist scare piece in that same era warning the nation about the effect of cocaine on blacks. It said cocaine was turning blacks in to monsters.

"NEGRO COCAINE FIENDS ARE A NEW SOUTHERN MENACE" read the headline of a 1914 *New York Times* article written by a doctor. The sub-headline said, "Murder and Insanity Increasing Among Lower Class Blacks Because They Have Taken to 'Sniffing' Since Deprived of Whisky by Prohibition."

Putting aside for a moment the shock of something like this appearing in the august and oh-so-proper *New York Times*, the sub-headline hit upon a key failing of Prohibition and indeed the efforts throughout history to legislate the appetites of humanity. *They Have Taken to*

Vince Wade

'Sniffing' Since Deprived of Whisky by Prohibition."
(Underlining added for emphasis.)

The article claimed "...the negro drug 'fiend' uses cocaine exclusively." It explained the use of cocaine by blacks this way: "*The 'fiend' when questioned, frequently gives his reason in this brief sentence: "Cause I couldn't git nothin' else, boss.' That seems to be the crux of the whole matter."*

To drive the point home, the author wrote: "Hospital and police records show that during the prohibition period drug habits have increased with alarming rapidity. Physicians, officers, and 'fiends,' with very few dissenting opinions, attribute the rise of cocainism to the low-class negro's inability to get his accustomed beverages."

The *New York Times* piece was not unique in the media reporting of that era. Blacks were routinely portrayed in the news as dangerous predators.

Fear of sexual conquest of white women by blacks and Asian and/or Hispanic immigrants bubbled just below the surface. Many white men feared white women would be seduced by the mind-numbing drugs to be had by consorting with non-white immigrants and black men, a worry that has endured over the years. One political cartoon from the 1950s entitled Conquer and Breed featured a white woman with cleavage bared in a plunging neckline dress featuring a thigh-high leg slit. She was looking anxiously over her shoulder and she appeared to be fleeing while being stalked by a muscular monster with a black face.

The *Baltimore Sun* in the late 1880s wrote of "negro disorder" and "negro rowdyism."

A 1906 article in the *Afro-American Ledger*, a black newspaper in Baltimore, said harsh police tactics against

28

blacks were common in the South and proclaimed criminal justice in the South was engaged in the "wholesale manufacturing of Negro criminals."

Blacks and Mexicans weren't the only ethnic groups in that era linked to and ostracized for using feel-good substances. German immigrants were condemned, too, for drinking beer. The Temperance movement was on the rise in the United States. The Volstead Act of 1919 and the Eighteenth Amendment brought in the era of Prohibition, the nation's first official, futile effort to control personal pleasure.

Chapter 3 – Prohibition: The Racketeering Enabler

"Nothing so needs reforming as other people's habits."
—Mark Twain

Prohibition has never worked. In the Garden of Eden, Adam ate the apple Eve proffered and it's been downhill ever since for forbidden fruit of one kind or another.

Throughout recorded history humans have enjoyed the relaxation and euphoria-inducing effects of mind-altering substances. Stone Age jugs and containers indicate man has been enjoying alcoholic beverages for at least ten thousand years. From time to time segments of society have tried to change the behavior and habits of others through prohibitions, usually justified by some group's moral code that they tried to impose on others. It has never worked. Ever.

People accept that humans need air, water, food, clothing and shelter. These things are what psychologist Abraham Maslow calls the physiological and most important components of the human Hierarchy of Needs. Without them the human creature ceases to exist. Safety is the next most important human need and "belongingness" ranks third. Humans are social animals and usually align themselves with others of the same race, religion, nationality, etc. We like people who are like us, who live as we live, who think as we think, who believe as we believe.

For some, the need to feel superior or of higher morality is a powerful driver of belongingness. It is commonly known as holier-than-thou. The self-righteous believe they are special because they believe so-and-so, and non-believers, the "unsaved," do not. "We're special and you're not" seems to be a tenet of many religions.

One of the curiosities of Christianity is how many Christians pick and choose the teachings of Jesus to live by. From the sadistic torture of the Inquisition to the Salem Witch Trials, to the mandatory-morality-through-legislation of the modern Religious Right, the admonition from Jesus to not judge others has been widely ignored through the ages.

Passing judgment is certainly not limited to Christians. The mass murders by radical Islamic fundamentalists in modern times are gruesome proof that judging others is cherished by believers of all stripes. A favorite pastime of religious zealots is to find fault with substances or activities that give others enjoyment. Self-indulgence flies in the face of their belief that denial of pleasure and punishment for sins somehow leads to a more virtuous life. Morality arbiters have equated human pleasure with human sin throughout human history.

H.L. Mencken, a famous early 20th century satirical humor columnist was fond of sticking rhetorical pins in the puffed-up morality of the holier-than-thou crowd. He defined dour Puritanism as "the haunting belief that someone, somewhere, may be happy." He also wrote, "immorality is the morality of others who are having a better time."

The deep-seated need of some to find fault with the habits of others was the driving force behind the passage of the National Prohibition Act, also known as the Volstead Act but more commonly known simply as Prohibition. Drinking and drunkenness have long been viewed as vices and a fundamental belief of puritanical judgment-passers is that sin and sinners must be punished. Ethnic prejudice played a role, too. Many rural American white Protestant teetotalers viewed Irish immigrants as drunkards and they disapproved of German immigrants and their fondness for beer and making beer.

In modern times the immigration boogeymen have been Middle Eastern Muslims and Hispanics from Mexico and Central America. But before them, the WASPS (White Anglo-Saxon Protestants) despised Irish and German immigrants, followed by Italian immigrants. Many of the immigrants were Roman Catholics, not Protestants, and that was enough to make them not-as-holy-as-us for many.

In the mid-1800s roughly half of the population of Ireland immigrated to the United States due to a severe famine that claimed over a million lives. At about the same time, roughly a million Germans fled economic hard times and a political revolution in their home country. They sought a better life in the United States. Fear and hostility among Protestant whites flourished. In those days, there were numerous signs around the country proclaiming NINA: No Irish Need Apply. Then, as now, much of the anxiety about the new immigrants centered around jobs. The xenophobia was so pervasive there were riots in some cities over the new, non-Protestant arrivals.

The German and Irish waves of immigration were followed in the 1880s by Italians. As with the émigrés that preceded them, the Italians were fleeing massive crop failures and bad economic conditions in their native country.

To cope with the anti-immigrant hostility, the Irish and Italians gravitated to big cities where they formed neighborhoods filled with others like themselves. Most were law abiding, but the ethnic enclaves gave rise to Irish, Italian and Jewish gangs. These early gangsters quickly became involved in vice crimes like gambling and prostitution. Some of the young ethnic hoodlums of that era later became notorious chieftains of organized crime in America.

In Detroit, the so-called Purple Gang of Jewish hoodlums was the earliest manifestation of organized racketeers. Later, when the Purple Gang faded, rival Sicilian gangsters battled one another and eventually founded what would become one of the nation's major Mafia factions. Early members of the Detroit Mafia included Giovanni "Papa John" Priziola and Raffaele "Jimmy Q" Quasarano who used their connections in Europe to become major heroin smugglers.

While the Chinese operated opium dens on the West Coast and early Mafia entrepreneurs got involved in smuggling heroin, the "immorality" that got the most attention was the consumption of alcohol. Cocaine, due to its cost, was a sin for rich whites. Cole Porter had a line about it in a popular 1934 song about how substances like cocaine don't appeal to him but he gets a kick out of you.

Anti-sin zealots were determined to rid the nation of "demon rum." The Anti-Saloon League (ASL) was the leading force behind Prohibition, but it did not achieve success overnight. The temperance movement got its start before the Civil War but it became a national organization in 1893. Some say it was the nation's first political pressure group. Their belief that an entire nation should live by their religious and cultural code was unshakable, as it has been with many historical "Prohibitions" including the War on Drugs. The Anti-Saloon League was populated by people—mostly white, rural Protestants and women of various beliefs—who wanted to stamp out the sin(s) associated with drinking alcohol.

Prisoner of War:
The Story of White Boy Rick and The War on Drugs

Through the 1800s, temperance movements began to appear in various locales. A temporary nationwide alcohol prohibition began in 1917 as a World War One rationing effort to save grain, a key ingredient in liquor, for food. Also, in 1917 Congress submitted the 18th Amendment to the states for consideration. It passed in less than a year.

Prohibition quickly became the incubator for real organized crime in America. It gave rise to crime legends like Lucky Luciano, Meyer Lansky and Chicago's Al Capone. Alcohol smugglers like Capone became wealthy. "When I sell liquor, it's called bootlegging; when my patrons serve it on Lake Shore Drive, it's called hospitality," Capone once said. The term bootlegging refers to the practice of hiding flasks of liquor in boot tops.

The smuggling of foreign-made liquor by ship and over the borders with Canada and Mexico was a complex business requiring sophisticated logistics and the ability to bribe the police and judges to avoid the disruption of the illegal booze pipeline. Some crime gangs, particular the Mafia, organized to meet the need. The profits were so vast organized crime racketeers widened their portfolio to include prostitution, labor extortion, loan sharking and gambling. Organized crime endured long after Prohibition ended.

The Volstead Act did not seek to prevent drinking directly. It focused, instead, on the *business* of drinking. It stated: "no person shall manufacture, sell, barter, transport, import, export, deliver, or furnish any intoxicating liquor except as authorized by this act."

Prohibition lasted from 1920 through 1933. It came to be known as The Noble Experiment. The Noble

Experiment was, by any measure, a colossal failure. Illegal drinking establishments sprouted like dandelions in springtime in cities across the country. Hundreds of thousands of Americans got an added thrill out of drinking alcohol clandestinely. Prohibition spawned its own lingo. Hooch was low-quality liquor. So was bathtub gin and white lightning. Illegal drinking establishments were speak-easies because a patron had to speak softly at the door when seeking admittance. In Detroit they were known as "blind pigs," so named because proprietors got around the Prohibition laws by charging patrons admission to view some displayed live animal such as a pig. They would give the gathered animal lovers alcoholic drinks supposedly at no charge, when in fact, the admission fee covered the cost of the drinks. In 1928 the *Detroit News* estimated there were as many as twenty-five thousand blind pigs operating in the city.

Humorists made fun of Prohibition without mercy. "Prohibition is better than no liquor at all," said Will Rogers. W.C. Fields, a comedian who made a living portraying a drunk said, "Once, during Prohibition, I was forced to live for days on nothing but food and water."

A question posed by Will Rogers underscored the total failure of Prohibition: "Why don't they pass a constitutional amendment prohibiting anybody from learning anything? If it works as well as Prohibition did, in five years Americans would be the smartest race of people on Earth." In a more serious observation, H.L. Mencken noted none of the goals of Prohibition were achieved. "There is not less drunkenness in the Republic, but more. There is not less crime, but more. There is not less insanity, but more. The cost of government is not smaller, but vastly greater. Respect for law has not increased, but diminished," Mencken wrote.

The hopelessness of trying to stop a popular habit through law enforcement can be seen in the rise in the number of pharmacies in the United States in that era. The Volstead Act allowed pharmacies to sell liquor for "medicinal" purposes with a prescription. Prohibition-era gangsters were soon opening pharmacies everywhere. The number of pharmacies in the nation tripled as a result of Prohibition.

One major downside of this attempt to legislate morality was the tremendous economic cost. Restaurants, breweries and legitimate saloons went out of business, taking thousands of jobs with them. Other jobs were lost in businesses providing the logistics of the previously legitimate alcoholic beverage industry, such as warehouses and trucking companies. The modern War on Drugs dwarfs Prohibition in its unjust failures and economic and human costs.

One consequence of Prohibition was widespread police corruption. When the sale of liquor became illegal, thousands of cops around the country went on the take. Some took bribes to *not* raid the bribe-payer's operation. They raided the warehouses and speakeasies of competitors, instead. Other lawmen provided protection for liquor shipments. More than a few Coast Guardsmen lined their pockets for looking the other way as shipments arrived by boat from Canada via the Great Lakes and coastal areas.

In his book, *Last Call: The Rise and Fall of Prohibition*, Daniel Okrent tells the story of a Detroit prosecutor who showed up in court and complained to the judge that a large quantity of evidence in a bootlegging case had disappeared from Detroit Police headquarters.

"That's a poor place to bring liquor," Okrent quotes judge Edward J. Jeffries as responding.

The same book tells the story of New York's legendary mayor Fiorello LaGuardia commenting in the early 1920s when Prohibition was getting started that the city would need 150,000 law enforcement agents to enforce the law, adding: "…you will have to have 150,000 agents to watch the first 150,000."

Yet, Prohibition-era police corruption pales in comparison to the dirty cops who have been among the warriors in the War on Drugs.

The parallels between the failure of Prohibition and the failure of the War on Drugs are unmistakable. Both failed miserably to combat a perceived public menace rooted in personal consumption. The only difference is Prohibition lasted 13 years while the War on Drugs has arguably never stopped since the late 1800s.

In writing about Prohibition for PBS, historian Michael Lerner could have been writing about the War on Drugs, too, when he said: "For over a decade, the law that was meant to foster temperance instead fostered intemperance and excess. The solution the United States had devised to address the problem of alcohol abuse had instead made the problem even worse."

The failure of Prohibition did not deter the teetotalers and those who believed themselves to be morally superior. One in particular turned his attention from booze to marijuana.

Harry Anslinger, a staunch Prohibitionist and the head of the Treasury Department's small Federal Bureau of

Narcotics (FBN), used the repeal of Prohibition to focus public attention on the danger of marijuana.

Anslinger was a bureaucratic empire-builder and he saw marijuana as the leverage needed to expand the size and power of the Federal Bureau of Narcotics. He railed against the use of reefer, weed, or pot by blacks, particularly black entertainers. Anslinger hated jazz with its free-wheeling lack of rigid structure and he equated it with what he viewed as black depravity. Black bandleader Cab Calloway had a 1933 hit song called *Reefer Man* featured in the movie *International House*. Anslinger must have been furious.

Anslinger kept a dossier on black jazz musicians and he singled out some popular ones for law enforcement pursuit. Among them were Louis Armstrong, Charlie Parker and singer Billie Holiday. Anslinger was determined to bring Holiday down and he did. Some say her anti-lynching song, *Strange Fruit,* marked her for pursuit by the FBN.

Anslinger tasked Jimmy Fletcher, one of the few black agents in the Federal Bureau of Narcotics, with making a case against Billie Holiday. He did. Holiday reportedly asked her trial judge to send her to a hospital for drug rehabilitation. The judge sent her, instead, to prison for a year. It didn't end there. Anslinger hounded Holiday until her career was destroyed.

In his 1964 memoir, *The Protectors*, Anslinger has a chapter entitled, "Jazz and Junk Don't Mix." In it, Anslinger says "Jazz grew up next to crime, so to speak."

Anslinger spent most of the Depression years building support for criminalizing marijuana. Anslinger—arguably the nation's first narc—was tireless in his tirades against the evils of marijuana. His marijuana-is-the-road-to-hell rants were frequently in the news. Anslinger mimicked the public relations and policy marketing moves of his rival, J. Edgar Hoover of the FBI.

Anslinger gave speeches, testified before congressional committees and wrote articles for magazines warning of the devastating danger of marijuana. There was no medical or scientific evidence that marijuana was dangerous, but it didn't matter to Anslinger. In a 1937 Senate hearing Anslinger testified:

- "... the primary reason to outlaw marijuana is its effect on the degenerate races."
- "Marijuana is an addictive drug which produces in its users insanity, criminality, and death."
- "There are 100,000 total marihuana smokers in the US, and most are Negroes, Hispanics, Filipinos and entertainers. Their Satanic music, jazz and swing, result from marijuana usage. This marihuana causes white women to seek sexual relations with Negroes, entertainers and any others."

Anslinger never missed an opportunity to link marijuana to his racist views and certainty that weed was a destroyer of minds.

- "Marihuana influences Negroes to look at white people in the eye, step on white men's shadows and look at a white woman twice."
- "Reefer makes darkies think they're as good as white men."
- "Marihuana is a short cut to the insane asylum."

The racist, inflammatory scare talk worked. In 1937
Congress passed the Marijuana Tax Stamp Act. In practice,
it prohibited the possession or use of marijuana. It was
repealed in 1970 and replaced with the Comprehensive
Drug Abuse Prevention and Control Act.

In 1937, the same year Anslinger was pushing all-out
for a federal anti-marijuana law, Richard Nixon graduated
from Duke Law School. He tried to join the FBI but he was
turned down due to a hiring freeze. The conservative
young attorney undoubtedly took note of the new federal
anti-marijuana legislation and the baleful warnings of the
head of the Federal Narcotics Bureau about the link
between marijuana and the "degenerate races." Three
decades later, he would become President of the United
States. He regarded blacks as a national problem and
among his "enemies."

Chapter 4 – Nixon starts a Hamster Wheel War

*"You don't know how to lie. If you can't lie, you'll
never go anywhere."*
—Richard Nixon comment to a political associate

1967 was a pivotal point in history for the City of
Detroit, for Michigan, for the United States and the yet-to-
be-declared War on Drugs that could have been called
Prohibition: The Drug Edition.

Richard J. Wershe, Jr. wasn't born yet, but events in
1967 and in the next few years would have a profound
influence on his life in the 1980s.

In July of that year a deadly and destructive riot
erupted in Detroit. *Light My Fire* by the Doors was one of
the top hits on the radio as flames swept through large
sections of the city. The riot began on 12th Street in the
heart of Detroit's near-west side black community. A fight
broke out outside a blind pig, the Detroit term for an after-
hours joint where night people could drink, gamble and
score drugs.

The summer night of July 23, 1967 was a hot one in
Detroit. Windows were open to catch whatever breeze
might stir the air. The sounds of the fight outside the blind
pig reverberated through the neighborhood. More police
arrived and so did a crowd. The combination of cops and
ghetto-dwellers and a hot summer night was combustible.
It exploded and exploded and exploded in ever-widening
fire lines across the city.

The riot led to widespread looting, fires, shootings and National Guard troops. It resulted in 43 dead, 342 injured and several thousand businesses and dwellings gutted by flames. It left a major U.S. city so devastated it has not fully recovered to this day. The Detroit riot was bad but it wasn't the only one that summer. Newark, New Jersey endured a similar trauma. Two years earlier the mostly black Watts section of Los Angeles was aflame in a riot that left 34 dead and over a thousand injured. For many blacks the promise of the Civil Rights Act of 1964 remained just that—a promise. Frustration turned to rioting—and looting.

Blacks in Detroit had been seething with anger and resentment long before the 1967 riot. After World War Two the white political and economic power structure destroyed Black Bottom and Paradise Valley, two predominately black communities near the downtown district. Those neighborhoods were bulldozed to make way for freeways to and from the fledgling suburbs.

High-rise, low-income housing projects replaced individual homes in the name of progress and urban renewal. Black Bottom was not a racist anatomical reference. The area had been known by that name since French explorers founded the city in the 1600s. Black Bottom referred to the rich black top soil that was a fertile by-product of the Detroit River, a short distance away.

The lively neighborhoods of Black Bottom had been home to thousands of blacks. There were shops, schools, restaurants and night spots. Legendary black jazz figures such as Duke Ellington, Ella Fitzgerald, Pearl Bailey and Count Basie entertained there. Many blacks viewed the forced "urban renewal" of Black Bottom and Paradise Valley as an effort to drive them out and corral them in prison-like housing projects. "The Projects" amounted to high-rise internment camps. It was mass incarceration but no one called it that. Black neighborhoods, were demolished by the local mostly-white government with the help of the federal government. From a black perspective the causes of the 1967 riot had been stewing for a long time.

Many whites saw the big-city riots as nothing more than opportunistic mass crime sprees conducted under the cover of civil rights grievances. What, many whites wondered, did smashing store windows and looting merchandise have to do with civil rights? In the last years of the 1960s seething white resentment and anger matched black hostility but it was directed toward affirmative action in jobs and "entitlements", that were seen as endless Washington giveaways of white tax dollars to minorities.

It was a time when many whites listened with approval to radio commentator Paul Harvey, a progenitor of conservative evangelists such as Rush Limbaugh and Sean Hannity. Harvey would frequently feign frustration about all of the "Help Wanted" ads he would see in the papers for minimum-wage jobs at fast food restaurants in the suburbs. He would compare such ads to high unemployment in the inner cities. There would be several seconds of silence as he let the thought sink in. The implication was, unemployed minorities have plenty of job opportunities, but they refuse to take them. It wasn't white discrimination, Harvey seemed to be telling his audience, it's that minorities are lazy.

It is doubtful Paul Harvey or any of his listeners ever tried to take a bus from, say, 7 Mile and Woodward in Detroit in the pre-dawn darkness of a snow-whipped winter morning and change buses multiple times over the course of several hours to reach a 7:00 a.m. minimum-wage job at a fast food joint in a suburb. For whites—with a car—this might be a 30-minute drive. For poor inner-city residents without a car, it's a time-and-spirit sapping logistical struggle each way because in the Detroit region, public transportation is spotty. It is spotty because it is significantly underfunded. It is underfunded because politicians know mostly poor minorities use public transportation and the poor don't have the political clout to demand better service.

Nineteen sixty-seven was a time of campus unrest as well. It was the Age of Aquarius and the Age of the Baby Boomer. Thousands of American college kids were protesting the war in Vietnam and showing contempt for the keep-up-with-the-Joneses society their parents built. The men and women who fought in World War Two had come home and started peacetime lives. They went to college and got an education on the GI Bill. They bought homes with federal government-subsidized mortgages. They liked to say they did it on their own.

They started families and careers. They created suburbia, where conformity was a virtue, where front porches shrank, sidewalks disappeared and back yards provided privacy and patios which enabled avoidance of the neighbors. Suburbia was where whites minded their own business and often didn't know the names of the people next door. "Good fences make good neighbors" was a popular saying. For the veterans of World War Two and their spouses this was the good life. In later years, many of them would forget their government-subsidized start down the road to the Middle Class. Many aging members of "The Greatest Generation" disapproved of government help for later generations, especially minorities. To their way of thinking these people hadn't earned government subsidies, but they had.

Prisoner of War:
The Story of White Boy Rick and The War on Drugs

In 1967, many Americans believed the fabric of the country was fraying rapidly. The entire nation was going to hell, or so it seemed. Heroic movies romanticizing the battles of World War Two, light musicals and Doris Day movies had to compete with teen angst films like *Rebel Without a Cause* and *The Graduate*. Dramatic films such as *Days of Wine and Roses* and *The Man with the Golden Arm* intruded on the mythical good life. These films were uncomfortable reminders of substance abuse by adults in White America.

The music of crooner Perry Como and band leader Lawrence Welk was becoming passé. The kids were excited by a dangerous-looking singer from Mississippi named Elvis Presley, a young white man who was suggestively swiveling his hips and singing "race" music accompanied by loud guitars and drums. Before long, white teens were listening to black singers, too; artists like Chuck Berry, a devilishly handsome ex-con who was a lively showman. Respectable adults kinda, sorta liked the tunes but they abhorred rock and roll and rhythm and blues because it was so…so…black. And raucous. And rebellious.

So, each week many adults would tune in to a TV show called *Your Hit Parade*. White male singers in conservative suits or female singers in modest dresses with pearl necklaces, would croon white-bread "covers" of the rock and roll the kids were listening to on the radio. These "wholesome" constantly-smiling singers would stand in front of a 1940s-style orchestra and snap their fingers while rocking side to side mimicking a metronome as they carefully enunciated each syllable while the orchestra took care not to overpower the singer. This was so the adult TV audience could understand the lyrics. While Elvis was on the radio growling about " *uh houn' dawg"* over pounding drums and loud guitars, Gisele MacKenzie or Snookie

Lanson were on TV crisply pronouncing each word and bobbing woodenly as they sang, about *"a hound dog."*

The Vietnam War was sold to the American voter as essential to avoiding a Communist domino effect in the countries of Southeast Asia. Most Americans had never heard of Vietnam but they were being told it was vital to the national security of the United States.

These chaotic times provided fuel for the fire of political ambition that burned within former Vice President Richard Nixon who planned to run for President in 1968. Nixon was proud to be a square. As a conservative, he firmly believed if you are a good American you follow the rules and you don't step out of line. He was an enthusiastic believer in what came to be known as law and order.

Nixon was quick to embrace an emerging Republican idea called the Southern Strategy. He had a natural affinity for law and order. Blending the two looked like a recipe for winning the Presidency.

The Southern Strategy was a scheme to draw resentful southern whites away from the Democratic Party and turn them in to Republicans. President Lincoln, the freer of slaves, had been a Republican. As a result, most segregation-minded southern whites had been Democrats since the Civil War. Many hated the federal government. They believed the South should be able to write and follow laws consistent with their pre-Civil War society and economy. They came to be known as Dixiecrats. Their agenda was in contrast to the increasingly liberal Democratic Party.

After the passage of the Civil Rights Act of 1964, Republicans like Nixon saw an opportunity to reverse years of voting history. Appealing outright to white racism was unacceptable. It risked alienating outside-the-South

moderate conservatives. Political cover was needed. Law
and order was just the ticket, along with party support for
"states' rights." The latter was widely understood to mean
resistance to the Civil Rights Act and all programs initiated
by the federal government, except defense spending.
States' rights and law and order became "dog-whistle
politics", code terms the white faithful would understand as
calls to keep blacks, Latinos and anti-war leftists under
control and keep Southern segregation alive through a
debate over states' rights and "local control" versus federal
law. As Conor Lynch wrote for *Salon*, "*...the Republican
party made a conscious decision to become the party of
white men.*"

The notion of a national drug menace was vital to the
law and order agenda. Annual crime statistics were too
varied. They went up. They went down. An enduring law-
and-order problem was needed.

The evidence was thin that drug abuse was a
widespread national problem. It was a problem, but it
wasn't widespread. The evidence was equally thin linking
drug use to crime. Statistics showed the issues did not
move in lockstep. Most experts agreed drug abuse was a
public health concern, not a crime problem. That didn't
matter to Richard Nixon.

Illegal drug use was an ideal sin and campaign issue
for Nixon. He knew many whites, particularly in the South,
believed minorities were lazy drug addicts and he knew
"law-abiding" whites everywhere were alarmed by the
sudden popularity of marijuana among hippies and young
campus protestors, many of them the children of white
suburbanites.

Reports and studies showing there was little evidence linking the rise in overall crime to the use of drugs were dismissed or ignored when Nixon occupied the Oval Office. Moreover, his team figuratively covered their ears when told there was scant evidence that marijuana was a "gateway" drug to the use of more hard-core substances.

"People react to fear, not love—they don't teach that in Sunday School, but it's true."—Richard Nixon

Nixon knew it wouldn't take much to scare people in to believing their children were on the road to becoming dope fiends. For many parents, blaming drug abuse for their struggles with normal teen rebellion was comforting. It gave them a malevolent and sinister outside evil they could blame. Studies and research showed most American teens were not part of the drug culture. It didn't matter to those who *wanted* to believe drugs were the source of conflict for the families of adolescents.

One of the believers was singer/actor/pop star Elvis Presley. Elvis showed up at the White House one day, unannounced, with no appointment. His stardom got him a few minutes with the President. Elvis had brought Nixon a World War Two Colt .45 in a commemorative case, and he announced he wanted to become an agent of the Bureau of Narcotics and Dangerous Drugs, (BNDD), the predecessor agency of the DEA. He told Nixon he could help with the "hippie elements" and the Black Panthers. Elvis got a grip-and-grin photo with the always-stiff Richard Nixon and eventually he got his wish to at least have a BNDD badge. When Elvis died in 1977, chronic drug abuse was listed as one of the causes of death.

Nixon did some political calculus and figured if he could intertwine blacks, marijuana, hard drugs, campus

unrest and crime in the minds of his Silent Majority, he would have a hot campaign theme he could use to win the election and occupy the Oval Office. He was right.

Post-Watergate revelations confirmed this was indeed the thinking of Nixon and his loyalists. After Nixon won the 1968 election, a 1969 diary entry by H.R. Haldeman, President Nixon's chief of staff, summarized an Oval Office discussion: "Nixon emphasized that you have to face the fact that the whole problem is really the blacks."

Yet, when President Nixon declared a War on Drugs in June, 1971, he had strong support from an unexpected source: the black community.

Books, articles, documentaries and discussions of the War on Drugs often overlook this truth. Black leaders had been pushing for something like the War on Drugs well before it became a national political initiative from the Nixon White House. Like many movements in American politics, black resistance to illegal drugs began at the grass roots with mothers in New York City forming ad-hoc groups to fight the heroin that was enslaving their children and, in many cases, killing them.

They found a champion in Harlem's Rev. Osperia Dempsey, who became an anti-drug activist before it was popular to do so. Rev. Dempsey would identify drug-dealing locations and point them out to the police. If that didn't work Dempsey and his supporters would show up and cause a commotion that prompted the drug pushers to leave the area.

Rev. Dempsey favored harsh penalties and action, such as the creation of national "health camps" where drug addicts could get help kicking the habit.

In June, 1970, *Ebony* magazine published an article headlined, "Blacks Declare War on Dope." This was a full year before Richard Nixon declared his War on Drugs. The magazine quoted Rev. Dempsey as saying, "All hard-core, older addicts should be involuntarily removed from the streets."

Dempsey and other black leaders viewed illegal drugs as a weapon to control and oppress blacks. While they favored law and order and crime-free communities, their larger concern was the subjugating nature of drug addiction.

"The flooding of black communities with drugs, especially heroin, is nothing less than a program of genocide against black people," activist Stokely Carmichael told the magazine. He called it a weapon of the oppressors.

It was Carmichael who popularized the term "Black Power" in a speech in 1966. "We have got to get us some Black Power," Carmichael said in remarks in Greenwood, Mississippi, after his arrest for participating in a civil rights march. "We don't control anything but what white people say we can control."

The Congressional Black Caucus had a rocky relationship with President Nixon, so much so they boycotted his State of the Union speech in 1971. But the black politicians soon decided they should pressure Nixon to address their policy concerns. That led to a meeting between Nixon and the Congressional Black Caucus in March, shortly before Nixon declared what would become an endless hamster wheel-like war to combat illegal drugs.

At the White House meeting the Congressional Black Caucus presented a list of 60 "recommendations" for the President. The list included: "Declare drug abuse and addiction a major national crisis and use all resources to stop the illegal entry of drugs."

One of the most vociferous voices in the meeting with
Nixon was Representative Charles Rangel of New York.
His district included Harlem, ground-zero for black
activism against illegal drugs. Rangel urged the President
to get tough on drugs, to combat them more aggressively
and to take action right away. The New York congressman
even urged bringing the Pentagon into the fight to stop the
flow of illegal drugs entering the country. Rangel
maintained his hardline stand on drugs throughout his
career, even when criticism mounted against the War on
Drugs.

The black politicians who met with Nixon were
reflecting the concerns of their constituents in the nation's
inner cities. Law-abiding blacks wanted the same thing
white citizens wanted: safe communities. They felt ignored
by the police and the courts. They saw a crackdown as a
way of making their neighborhoods more livable. They had
no way of knowing they were supporting a plan of action
that would later be considered a war on America's blacks.

In the minds of many white Detroiters, an incident in
early 1969 validated the wisdom of Nixon's tough-on-
crime strategy. Late on Saturday evening, March 29, 1969,
a police patrol car in the inner city 10th Precinct happened
upon a group of black men in combat fatigues carrying
rifles. Officers Michael Czapski and Richard Worobec
radioed in what they observed:

"Scout 10-5. We got guys with rifles out here,
Linwood and Euclid." Officers Czapski and Worobec got
out of their police car to investigate.

Moments later the police radio crackled with desperate
cries and screams for help. A honking police car horn
nearly drowned out the terrified voice on the radio. "10-5

Help! 10-5 Help! 10-5 Help!" It was Officer Richard
Worobec, lying on the floorboard of his police car,
frantically trying to steer, honk, accelerate and escape as a
fusillade of rifle fire riddled the car. Thwack! Thwack!
Thwack! The sound of the rifle bullets hitting the police car
could be heard over the police radio amid Worobec's
screams. His partner, Michael Czapski lay dead on the
sidewalk, shot seven times.

Scout car 10-5 had happened upon people leaving the
church after a meeting of the Republic of New Africa or
RNA, a militant Detroit-based national black separatist
group that wanted five Southern states—Alabama,
Georgia, Louisiana, Mississippi and South Carolina—to
become the core of a new all-black nation, exclusively for
blacks and controlled by blacks—within the United States.
In addition, the RNA wanted the United States to pay the
nation's blacks $400 billion in reparations for slavery.

The Detroit police responded forcefully to the shooting
of two of their own. Arriving officers claimed they were
fired upon by people inside the church. The police stormed
the church, spraying it with heavy gunfire as people inside
took cover under church pews. The police arrested 135
people inside the church and hauled them to police
headquarters. A local black judge showed up in the middle
of the night and ordered all released on low bond or their
personal recognizance. The Police Commissioner was told
he would face contempt of court charges if he didn't
comply.

The shooting and its aftermath sparked more tension
between the white and black communities. Blacks were
furious and whites were outraged. The New Bethel Baptist
Church incident was, in a political sense, tailor-made for
President Nixon's Southern Strategy.

Prisoner of War:
The Story of White Boy Rick and The War on Drugs

In the summer of 1981, the racism underlying the
Southern Strategy (and the War on Drugs) was verified in
stark terms by Lee Atwater, a Republican political
consultant, strategist and an adviser to then-President
Ronald Reagan. Atwater died in 1991.

"You start out in 1954 by saying, 'Nigger, nigger,
nigger,' Atwater explained. 'By 1968 you can't say 'nigger'
— that hurts you. Backfires. So you say stuff like forced
busing, states' rights and all that stuff. You're getting so
abstract now [that] you're talking about cutting taxes, and
all these things you're talking about are totally economic
things and a byproduct of them is [that] blacks get hurt
worse than whites. And subconsciously maybe that is part
of it. I'm not saying that. But I'm saying that if it is getting
that abstract, and that coded, that we are doing away with
the racial problem one way or the other. You follow me —
because obviously sitting around saying, "We want to cut
this," is much more abstract than even the busing thing,
and a hell of a lot more abstract than 'Nigger, nigger.'"

Atwater's comments are on an audio recording by the
late political science researcher Alexander P. Lamis.
Atwater's blunt explanation of the Southern Strategy was
not unique among Nixon loyalists.

In an amazingly candid interview featured in the April,
2016 issue of *Harper's* magazine, Dan Baum, author of
Smoke and Mirrors, a book about the failed War on Drugs,
quotes John Ehrlichman, Nixon's White House counselor
and chief of domestic policy, on the Nixonian view of
blacks and the anti-war movement:

"The Nixon Campaign in 1968, and the Nixon White
House after that, had two enemies: the antiwar Left, and
Black people. You understand what I'm saying? We knew
we couldn't make it illegal to be either against the war or
Black. But by getting the public to associate the hippies

with marijuana and Blacks with heroin, and then criminalizing both heavily, we could disrupt those communities. We could arrest their leaders, raid their homes, break up their meetings and vilify them night after night on the evening news. Did we know we were lying about the drugs? Of course we did."

It wasn't until Jo Haldeman, H.R. Haldeman's widow, released her autobiography in 2017 that we learned that at the height of the Watergate scandal, with reporters staking out their home, the Haldemans discovered one of their college student sons was growing marijuana in a mini hothouse in his bedroom. Jo Haldeman wrote that she thought he was growing wax begonias.

Nixon didn't have the angry white vote all to himself. He had competition on the right in the 1968 presidential race and again in 1972 from George Wallace, a stand-in-the-school-door segregationist who was every bit as skilled as Nixon at manipulating white anger and resentment toward the civil rights movement. Wallace was the governor of Alabama for twenty years and he ran for president four times. Some say his positions were precursors to the social issues that crystallized in the Reagan Revolution and have continued to reverberate through the nation's politics and culture.

There was no doubt where Wallace stood. In his 1963 inaugural gubernatorial speech Wallace said, "...segregation now, segregation tomorrow, segregation forever."

A central element in the politics of George Wallace was his gut-level appeal to whites who felt they were losing power to minorities and therefore losing the United States of America. Wallace tapped in to a belief by many that the main political parties regarded aggrieved whites with contempt: "…they've looked down their nose at you and me a long time," Wallace said in his 1968 presidential campaign. Forty-eight years later, these people were scorned as a "basket of deplorables" by Democratic Presidential candidate Hillary Clinton.

Wallace discovered, as Nixon had, that a significant segment of the population was open to linking crime and drugs to the civil rights movement. Wallace was fond of bemoaning the loss of "law and order" in the United States.

Stoking white fear, Wallace manipulated it: "It is a sad day in our country that you cannot walk even in your neighborhoods at night or even in the daytime because both national parties, in the last number of years, have kowtowed to every group of anarchists that have roamed the streets of San Francisco and Los Angeles and throughout the country. And now they have created themselves a Frankenstein monster, and the chickens are coming home to roost all over this country."

Unsurprisingly, there were frequent protests at Wallace rallies. When that happened Wallace would invariably say, "Let the police handle it." This accomplished two things; it fortified his image as a law-and-order man and it won him many admirers in the police departments of cities where he campaigned.

Wallace found a receptive audience in the blue-collar enclaves of Michigan, that is to say, most suburbs in the state. Before President Ronald Reagan and his seemingly new Reagan Democrats of blue-collar Macomb County, Michigan, there was George Wallace. He drew some of the same people to his campaign rallies.

In the 1972 campaign, a mentally unbalanced stalker named Arthur Bremer shadowed Wallace and attempted to assassinate him at a rally in Laurel, Maryland. He fired six shots at Wallace. Four of the bullets hit their target. Wallace survived but he was left paralyzed from the waist down for the rest of his life. In later years Wallace changed his views on racial issues. He went so far as to ask for forgiveness from blacks.

Nixon had competition for the law and order vote closer to the political center, too. New York Governor Nelson Rockefeller, a Republican centrist, had political ambitions to be President. He concluded an essential element in a winning campaign was to be tough on crime, the same as every other candidate for major office in either party. No one ever wins office in the United States by advocating the coddling of criminals

Even Rockefeller's centrist supporters were startled by the so-called Rockefeller Drug Laws. New York became the toughest state in the nation regarding criminal penalties for drug convictions. New York pioneered the view of drug abuse as a crime as opposed to a public health issue. Addiction was no longer an illness to be treated, it was a law violation to be punished and punished severely. While studies claimed drug abuse is roughly equal among the races, enforcement under the Rockefeller drug statutes focused disproportionately on minorities.

Lawmakers in Michigan were impressed by the hard-ass Rockefeller drug laws and a few years later they enacted the so-called 650 Lifer drug law. Anyone convicted of possessing over 650 grams (almost a pound-and-a-half) of illegal drugs was automatically sentenced to life in prison without parole. If the accused was a juvenile in a non-violent case, it didn't matter. It was a fate that befell Richard J. Wershe, Jr in 1988, to be explored in Chapter 15. Michigan's moderate Republican governor,

Prisoner of War:
The Story of White Boy Rick and The War on Drugs

William Milliken, later said signing the 650-law was the biggest mistake of his political career.

Eventually, the harsh drug laws in New York and Michigan were revised, but not before thousands of young men were thrown in prison for most of their adult lives.

The Republican Southern Strategy was about more than exploiting southern white animosity toward sharing lunch counters, restrooms and drinking fountains with blacks. Plenty of whites outside the Old South resented the federal government spending tens of millions of dollars on programs they viewed as coddling minorities. These non-southern whites were caricatured by the cranky, bigoted character Archie Bunker on a provocative and mocking TV sitcom called *All in the Family.*

In one episode, Archie, who had a New York dialect and was the archetype of white working-class 1960s American conservatism, is lecturing his liberal son-in-law about the Statue of Liberty and why that symbol in the New York harbor makes America great. He talked of her torch held high: "…screamin' out to all the nations of the woild. Send me your poor, your deadbeats, your filthy." Bunker says other nations answered the call and immigrants arrived. He likened them to a swarm of ants. He listed what he regarded as human refuse that immigrated to America: "The Spanish PRs from the Caribboen, yer Japs, yer Chinamen, your Krauts and your Hebes and your English fags." According to the Bunker character, the immigrants to America, are: "…free to live in their own separate sections where they feel safe and they'll bust your head if you go in there. That's what makes America great, buddy!"

Vince Wade

In June, 1971, as the Pentagon Papers were stunning
the nation with details about years of U.S. government lies
about the bloody war in Vietnam, President Nixon started a
new war.

It would become a war without end. Like Vietnam, the
rationale for the War on Drugs was largely built on official
lies.

By all indications, the War on Drugs was a fraud from
the beginning, political cover for suppressing the two
groups President Nixon regarded as enemies; the mostly-
white liberal anti-war movement and the black-dominated
civil rights movement.

The War on Drugs provided fuel for another growing
national problem; police corruption. At the end of 1971,
the same year President Nixon declared a War on Drugs, a
New York City cop named Frank Serpico was testifying
before a commission about widespread and deeply
entrenched drug corruption in the NYPD. Serpico had been
an undercover narc who was shot in the face during a drug
raid. Many believed, and still do, the raid was a set-up by
other narcs to have Serpico killed for refusing to take
bribes like other police officers.

His story became such a sensation it was made in to a
movie starring Al Pacino as Serpico. The tag line on the
movie poster read: "Many of his fellow officers considered
him the most dangerous man alive—an honest cop."

The Democrats weren't about to let the Right keep
sure-fire issues like Law and Order and the War on Drugs
all to themselves. A decade after Nixon launched his War
on Drugs, about the time the federal government was
recruiting Richard J. Wershe, Jr to be a combatant in this
hopeless new iteration of Prohibition, the Democrats would

join the fight with gusto with a new set of tough laws that led the United States to have the highest prison population in the world. In between, Detroit political power changed color and the man who led the political struggle confirmed the worst fears of whites about Black Power.

Chapter 5—Coming of Age in a Fading City

"The darkest hour is just before everything goes completely black."
—A popular police saying after the election of Detroit's first black mayor.

The story of how the teenaged crime legend known as White Boy Rick came to have enemies in the political and criminal justice systems of a major city, is rooted in what happened to the City of Detroit and its police department as he was growing up.

Detroit put America on wheels and was proud of it. The city was tough and gritty but vibrant and humming like a well-tuned V-8 engine.

The children of the World War Two generation embraced car tunes—odes to the Rocket 88, Chevy 409s, Little Deuce Coupes, Little GTOs, and Little Cobras. These "little" cars had monstrous horsepower and pop musical groups sang anthems to their muscular hot wheels.

On nice weekends, the Detroit River became a playground. Fishermen watched hulking Great Lakes freighters silently glide past while pleasure boats and yachts cruised around Belle Isle, a large, woodsy strip of land in the river that was a natural recreation treasure.

On summer weekends in the southern riverside suburbs, boat owners would stock their craft with beer, booze and food and navigate across the fast-moving river to placid coves on the Canadian side. They would tie up alongside other boats and initiate large, ad-hoc Friday-night-through-Sunday-evening parties with bikini-clad revelers hopping from boat to boat while Motown music reverberated into the night. Many boaters didn't know one another, but in the festive weekend atmosphere, no one cared.

In the 1970s, there was a growing appetite for heroin in Detroit's ghetto which brought forth black drug entrepreneurs like Henry Marzette, John Classen and Eddie Jackson.

Marzette was first among equals, although it's debatable that Marzette had any equals. He was a celebrated Detroit narcotics cop. Newspapers published stories about Marzette's exploits as a narcotics officer.

Then he went to the other side.

He built a robust heroin empire, paying former police colleagues as needed and ruthlessly murdering rivals who got in his way. Marzette took the bold step of traveling to Southeast Asia where he persisted until he made the right connections with global drug smugglers. By the time Marzette returned to Detroit he had his own heroin smuggling pipeline from the Golden Triangle in Burma, Laos and Thailand.

In the spring of 1972 kidney failure ended Marzette's life and empire. A bloody battle for control of Detroit's heroin market ensued. Bodies piled up on stainless steel slabs at the morgue. The community was horrified by the cold-blooded execution murders as drug entrepreneurs vied for market dominance.

Prisoner of War:
The Story of White Boy Rick and The War on Drugs

In 1973, there was a seismic upheaval in Detroit politics. The tectonic plates of governance shifted. The color of power changed from white to black.

In a bitterly fought mayoral race, a black politician named Coleman A. Young defeated former Detroit Police Commissioner John Nichols, a white Patton-like law-and-order candidate with a crew cut who had been a no-bullshit, keep-the-lid-on police boss. In the years preceding the 1973 election, many Detroit blacks viewed the police department as a mostly-white occupying army. The 1967 riot accelerated white flight to the rapidly expanding, freeway-accessible suburbs. Detroit's fast-shrinking white population shuddered to think of the city under black rule. Nichols was Detroit's political version of the Great White Hope.

Coleman Young and his supporters did nothing to assuage white fears. He had been a Tuskegee Airman, a racially segregated fighter and bomber unit that served with distinction in World War Two. After the war, Young was a union organizer, and a state senator. He had a reputation as a militant long before black militancy and talk of black power came in to vogue. He promised significant and substantial reform of the Detroit Police Department. Everyone knew it was code talk for saying blacks were going to be in charge.

Young said if elected mayor, one of his first acts would be to abolish a controversial, mostly white, undercover police unit known by the acronym STRESS. It was shorthand for Stop The Robberies, Enjoy Safe Streets.

STRESS was the police response to a crime problem that was out of control. In 1970 there were 23,038 armed robberies on the streets of Detroit. Eighty-five of the stick-up victims were killed.

Formed in 1971, the covert unit's methods often involved a decoy officer posing as a drunk. Backup officers were in a nearby van. If a mugger accosted the undercover officer, there would be an arrest, often involving police gunfire. There was a joke that the STRESS unit's standard tactics were to start shooting, announce they were the police, then resume firing.

STRESS wasn't just a decoy unit. They conducted surveillance and executed search warrants, too. STRESS cops kicked doors and kicked ass. They were widely viewed as a shoot-first, ask-questions-later squad. Over two-and-a-half years, STRESS teams killed nearly two dozen civilians. All but one was black.

But STRESS got results. During the STRESS-era street robberies dropped dramatically. STRESS made nearly eight-thousand felony arrests and took thousands of guns off the streets.

Other cities with decoy units did not have the trouble Detroit had. Critics blamed the problem on poor supervision and a flawed system for selecting the officers to serve in the unit. To a significant degree, STRESS was the catalyst for a change in city leadership.

The precursor to STRESS was a citywide policing concept called Precinct Support Units, known on the streets as the Big Four or the Big Foh, in ghetto-speak. They were so named because there were four burly, fight-ready, armed-to-the-teeth police officers riding around in a big, unmarked four-door sedan. One officer was always in uniform and usually he was the driver. The others were in plainclothes. The Big Four were known to bail out of their cruiser brandishing pump-action shotguns and old-style Thompson submachine guns. They backed up the patrol units if needed. Otherwise, the Big Four went looking for trouble.

Prisoner of War:
The Story of White Boy Rick and The War on Drugs

One Big Four officer, Jack Rogers O'Kelley, was known on the street as Rotation Slim. He was six-foot-five, clean shaven and weighed 190 pounds. O'Kelley, now deceased, was a legend among street people and other cops.

The *Detroit Free Press*, in a profile story about Rotation Slim, quoted George Richmond, the proprietor of what used to be the Willis Show Bar in Detroit's Cass Corridor near downtown. The Willis Show Bar was notorious as a base for ladies of the evening. For the Big Four, the bar was often a good source of street intelligence.

"That man (Rotation Slim) wasn't afraid of nobody," Richmond recalled. "When Rotation come around and the punks seen him coming, they'd run. If we had more cops like that now, there'd be less trouble on the street."

The Rotation Slim legend includes several versions of the origin of his nickname. One says it came from his habit of jumping out of a Big Four cruiser and confronting a loitering crowd of young black men. Rotation Slim would tell the group he was going to "rotate" around the block with his cruiser team and when he came back, if any of the guys on the corner were still there, he would administer a bare-fisted ass-whupping they would never forget. He cleared a lot of street corners that way.

This kick-ass cop mentality carried over to some in the new STRESS unit, which quickly earned a reputation for trigger-happy policing. This became painfully clear in a deadly shoot-out in March of 1972 between a three-man STRESS team and several off-duty Wayne County Sheriff's deputies. All involved were black.

It was a Saturday night and five deputies were gathered in an inner-city apartment playing cards on their night off.

One of them arrived late in the evening. The STRESS team was watching. They noticed the man appeared to have a gun. Off-duty cops usually carry their weapons during their time off, especially in cities like Detroit. The STRESS team quietly followed the man up an outdoor staircase to the apartment where the door was open on a mild spring night.

There are conflicting accounts by the participants about what happened. There were shouts and a lot of shooting. Over 30 shots were fired, all or nearly all, by the STRESS officers. The deputies ducked for cover and tried in vain to reach for their guns. One deputy was killed, three were wounded, one critically. The incident became known as the Rochester Street Massacre.

In a high-profile trial, the three STRESS officers, Virgil Starkey, Ronald Martin and James Harris, were charged with assault with intent to commit murder. A jury acquitted the three officers. Afterward, Harris announced he would seek transfer to another assignment. Years later, the lives of Harris and Richard Wershe, Jr. would intersect fatefully.

In December, 1972 four STRESS officers working surveillance stopped a car they saw leaving a suspected dope house. The three occupants of the car bailed out with guns blazing at the unmarked police unit. All four officers were wounded, one quite badly. Later that month, two other STRESS officers working surveillance were ambushed by the same trio. One officer was killed, the other seriously wounded.

The shooters were Mark Clyde Bethune, John Percy Boyd and Hayward Leslie Brown.

The Detroit Police Department launched the largest manhunt in its history, spanning 86 days. Brown was captured in January after a firebombing, but Boyd and Bethune got away. They surfaced in Atlanta, Georgia the next month. Both died in a shootout with the police. Brown was eventually tried and convicted in the firebombing but his sentence was later overturned.

Bethune was identified as the leader of a self-styled black vigilante trio. Bethune was influenced by the pronouncements of black radical H. Rap Brown who famously said violence is as American as cherry pie.

Many in the black community expressed support for the trio, with some viewing them as avengers battling a white army. There were public protests, noisy and crowded city council discussions and several lawsuits.

By the time the STRESS unit was disbanded 22 people had died from gunshots fired by the plainclothes police unit. Many blacks believed STRESS was acting as judge, jury and executioner. STRESS-related shootings cost the city's taxpayers over a million dollars in settlements. Many white police officers and white citizens regarded the STRESS unit as a sensible, effective response to violent street crime.

In the fall of 1973, Young was elected Detroit's first black mayor. Rick Wershe, Jr. was a preschooler at the time. Through the '70s, as Wershe grew, so did Detroit's problems with street crime, including illegal drugs.

It wasn't widely known, but Young was involved in crime when he was a young man. In his younger days, the police vice squad viewed him as a black organized crime figure—what the police call an associate. He was a numbers man. Numbers was a popular illegal gambling racket in the inner city. It was an illegal version of today's state-run lotteries. In the inner city, numbers runners would collect bets and cash and bring them to what might be called betting parlors or numbers banks. Coleman Young was a numbers runner in the late 1940s.

One of Detroit's few black police officers in that era was working surveillance in the Organized Crime Section's rackets squad. He worked on foot, loitering near gambling joints, noting the numbers operators. One of the numbers men he was watching was identified as Coleman A. Young. The black police surveillance officer was young, quiet, and good at blending in, at not drawing attention. This surveillance cop was Patrolman William Hart. His surveillance notes about Young were in a confidential Detroit Police vice squad folder that came to be known as File 88. That number was undoubtedly part of a longer identifier, but that's how the file came to be described by those who didn't want its existence known.

When Coleman Young was elected mayor, one of his early priorities was to "reform" the Police Department, which included gutting the Organized Crime Section. Young was aware of the section's history of making arrests in the black gambling community. He was one those they arrested. Years of hard work, detailed criminal history and sensitive police investigative files vanished one day.

A white cop who knew what was in File 88 arranged to get the surveillance notes of the file to me. They were on the slick coated paper used in early photocopy machines. I was not given the complete illegal gambling case file. There was a hard-to-read handwritten note on the top of the first page. I thought it said "Lt. Giebic's Case." Veteran cops drew a blank when I inquired about Lt. Giebic.

Determined to find out more about Coleman Young's numbers racketeering, I got the idea to contact an old

friend, Kalliope "Kae" Resh, a key employee for decades
in the Detroit criminal court clerk's office. The criminal
court in those days was called Recorder's Court. Some
called Resh "the conscience of Recorder's Court" because
of her reputation for honesty and integrity. When I
contacted her, she was frail and in her nineties, but her
mind was still sharp. She was a human encyclopedia of the
criminal courts and much of the criminal history of Detroit.
I mentioned File 88 and my struggle to find out more about
the case assigned to Lt. Giebic.

She thought about it for a minute or two. "Oh, you
mean Lt. Giesig," she said. "Eugene Giesig. He was a
lieutenant in the vice squad years ago."

I told Resh about the surveillance notes in File 88. To
my astonishment, she knew what I was talking about.

"I know about that case," she said. "That file goes back
to the late 40s, 1947 or 1948. I was a rookie at the court in
those days." Resh went on: "I handled it when it came to
Recorder's Court," she said. "I remember one day a young
black officer came in to get warrants after a raid on a
gambling joint on Livernois Ave. in the 10th Precinct. It
was Bill Hart."

The criminal warrant against Coleman Young featured
the usual law enforcement accusation for gambling houses:
engaging in an illegal occupation.

"I remember I asked Bill how he managed to do
extensive foot surveillance in this case without being
discovered," she said. "He told me he was so skinny he
could stand behind a telephone pole and not be seen. We
both laughed."

Ever the court professional, Resh noted: "What I'm
telling you is not hearsay. It's a conversation I had

personally with Bill Hart." Kae Resh passed away in March, 2017.

In one of life's ironies, Young eventually named Bill Hart as his chief of police in September, 1976. Hart had worked his way up through the ranks. Philip G. Tannian, Hart's white predecessor, ran afoul of Young for not informing him about a secret DEA investigation of possible high-level police drug corruption involving the mayor's brother-in-law, Willie Volsan. The mayor fired Tannian and replaced him with the man who once collared him for working in the numbers racket—William Hart. Tannian had been sworn to secrecy but that didn't matter to Young. He demanded to know anything and everything police-related that might involve his family or relatives.

Hart realized he owed his new job as police chief to his predecessor's failure to keep Young informed. Young's demand for police information involving his family would become a key issue in the Richard Wershe, Jr. story.

Sixteen years after he was named Chief of Police in Detroit, Hart would be convicted in federal court on charges he embezzled over two million dollars from a secret police fund intended for the War on Drugs. Hart's embezzlement trial is explored in more detail in Chapter 16.

In his days as an illegal numbers runner, Coleman Young got to know another young black gambling racketeer named Willie Clyde Volsan. Both men are deceased so there is no way of knowing the details of how they came to know one another. What we do know is Young moved on to a job in the organized labor movement and eventually got in to politics. Volsan remained in the criminal underworld his entire life. He was in the numbers rackets for years. When heroin became a money-making ghetto commodity, Volsan got involved.

In the 1970s, Volsan was publicly linked to Kenneth Garrett, a major white heroin dealer. DEA surveillance agents observed that Garrett was a frequent patron at a lounge owned by Coleman Young and his brother. Willie Volsan was believed to be selling heroin at the lounge but no charges were ever brought against him.

Volsan always seemed to lurk on the fringes of Detroit's crime community and made money doing it. He had the savvy, or luck, or both, to avoid getting caught by the police.

Eventually, Coleman Young and Willie Volsan were related through marriage. Juanita Clark, one of the mayor's sisters, became Volsan's common-law wife. They had a daughter, Cathy Volsan, who was said to be the mayor's favorite niece. In the 1980s and 90s, Willie Volsan and his daughter Cathy would figure prominently in the life of Richard Wershe, Jr.

Volsan played all the angles. In the 1970s, he was an FBI informant. Media reports speculated he was spying on Young. Agents familiar with Volsan's snitching say he was reporting on black organized crime figures. Volsan apparently thought this would win friends in the FBI. He was wrong.

Coleman Young was not paranoid in his distrust of the FBI. They <u>were</u> out to get him—for decades. "He viewed us as the enemy and we viewed him as a priority investigative target," is the way retired FBI special agent Herman Groman describes the lifelong struggle between Young and federal law enforcement.

Young was defiant when called to testify in 1952 before the House Un-American Activities Committee (HUAC) during the Red Scare hearings. When asked if was or ever had been a Communist, Young said "…I have no purpose being here as a stool pigeon." It was street slang for a police informant. That alone was enough to put Young permanently on the radar of J. Edgar Hoover's FBI.

When Young was elected mayor, he gave a speech that accelerated white flight. Young said: "I issue a warning to all those pushers, to all rip-off artists, to all muggers: It's time to leave Detroit; hit Eight Mile Road!" Young went on: "And I don't give a damn if they are black or white, or if they wear Superfly suits or blue uniforms with silver badges. Hit the road!" Eight Mile Rd. is the dividing line between Detroit and suburbia.

Many white citizens interpreted it as a warning to get out of town. They did, by the thousands.

A fact that has been under-reported over the years is that uncounted numbers of Detroit's middle-class blacks hit the road for the suburbs, too. Like whites, they were not just fleeing crime. Declining property values and rising taxes were factors, too. Young raised income taxes to cover the loss of taxes from businesses that had abandoned the city after the riots. Hammering individuals and homeowners with higher taxes gained nothing. Those who left Detroit—white and black—took a sizeable chunk of the city's tax base with them.

Young was unapologetic about what his white critics viewed as a reverse-racism, anti-white attitude. Detroit was on its way to becoming one of the mostly racially divided big cities in the nation.

One of Young's contradictions was his fondness for hobnobbing privately with wealthy white men. Publicly, Young scorned the mostly-white suburbs, yet he was known to quietly slip away to dine in the private rooms of pricey suburban restaurants with men like industrialist and business magnate Max Fisher, a liberal Republican. Young was forever searching for splashy building projects requiring big money, as the infrastructure of the city fell apart around him.

Despite the massive white and black migration out of Detroit, the criminals Young referred to in his inaugural address, didn't hit the road. They stayed.

Young's "reform" of the police department seemed limited to hiring and promoting blacks. Police corruption escalated substantially during the Young years. In May, 1988, for example, the *Detroit News* reported some 100 Detroit police officers were under investigation at one time for narcotics corruption. The article quoted a veteran cop as saying, "Some nights it's like the Wild West out there, but our guys (police) are the ones doing the robbing."

Corruption was rampant in other city departments, too. Young's attitude about graft and bribe-taking among his mostly-black appointees seemed to be: 'It's our turn.'

Many of the FBI agents assigned to Detroit in that era would agree that Young had an 'It's our turn' attitude about looting the city's finances.

"Detroit has been and continues to be the gold standard for public corruption in the United States," said Gregg Schwarz, a retired FBI agent who worked briefly with Rick Wershe, Jr. in the late 1980s. "Mayors, city officials, judges, police, it's all there."

As the scandals, budget mismanagement and the occasional convictions piled up, it is reasonable to say Coleman Young ran a corrupt administration. But the belief by many—mostly white—that Coleman Young was personally on the take has never been proven. The suspicion that Young was corrupt was largely a self-inflicted wound. He didn't seem to pay much attention to those in his administration who had their hand in the cookie jar, as long as the thieves showed loyalty to him. The FBI, for its part, thought they almost had Young for kickbacks on a lucrative city sludge hauling contract in the 80s, but they couldn't accumulate enough evidence to be sure a jury would agree. As will be shown in another important Detroit case, the Justice Department attitude was, don't indict unless you're absolutely sure you're going to convict. Young was never prosecuted by the federal government.

Police corruption in Detroit and many other cities increased as illegal drugs flooded the streets. It was similar to the nation's experience with cops on the take during Prohibition. The year Young took office, the local prosecutor and a county grand jury indicted 12 Detroit police officers and 14 civilians on charges they conspired to sell heroin in Detroit's 10th police precinct in the heart of the ghetto. The civilian defendants included dope gangsters like Milton "Happy" Battle, George "Texas Slim" Dudley and Harold "Boo" Turner. Other characters in the case had names like Snitchin' Bill and Alabama Red McNeal. The latter had an entrepreneurial flair. According to prosecution court documents: *"McNeal posted signs on telephone poles saying, 'Buy one cap, get a free dinner,' signed Alabama Red. When the heroin consumer purchased the narcotics, he was treated to barbecue spare ribs, potato salad, pork*

*and beans and white bread, with a Sunday special of turkey
and dressing."*

The prosecution said the 10th Precinct Conspiracy,
controlled by corrupt narcs, was a total service enterprise:
"Besides selling narcotics, they would sell and rent needles
and droppers to the users, provide 'hit men' to find the
veins of those addicts who could not do it by themselves,
and were prepared to give emergency medical treatment in
case of an overdose."

The prosecution claimed the 10th Precinct narcotics
crew conspired with favored heroin dealers like Battle and
McNeal to raid the dope houses of competitors and drive
them out of business in exchange for payoffs from their co-
defendants. Most of the accused were convicted, including
the white precinct narcotics crew chief, Sgt. Rudy Davis.

I covered the trial aggressively, much to the irritation
of the defendants. One of them was named Bobby Neeley.

During a court break one day, Neeley, a dope gangster
who always dressed the part, sauntered up to me with a
wicked grin on his face.

"Hey, Vince," Neeley said. You wanna join the pool,
man?"

"What pool is that, Bobby?" I asked.

His face turned menacing.

"The pool on when you're gonna get hit, muthafucka."

This was a test. A verbal mano-a-mano test to see if I
would flinch.

"Sure, Bobby," I said, pretending to reach for my
wallet. I managed a grin of my own.

"I'll take some of that action," I said. I paused for a beat, then continued with a serious demeanor of my own: "But you better get it right the first time, mutha."

Neeley broke out laughing. He bent over, slapped his leg, gave me a big grin and walked away. We got along after that.

Over time it became obvious the police corruption exposed in the 10th Precinct case was not an anomaly. Street crime flourished and police complicity in the drug trade did not stop with the 10th Precinct convictions.

Not everyone charged in the 10th Precinct case went on trial. Chester Wheeler Campbell eluded capture for a long time. Campbell was a stone-cold hitman. He was a middle-aged black man with a salt-and-pepper goatee, always stylishly dressed, but with a blood-chilling gaze. He had a fearsome reputation. The word on the street was he was gunning for Wiley Reed, the star prosecution witness in the case.

One night, Campbell's luck ran out on a twisting suburban road adjacent to a major lake. It was 3:30 in the morning and Campbell had been drinking. He was a black man in a Cadillac in lily-white suburban lake country. He side-swiped a police patrol car. The cop did a fast U-turn. Campbell tried to escape but his car hit a bridge abutment. The shaken cop saw a semi-automatic .45 caliber pistol on the front seat of Campbell's car.

Other cops arrived quickly. Impulsively, they searched Campbell's vehicle and opened the trunk. They were stunned. Campbell had two pistols, a sawed-off shotgun, surveillance equipment, transcripts of secret grand jury testimony and 29 notebooks including more than 300 names of drug figures and some murder victims accompanied by crude drawings of birds with the eyes x'ed out.

More disturbing was the fact the notebooks contained the names, home addresses, unlisted phone numbers and the names of family members of numerous narcotics cops. Included were descriptions of the officers' personal vehicles and in some cases what churches they attended. The cops at the Chester Campbell traffic stop were so rattled by what they found they decided they should get a legal search warrant.

One of the names in Chester Campbell's notebooks was mine. There was a notation that read, "Vince Wade— TV 7—case conspiracy." At his arraignment, I asked Campbell why my name was in his notebooks. He said he wanted to "assess my credibility." The prosecutor allowed my cameraman to film the notebook and the page with my name in it. It made quite an impression on TV viewers. For years afterward, people would stop me occasionally and ask: "Weren't you the reporter in the hitman's notebook?" Contract murderer Chester Campbell, now deceased, did a lot for my career.

Despite all his swagger and street-guy posturing, ("I'm the head muthafucka in charge.") Coleman Young was just as powerless as any white politician in bringing street crime under control. It was on Coleman Young's watch that the Motor City came to be known as the Murder City.

Rick Wershe, Jr. grew up against this backdrop of rampant crime on the streets of Coleman Young's Detroit.

When Richard Wershe, Jr. was in grade school, heroin—often pronounced hair-oh-wahn in the ghetto— was the narcotic of choice in the inner city. In the Detroit of the 1970s, drug-related murders were as plentiful as burned-out houses.

There were so many murders in Detroit, my TV news director, the late Phil Nye, got the idea to do a daily body count report on the evening news for a year. He assigned a camera crew and me to an early weekday schedule to coincide with the day shift of the Wayne County morgue.

When the morgue wagon showed up at its first assignment of the morning, we were there, too. The year we were on the weekday morgue wagon beat we reported on over 380 dead bodies. The Detroit body count for the year was much higher than the total in my assignment log because many murders occurred on Friday and Saturday nights.

That year I learned the importance of keeping a jar of Vicks VapoRub and a small packet of tissues in my briefcase. The stench from a rotting human body can be so overpowering it can cause you to vomit involuntarily. A way around such a fate is to pack your nose, really pack it, with Vicks VapoRub jelly if you are anywhere near a decaying body. After you depart the scene, you use tissues to clean the mentholated petroleum jelly out of your nostrils. Even the cadaver business has its tricks of the trade.

Detroit—the Motor City turned Murder City—had daily body-bag proof that the War on Drugs was failing.

There was an episode in 1980 that had a significant impact on police thinking and attitudes in Detroit during the Coleman Young years. It likely had an effect on an important homicide case in 1985 in which Richard Wershe, Jr. was the FBI's key informant.

Prisoner of War:
The Story of White Boy Rick and The War on Drugs

In January, 1980, several of Mayor Young's relatives were involved in a parking altercation requiring police intervention. Mayor Young's sisters, Bernice Grier and Juanita Volsan, and Grier's daughter, Sidni Jacobs, got in to a dispute over an apartment building assigned parking spot. Jacobs was being evicted from the apartment building. The police were called twice. When they arrived the second time, the mayor's relatives became belligerent and combative. The police started putting Sidni Jacobs in handcuffs and a confrontation ensued. Jacobs punched an officer and kicked him in the groin. The two older women tried to block the arrest and they, too, were arrested. All three were taken to the local police precinct.

The apartment owner told the police Ms. Jacobs had bragged she was carrying a gun, so as a precaution, the women were forced to disrobe down to their underwear and they were strip-searched for weapons by two female officers, and then held in custody. There was a mix of black and white police officers involved in the incident.

Detroit city government went a little berserk that night. The police precinct commander, Anthony Fiermonti, was called at home where he was recovering from a head injury and ordered by a deputy chief to go to the precinct immediately. TV news crews descended on the precinct police station. Fiermonti ordered the women held until he could get there. There were conflicting orders from police headquarters and the mayor's office. Do not parade the women before the TV cameras, but release them immediately.

Mayor Young's female relatives were fond of behaving like royalty—rude, ill-mannered royalty. They didn't have to follow the rules everyone else followed. They were relatives of *The Mayor*.

If they received tickets for expired parking meters, speeding, even reckless driving, the tickets were routinely fixed by loyal police officers.

Commander Fiermonti was highly regarded by his fellow cops and the 12th Precinct citizens, black and white. He had received the Spirit of Detroit award from the city council. Many citizens spoke out in Fiermonti's behalf. It didn't make any difference. Mayor Young ordered Fiermonti demoted two ranks and a police lieutenant and sergeant were also busted down in rank. Several officers were suspended without pay.

Several months later the demotion was rescinded and Fiermonti was allowed to take a disability retirement at the rank of commander.

Fiermonti's ordeal with the Mayor's relatives and the firing of the police chief a few years earlier for not informing Young that someone in his family was under federal investigation for drug trafficking, sent a powerful message to the Detroit Police Department.

The Mayor's family was above the law.

The Mayor was to be fully informed no matter what investigative secrecy rules applied. Any law enforcement trouble for the Mayor's family was likely a career-ender.

Sidni Jacobs eventually discovered her uncle's power stopped at the city limits.

Sgt. James Harris, mentioned earlier as a STRESS officer, was by 1980 a homicide detective who sometimes did dual-duty as a trouble-fixer for the mayor's family. Harris eventually got caught up in an FBI corruption investigation as detailed in Chapter 16.

Harris told me he was ordered on one occasion to travel to Puerto Rico to bail Sidni Jacobs out of jail. He traveled, he said, using funds provided to him from the Detroit Police Secret Service Fund, which was earmarked strictly for narcotics enforcement. Harris said Jacobs had been stopped for speeding and got arrogant and belligerent with the Puerto Rican cop who pulled her over. He threw her in jail.

Using police department narcotics enforcement funds to bail the mayor's mouthy niece out of jail in Puerto Rico was illegal. But this was Detroit and this was the mayor's family. And Mayor Coleman Young was the absolute ruler of Detroit.

Chapter 6 – A Coast to Coast Snowstorm

"I said no to drugs but they just wouldn't listen"
— Joke mocking Nancy Reagan's 'Just Say No' campaign against drugs

Through most of the 1970s, heroin was the "serious" narcotic of choice in the world of illicit drugs. Even so, politicians and law enforcement kept flogging marijuana. Mainstream Americans had been convinced by relentless political propaganda and unquestioning media coverage that pot use was rampant among the under-21 crowd and posed an ominous danger. President Nixon had appointed the bi-partisan Shafer Commission to examine the problem, but when the Commission recommended that personal use of marijuana be decriminalized, Nixon rejected the recommendation as did some powerful conservative parents' groups.

As the 1980s began, Gallup national opinion surveys showed most Americans didn't rate drugs high on the list of national problems, but just as in the Prohibition era, significant numbers in the heartland *wanted* to believe it was so. White America was ready to believe reports of an "epidemic" of marijuana because many had experienced their kids smoking pot. They took comfort of sorts in the belief that the family pot smoker was swept up in a national crisis. Politicians were only too willing to propose tougher laws and law enforcement.

For the police, marijuana was easier to pursue because it was so plentiful. Marijuana was like bootleg booze in Prohibition—it was everywhere. Nixon's Silent Majority didn't like it because they associated it with the habits, the music and the political/social views of blacks, Latinos and liberal young whites.

In the latter half of the 70s, Hollywood stars and other lesser luminaries in the film and music industries discovered the potent high of smoking cocaine in a process known as free basing. Users described the high as more intense than snorting powdered cocaine, but the buzz was shorter. Freebasers who indulge frequently can't wait to do it again. And again. And again. Perhaps the most famous example was the late comedian Richard Pryor who once spent several days free basing. He reached for a cognac bottle on a table and casually poured the liquor all over himself. As he went to light up another hit of freebase cocaine, the cognac caught fire and Pryor ran out of his house and down the street in flames. He died of a heart attack in 2005.

Even Santa Claus got caught up in the infatuation with cocaine. More specifically, actor/comedian Tim Allen, who became famous for playing Santa Claus in the movies, was busted in 1978 in the Kalamazoo/Battle Creek, Michigan airport with about a pound and a half of coke. Like so many dopers before and since, Allen pleaded guilty and rolled over in a plea deal. He was facing a possible life prison term, but he snitched on others who were involved with him in the cocaine biz and he received a sentence of three to seven years. He did two years in a federal penitentiary in Minnesota.

As the 70s gave way to the 80s, cocaine was leaving heroin in its dust as America's favorite illicit drug of choice. The big players changed from the Mafia, with its Corsican smuggling connections in Marseilles and heroin producers in Turkey to another ethnic group: Latinos. More specifically, Colombians and Cubans in Miami. Central and South America was where cocaine was sourced.

Miami began to resemble the Wild West as traffickers fought for market dominance and control. In the summer of 1979, gunmen in an armored "war wagon", a van with gun portals and a sign proclaiming Happy Time Party Supplies, rolled up to Miami's popular Dadeland Mall on a Wednesday afternoon. Gunmen bailed out, entered a liquor store, and began firing submachine guns, killing two men and wounding several store employees. The drug execution murders made national headlines. The *Chicago Tribune* called it the Shootout at the Cocaine Corral, a cynical play on the famous Gunfight at the OK Corral in Tombstone, Arizona in 1881.

Investigators learned the brazen hit at the shopping mall was ordered by Griselda Blanco, a grandmotherly Colombian woman who came to be known as the Cocaine Godmother. The terms godmother and grandmotherly fit Blanco only if those words conjure up a corpulent, jowly sociopath who viewed murder as the way to resolve problems with interpersonal relationships. She was implicated in a minimum of 40 slayings, including the deaths of three of her husbands. Some investigators estimate the number of hits she ordered was closer to 200. Blanco is said to have developed the motorcycle drive-by shooting as an assassination technique.

The woman known as a "queenpin", as opposed to a kingpin, was a pioneer of the cocaine trade in Miami. Her murderous rise to underworld power was partly behind the term "cocaine cowboys." She named one of her sons Michael Corleone, after one of the Mafia characters in *The Godfather* book and movies. She was busted by the DEA for drug trafficking and sent to prison for a long stretch where she continued to run her drug empire. Local authorities eventually charged her with three murders, but the case collapsed due to prosecutorial misconduct. In 2004, Blanco was deported to Colombia. She was gunned down in 2012 in Medellín, Colombia by an assassin who put two bullets in her head. The hitman was riding a motorcycle.

As the 1980s arrived, there was a change of administrations in Washington and a massive transformation in political attitude. It was the "morning in America" decade of Ronald Reagan.

The man adored and revered as Saint Ronnie by many conservatives was worthy of his nickname, the Great Communicator. He gave motivating speeches. He understood the power of images. But his deeds didn't always line up with his rhetoric.

For example, many of his fans fondly remember President Reagan as a "law and order" President. This was helped in no small part by his days as a movie actor. A publicity photo from one film shows Reagan in Old West attire with a six gun in one hand, a double-barreled shotgun in the other and a Deputy U.S. Marshal badge on his chest.

Yet, when he moved in to the White House, Reagan and his team took an axe to the budget, including federal law enforcement funding. "Government is not the solution to our problem; government is the problem," Reagan said in his first inaugural address.

As a result of Reagan's wide-ranging shrink-the-government crusade, DEA agents in Detroit resorted to digging in their own pockets for gas for their government cars. Agents on TDY—Temporary Duty—had to sleep on cots and one team from out of town reportedly used a hot plate to cook meals. Reagan's DEA didn't have any money for travel expenses. Reagan's budget cutters had chopped $35 million out of appropriations for the primary federal law enforcement troops in the on-again, off-again War on Drugs. The story was the same in other federal agencies. BATF, the Bureau of Alcohol, Tobacco and Firearms, was so starved for operating funds that agents in several field offices backed out of undercover buys of dynamite, machine guns and plastic explosives because they didn't have the cash.

President Reagan, seemingly unaware of the disconnect between his budget cutting and the cost of fighting crime, gave a speech in New Orleans in September raising the specter of what he termed "the ominous growth of crime in our nation."

"Crime is an epidemic," Reagan said, invoking one of America's favorite scare words. "It takes the lives of 25,000 Americans..."

That same year, in contrast, auto accidents claimed 49,301 lives—nearly double the number who lost their lives to crime. It didn't matter to the Reagan White House. The President wanted to significantly reduce the Federal government's role in highway safety, anyway.

If crime was an epidemic, drugs were the enforcement-resistant superbug. In November of 1981 the Knight-Ridder newspapers published a ten- years-later investigative report on the War on Drugs. "The federal drug effort—expensive, elaborate and well publicized—has been a multi-billion-dollar bust, a lopsided victory for the bad guys," the newspapers reported.

The Reagan Administration decided the answer was more of the same thing that had not been working, only in

Vince Wade

stronger doses. In December, the Military Cooperation with Civilian Law Enforcement Agencies Act was passed. The Posse Comitatus Act, which limits military intervention in domestic affairs, was amended to permit the military to join in the War on Drugs.

In 1982, Reagan's budget cutters took a back seat to the something-evil-is-going-to-get-you-if-we-don't-kick-ass law and order crowd.

In January, the White House announced the FBI was going to be the lead law enforcement agency in the War on Drugs. The DEA would report to the FBI.

The rival agencies would have concurrent jurisdiction for narcotics enforcement. A federal law enforcement tug of war was created that same day.

The same month, it was announced that a new South Florida Task Force would be created to stanch the flow of drugs pouring in to the country through the Sunshine state. Vice President George H.W. Bush was named to chair this bold new anti-drug project.

The South Florida Task Force was hastily conceived by politicians who were in a we-gotta-do-something frame of mind. The Task Force got off to a rocky start and its path stayed rocky.

Nothing gets the American public's attention like a shocking incident involving someone famous. Comic actor John Belushi reminded the nation that drugs were still a problem in March of 1982 when he died as a result of an injection called a speedball—a combination of heroin and cocaine.

In August, the move to involve the military in drug
interdiction took another step when Defense Secretary
Casper Weinberger gave the Navy authorization to join the
endless battle.

In October of 1982 Reagan declared drugs were a
threat to national security. Speaking in a national radio
address the President said: "We've taken down the
surrender flag and run up the battle flag." He added:
"Drugs are bad and we're going after them. And we're
going to win the war on drugs."

President Reagan shared the microphone with his wife,
Nancy. "I have to tell you," Mrs. Reagan said, "that few
things in my life have frightened me as much as the drug
epidemic among our children." The term "epidemic", when
paired with drugs and crime, got a real workout during the
Reagan years. The news media loved the word because it
gave urgency to any story that used it. Thus, reporters and
editors like it when politicians use "epidemic" to
characterize a growing problem. It lends itself to scare
headlines in the papers and ominous teaser lines by TV and
radio news anchors.

In remarks at the Justice Department later that month,
President Reagan affirmed Nixon's War on Drugs. It was
now the Reagan War on Drugs. He called for the formation
of 13 regional law enforcement drug task forces, patterned
after the largely unsuccessful South Florida Task Force. He
again used the word "epidemic" to describe the nation's
crime problem. In this speech, Reagan said the number of
lives lost to crime was 20,000. The previous year he said it
was 25,000. No one seemed to notice the President was
saying there had been a significant reduction in crime-
related fatalities. The media focused, instead, on the
"epidemic."

Reagan called for two significant changes that would escalate the War on Drugs. One was a plan to enlist the nation's governors in the battle to push for tougher state-level drug laws. The other was a suggestion for upping the stakes in federal laws for those prosecuted for drug crimes. He called for reforms of criminal statutes "dealing with bail, sentencing and criminal forfeiture." This was the opening salvo in what would eventually become a mass incarceration frenzy that devastated an entire generation of young minority men.

By 1983 the Democrats decided they couldn't let the Republicans dominate such a fertile campaign issue as the nation's drug abuse problem. Democrats viewed the Republican anti-drug efforts as splintered and unfocused. Their view was bolstered by a non-partisan General Accounting Office (GAO) report to the President essentially stating the War on Drugs was being lost. The GAO noted lack of coordination and antagonism between the competing federal law enforcement entities. The analysis noted the price of illegal drugs was dropping across the nation because the supply had increased.

Senator Joe Biden of Delaware jumped in the fray with legislation to create a federal Drug Czar, a bureaucrat with power over the entire federal anti-drug effort. President Reagan vetoed the legislation.

Like their predecessors in the Prohibition era, the anti-drug crusaders were not deterred by facts. California, under an ostensibly liberal governor, Edmund "Jerry" Brown, launched a storm-trooper-like program to wipe out clandestine marijuana growing operations in remote areas. The project known as CAMP—Campaign Against Marijuana Planting—featured law enforcement narcs and

Prisoner of War:
The Story of White Boy Rick and The War on Drugs

National Guardsmen crisscrossing the skies in helicopters, looking for marijuana plants to eradicate.

But the militarization of the War on Drugs didn't stop at helicopter sorties. The CAMP program deployed an Air Force U-2 spy plane to fly over northern California looking for marijuana crops. The surveillance aircraft, used in the Cuban missile crisis and flyovers of the Soviet Union at the height of the Cold War, wasn't looking for secret stores of heroin or clandestine cocaine production labs. It was deployed to find patches of marijuana plants in rural California. Page 12 of a 1984 report on CAMP operations contains a footnote about the program's expenditures. It says simply "$500,000 for U2 cost."

Ronald Reagan was a man of his times and his times included the nationwide Red Scare of the late 40s and early 50s. The late Senator Joe McCarthy was looking for Commies under every rock and behind every tree, as the saying goes. He had help from patriotic Americans like Ronald Reagan, who, it must be remembered, was FBI informant T-10 in Los Angeles. Reagan was staunchly anti-Communist all of his adult life. He, along with many others, saw Capitalism and Communism locked in a fight to the death. At stake was nothing less than which ideology would rule the planet.

When Reagan won the White House, it wasn't surprising that he was concerned with the Socialist movements afoot in Central America. He was worried about a Communist domino effect in America's back yard. The Nicaraguan Sandinistas were of particular concern because they were being supported by Communist Cuba and indirectly by the Soviet Union.

The Central Intelligence Agency, as it always does, got involved in the anti-Communist machinations in the region. It was done without Congressional approval. This irritated many in Congress, and in late 1982 the first so-called Boland Amendment was passed, prohibiting the use of U.S. funds to support a military effort by Nicaragua's Contras to overthrow that nation's leftist government. But the amendment had a huge loophole. It allowed U.S. aid to the Contras for other purposes. Suddenly, "humanitarian" aid for the Contras became a big thing in the Reagan White House. As the Detroit FBI would learn, the airlifts to the Contras also aided the importation of tons of drugs into the United States, as explained in Chapter 10.

In the early 1980s, crack swept through the drug user community of every big city in America, including Detroit. Powdered cocaine was favored by upper income whites, but the cost put it out of reach of most ghetto-dwellers. Crack, on the other hand, was the poor man's cocaine.

The Drug Enforcement Administration (DEA) reports the first crack house was discovered in Miami in 1982 but its significance was not immediately recognized. Caribbean immigrants taught the drug crowd in Miami how to cook cocaine with another mixing agent and turn it in to "rocks" that were called "crack." The rocks could be smoked, producing an intense high. The amount of cocaine needed was far less than the amount snorted from silver spoons by the partying white users. The profit margin on crack was stunning.

Community leaders described the popularity and use of crack as an epidemic—that favorite word again. Before long, there were demands from many quarters that law enforcement *do* something. They did. The War on Drugs shifted into a higher gear.

Prisoner of War:
The Story of White Boy Rick and The War on Drugs

As every federal employee knows, grand policy pronouncements in Washington seldom work as promised in the world west of the Potomac River. That was certainly true in Detroit when the FBI was given concurrent drug enforcement jurisdiction with the DEA.

The FBI had been investigating prescription drug fraud—pill cases—as part of its prosecution of white-collar crimes. But street drugs were a different matter entirely. Agency founder J. Edgar Hoover had resisted FBI involvement with drugs because he felt the potential for corruption was too great. Many of the old hands in the FBI agreed with "Jedgar" and shuddered at the thought of the Bureau getting its hands soiled interacting with the dirt bags of the dope business.

Younger agents, however, saw narcotics enforcement as a chance for some excitement, adventure and real police work. Unlike the old-school agents, many in the new generation didn't come to the job with law or accounting degrees. A number had been cops in local police departments for several years before applying for a more prestigious position as an FBI agent. That was the story with Herman "Herm" Groman an FBI special agent who played a key role in the Rick Wershe saga.

Agent Groman was assigned to the Detroit Division of the FBI just as the Bureau was getting concurrent drug jurisdiction with the DEA. Groman brought some experience with drug investigations to the job. Before joining the FBI, he had worked as an investigator for the Ohio Attorney General's office. His work had included drug cases and some undercover work. When he arrived in

Detroit, with drug investigations fresh on the FBI's plate, it made sense to assign Groman to the new drug squad.

Groman was an innovative and resourceful agent, but he and the FBI's rules and regulations only had a passing acquaintance. This got him in serious trouble from time to time in an organization that values a by-the-book work ethic. Groman played a key role in the adventures and misadventures of Rick Wershe, Jr. over the years, so it's worth profiling him.

One agent was in a unique position to see the highlights and lowlights of Groman's time in the Detroit Division.

Special Agent John Anthony (retired) was the Principal Legal Advisor, or PLA, for the Detroit FBI during this era. In his role as an FBI consigliere, Anthony was "in on" every important case and many personnel decisions. Anthony shakes his head and rolls his eyes upward when asked about Herm Groman.

"Rules and Herm are an oxymoron, if that's the way to say it," Anthony said, laughing. "Herm operated on a different wavelength. His whole career was right on the edge. (But) he's a great investigator. I like him."

In Anthony's view, Groman's excellent case work came at a price, administratively. "If I was his supervisor I would be extremely nervous," Anthony said, putting himself rhetorically in a supervisor's position. "He would have a short leash. There was nothing good that could happen from an administrative standpoint. He was a great investigator...(but) you'd be up at night wondering, 'What the hell is that sonofabitch doin'? Here I am and I don't have enough time in to get a pension." Anthony broke out in a big laugh at the thought, then continued. "Yet, the end result was always positive. I mean it was great. Great

information, great cases. Everything you'd want as a
supervisor, but getting to that point would drive you nuts.
That's why God invented Jack Daniels, because of guys
like Herm Groman."

Complicating matters was a mandate from Washington
to encourage local police departments to join the federal
War on Drugs. In designated cities like Detroit, Organized
Crime Drug Enforcement Task Forces were established
with minimal planning and minimal consultation between
the feds and the locals. Washington loves acronyms and the
term Organized Crime Drug Enforcement Task Force was
shortened to OCDETF, pronounced Oh-seh-Def.

The Hollywood image of the work space of a police
task force often features an abandoned warehouse with
stark industrial lighting, dark metal desks, large bulletin
boards festooned with notes and mug shots. Plus, empty
pizza boxes—an essential prop.

Compare that image with the Detroit OCDETF Task
Force, which didn't have any work space at all. It was
nothing more than a title bestowed upon an FBI supervisor
who already had a squad to manage. Agents and police
officers "assigned" to the OCDETF Task Force worked
from the desks they already had in their respective
workplaces. There was no action-filled room in an
abandoned warehouse. There were no empty pizza boxes.

Inserting the FBI in the War on Drugs was no easy
task. There was a learning curve. Groman remembers there
was a disconnect between headquarters marching orders
regarding the newly bestowed jurisdiction over drug
crimes, and the reality on the streets. FBI HQ said the
Detroit Division should focus on heroin cases.

"We were trying to develop these heroin cases," Groman said. "And really the problem was cocaine, more specifically crack cocaine. It was a brand-new type of drug that was on the street. I remember we would debrief informants and they would talk about crack, and somehow, we ended up thinking they were saying cracks. (We wondered) What the heck is cracks? Eventually we figured out that it was crack (cocaine) that they were talking about."

Bureau old-timers must have been dismayed beyond words when Washington added narcotics investigations to the FBI portfolio. Not only was the FBI spiraling downhill because it now had drug investigations, but the prestigious law enforcement agency had to somehow get along with DEA agents; lesser mortals from another federal cop shop. Even worse, (in the view of some) these mighty special agents of the Federal Bureau of Investigation were being told to work with local cops. The locals! What the hell! The FBI investigated and prosecuted local cops from time to time for public corruption. Now, with the Task Force mandate, local cops would be entering sacred FBI office space. It was bureaucratic blasphemy. Outsiders in the inner offices of the FBI just...wasn't...done.

"There was a lot of distrust," Groman said with abundant understatement. "We eventually did overcome those distrust issues and mainly it was because we developed friendships. Once we developed friendships and we were able to trust one another, we were able to successfully move forward with what we needed to do, and that was the mission of attacking the drug problem in Detroit."

What Groman said is true, up to a point. I covered Detroit law enforcement for years. Individual federal agents and local cops did develop good personal relationships from time to time, like professional athletes on rival sports teams. But on the playing field or basketball court or the gritty streets where crime festers, the teams, or law enforcement agencies, often dislike one another and compete fiercely. Some law enforcement agencies barely tolerate one another, but they are bound by the common bond of badges and guns and a mandate to uphold the law. It's always a hoot to see law enforcement news conferences where the heads of various agencies stand together, stiffly, telling the cameras they worked together to solve the big case du jour. In some cases, it's true.

The Task Force undoubtedly sounded like a good idea—in Washington. In the field, it had more failures than successes.

At the end of 1983 the GAO issued a report questioning the effectiveness of the OCDETF task forces. "...although task forces may be successful in destroying organizations, the potential profit in the business and continued drug availability and demand draw others into the business," the GAO report said. In other words, the illegal drug trade was (and remains) such a lucrative racket there was always someone waiting in the shadows to replace "Mr. Big" if Mr. Big was sent to prison. The War on Drugs is an endless game of whack-a-mole, with or without drug task forces.

In Detroit, the OCEDETF Task Force proved to be problematic in a big way in the case of soon-to-be FBI informant Richard Wershe, Jr. Before it was all over, the OCDETF case in which Wershe was the key informant resulted in crisis meetings at the very top echelons of the FBI and Justice Department. The meeting topic: what to do about the informant named Wershe.

While Special Agent Groman was chipping away at the ice floe between the Detroit offices of the FBI and DEA, another aggressive young FBI agent, William Don Tisaby, was doing his part in the War on Drugs out on the streets. Tisaby, who is black, grew up on Detroit's east side. He knew the city. He knew where the street players, the people of the night, hung out. He had family who knew about the streets, too.

Tisaby, now retired, embraced the FBI's new drug crimes authority and hit a home run in his first time at bat. He built a significant case against a doper named Gloyd Tyrone Singer and 23 others. They were indicted in a cocaine conspiracy. Singer was loosely associated with Frank "Frank Nitti" Usher, a ruthless drug dealer who became infamous in Detroit as a result of a triple murder at a ghetto club where the victims were beheaded. Usher's nickname came from a notorious Prohibition-era Chicago gangster, Francesco Raffaele Nitto—Frank Nitti—who was the top enforcer for Al Capone.

While working on the Singer case, Tisaby met Mae Mack, a woman who would become one of his most valuable informants. Ms. Mack, was the owner of Steppin' Out, a clothing store patronized by the wives and girlfriends of the biggest dope dealers in town.

Mae Mack seemed to know everybody in the Detroit drug underworld. She was not, however, a paid informant. She was what the FBI calls a Cooperating Witness. Mack would meet with Tisaby at McDonald's restaurants to pass along information, which was always free. She was never paid for her information. Tisaby recalled Ms. Mack always ordered a Big Mac. It wasn't lost on Tisaby that his snitch was a woman named Mack who was fond of eating Big Macs.

"Her information was always so precise and so distinct," Tisaby said. It enabled him to blend in at the doper's favorite night spots because he knew who everyone was. Mae Mack's information enabled him to develop a Who's Who of the Detroit drug trade.

Tisaby worked at keeping Mae Mack's cooperation confidential. One day, Tisaby says he was called to the U.S. Attorney's office. Mae Mack was there with an assistant United States attorney and a DEA agent. They wanted her to testify before a federal grand jury on a drug case, something she had never done. She trusted Tisaby and wanted his advice. Tisaby worried that such a move would expose her. Federal grand jury activity is not as secret as the government and the courts like to pretend.

"They turned around and burned her," Tisaby said. "They had a leak in the United States Attorney's Office then," Tisaby said. "I think it was a secretary."

A few weeks later Mae Mack was gunned down while trying to make a phone call in a convenience store near her dress shop. She was shot with an Uzi-type machine pistol. Some federal agents who knew her said Mae Mack put herself at risk by talking to too many people about the drug trade. Some say her estranged husband, Charles "Chuckie" Hardaway ordered the hit. The two filed for a divorce the previous month. Don Tisaby believes sloppy confidentiality by others in the federal criminal justice system led to her death. Chuckie Hardaway was shot to death some years later.

Tisaby's cover story was that he was David Louis Green, a recruiter of "runners" for shady doctors, pharmacists and clinic operators who were illegally peddling prescription drugs. The hardcore drug dealers

Vince Wade

accepted that he wasn't pushing cocaine or heroin. They
bought his story that he was in the illegal pill business. He
was in a different part of the narcotics trade, but they
thought he was a criminal who was in the know, so he was
cool.

Before long, Tisaby developed a drug intelligence
dossier with fodder for new cases for the Detroit FBI. "I
wasn't trying to be a player but I (got to know) most of the
players involved," Tisaby said. Tisaby rattled off some of
the big names of the Detroit drug scene of the 1980s. "I ran
in to Chuckie Hardaway, one of the main guys on the east
side," Tisaby recalls. "I ran in to Demetrius Holloway,
(Terrance) Boogaloo Brown, Maserati Rick (Carter), all
them folks."

Agent Tisaby quickly realized he couldn't frequent the
gangster hangouts alone. A guy by himself raised
eyebrows. It didn't fit the macho culture. The dope
gangsters would make the after-dark scene with sexy,
bling-bedecked women on their arm. A partyer by himself
would make the dopers wonder. So Tisaby enlisted the help
of Janis Famous, a female agent in the FBI office. Agent
Famous worked at various times on the FBI white-collar
crime and public corruption squads. At Tisaby's request,
she occasionally worked nights to help him with his club
prowling. Her cover story was that she was Tisaby's
fiancé, but she was attending medical school in New York
so she was only in town on occasion. Famous was from
New York so she could easily talk about the Big Apple if
anyone asked her about it. One piece of tradecraft
undercover agents use is to concoct cover stories about
themselves with elements they are familiar with, in case
they are challenged with questions. They sometimes use
their first names but change their last name to something
that sounds similar to their real name. That way, if they
accidentally run in to an old acquaintance while working

102

undercover they can make it seem that their old friend's memory is faulty regarding the last name.

The fiction that Agent Famous was Tisaby's out-of-state fiancé was sufficient to allow him to hob nob in the night clubs without a date most of the time.

Tisaby learned one of the fast-rising dope gangs on the east side of town was the Curry Brothers organization; Johnny, Leo and Rudell Curry, with some help from their father, Sam Curry. The Currys began by selling marijuana, then they moved to heroin. As crack took over the drug market, the Currys shifted to cocaine.

In terms of FBI interest, the Currys stood apart because Johnny Curry's fiancé and soon-to-be wife was Cathy Volsan, the attractive niece of Detroit Mayor Coleman Young. Her looks were such that she dabbled in modeling from time to time. She was always well dressed. One FBI agent dubbed her a ghetto princess.

If the mayor's niece was consorting with a rising drug slinger, what did that say about him? The FBI didn't know, but it was an intriguing question for a law enforcement agency that was convinced Young should be in prison. The Currys became a strong blip on the Detroit FBI radar.

Tisaby learned something else about the Currys in his intelligence gathering. There was a white kid hanging around with them. He was very street savvy for a white youngster. His name was Richard J. Wershe, Jr, and as a result of Tisaby's intelligence gathering, he was about to become the FBI's youngest recruit in the War on Drugs.

Chapter 7 – A Kid goes to War

*"Teacher asked me to turn in my essay. But I ain't no
snitch."*
—Joke about being a police informant.

Rick Wershe remembers standing in his family home
one day in June of 1984, watching and listening as his
father sat at the dining room table talking with two black
men who had come to the house unannounced. They were
showing Richard Wershe, Sr. some snapshots of other
black men. The elder Wershe said he didn't recognize
anyone in the photos, but he suggested his son might. He
asked Richard Wershe, Jr. to join the conversation.

The younger Wershe approached the men and looked
at the photos spread across the table. "That's Big Man,
that's Little Man, that's Boo," he said, pointing to the
photos one by one.

The visitors, FBI agents Jim Dixon and Al Finch, knew
they had hit pay dirt. The fourteen-year old was correctly
identifying, by street name, the Curry Brothers drug gang.
In the criminal underworld, street names are often the only
names used. It makes it harder for the police to figure out
the true identities of crime suspects.

"For a fourteen-year old kid, he had so much
information," recalled Jim Dixon, one of the FBI agents
who was there for the recruitment of Richard Wershe, Jr. as
an FBI CI—Confidential Informant. This was no random
house call by a pair of FBI agents. They started the
conversation with the father, but the agents knew it was the
younger Wershe who had the knowledge—and access to
the Currys—that they wanted. It was expedient to involve
the father. In a way, Richard Wershe, Senior had opened

the door by contacting the FBI looking for help with Dawn, his drug-addicted daughter—Rick's sister. She had taken up with a known burglar and the elder Wershe wanted the FBI's help in finding her. The FBI wanted something in return, a quid pro quo.

Even though he was an adolescent, Rick Wershe knew he was the real target for recruitment. The agents told his father they wanted to recruit him—Wershe Senior—as a paid Confidential Informant, but the teen knew from the outset he would be the real source of information. Asked when the agents recruited his father and when they recruited him, Rick Wershe says, "It was the same day, in that same meeting."

The FBI agents were not enlisting the help of some sweet, innocent *Leave It To Beaver* sitcom adolescent. Young Wershe had had numerous minor run-ins with the police. Dave Majkowski, Rick's lifelong friend, said they were always getting stopped by the police for juvenile misbehavior of one kind or another.

Three months earlier, the younger Wershe had been arrested and charged in Juvenile Court with Assault with Intent to Commit Murder.

One night in March, 1984, Rick Wershe and his sister were driving together but in separate cars when Rick stopped at a gas station to get a soft drink. He was driving his grandmother's car. He left it running while he went inside to get his drink. A thief saw an opportunity and jumped in the idling car and drove off. Dawn Wershe leaned on the horn. As Rick stepped outside he could see his grandmother's car was gone. He dashed to Dawn's car, jumped in and told her to chase the stolen car, now on a nearby freeway.

As they gave chase Rick asked Dawn if she had a gun.
She did. Rick found a .22 and began firing at his
grandmother's car. It was Rick Wershe's buzzard luck that
an off-duty Detroit police officer was in the traffic mix as
he was shooting at the fleeing car. Rick Wershe was
arrested. His grandmother's car was later found on the side
of a freeway with a gun inside.

Rick eventually beat the charge with the help of a
Detroit Police narcotics cop working with the FBI on the
drug task force. It took some months for the attempted
murder charge to make its way through the juvenile court
system. By the time the case came up, young Wershe was
making lots of undercover drug buys for the Detroit narcs.
When the case was called on the Juvenile Court docket, the
officer who had written the complaint wasn't at court. Case
dismissed.

Years later, a parole board attorney asked Wershe why
his sister had a gun he could fire at the stolen car. Rick
Wershe said guns were part of their world. "We played
with guns, we had guns," Wershe said. "I mean, I really
didn't have any parental supervision at that time. I was
basically raising myself and I went down some wrong
paths."

The FBI men were slightly acquainted with the senior
Wershe due to his work at a Detroit gun shop. They knew
he was a business hustler, always hungry for a fast buck.
Snitch pay was quick money.

Through intelligence work the agents knew young
Wershe was hanging out at the Curry house on a regular
basis. Rick Wershe had become friends with Rudell "Boo"
Curry, the youngest of the brothers. They would shoot

hoops at neighborhood outdoor basketball courts. Rick was good at baseball, too.

Agent Tisaby, a native east-sider, had a knack for getting people to tell him things without arousing suspicion that he was a cop. He worked diligently but Tisaby's first awareness of young Rick Wershe's relationship with the Currys came in over the transom, as the saying goes.

Tisaby remembers getting a call at home one snowy night from the Detroit FBI switchboard. The operator said there were two women on the line who claimed they had information they wanted to share about some dope dealers. They wanted to talk face to face with an FBI agent. Now.

When Tisaby sat down with the women, they were pissed off and a bit desperate. Straight away they admitted they were boosters, thieves who steal merchandise from retail stores and sell it on the streets. The women were from the Philadelphia area. They had hooked up with the Curry Brothers of Detroit who were helping them move stolen merchandise. Initially, their business with the Currys had been lucrative, but the women claimed they had given the Currys a substantial amount of merchandise and now the Currys were refusing to pay them for the goods they provided. They said they were double-crossed, broke and stranded in Detroit. They wanted to get even. They called the FBI.

As the East Coast women told him about drug dealing by the Curry brothers, the agent took detailed notes and made arrangements to put the women up in a downtown Detroit hotel for a few nights. In one of the debriefing sessions they mentioned a young white kid named Rick hanging out with the Currys, a fact they found curious. Agent Tisaby found it curious, too.

Tisaby learned the white kid was named Rick Wershe. After a little more investigation, he passed the info along to Special Agents Jim Dixon and Al Finch, who were at the beginning of their investigation of the Currys.

There were no formal FBI or Justice Department rules in 1984 against recruiting juveniles as paid confidential informants in criminal cases, apparently because no one had ever considered such a thing.

Still, the agents knew this was a dicey proposition. But they came up with a clever idea. They realized this was a fortuitous situation because the father and son had the exact same name; Richard J. Wershe—Senior and Junior. They decided to recruit the father, an adult, as an on-the-books paid CI—Confidential Informant—but they figured to use the father as their entre to the son, the one with the useful information.

On June 29, 1984, a teletype was sent from the Detroit Division to FBI headquarters stating a "suitability inquiry" was being opened on an individual named Richard J. Wershe. The message did not mention whether it was Richard J. Wershe Senior or Junior. The teletype to headquarters said this "subject is in a position to furnish information re drug distribution both hard and pharmaceutical on the east side of Detroit and information re Robberies, Prior Shootings, Bombings in the Detroit area." FBI headquarters approved the request to add Richard J. Wershe to the list of informants. He was given the code name Gem. There was no mention in any of the informant files of the Detroit FBI of Richard J. Wershe, Junior. Or Senior. Just Richard J. Wershe.

Most of the FBI's intelligence about the Currys came from the younger Wershe, but the paper trail didn't reflect that. Any internal Bureau audit of the informant files would

109

show information coming from "Richard Wershe"—code name: Gem.

In the years since the recruitment of 14-year old Richard J. Wershe, Jr. as an FBI informant, there has been considerable criticism of the use of a teenaged kid as a secret combatant in the War on Drugs. But the use of a teen as an informant was the least of the potential trouble for the Detroit FBI. By opening the father as an on-the-books informant, but using information from the son disguised as intel from the father, a felony was being committed each time intelligence from the kid was added to the file.

It's true there isn't any paper trail in the Detroit FBI indicating the Curry case information came from a juvenile. When the identity of the Curry case informant became an issue, all of the FBI paperwork and teletypes to FBI Headquarters maintained the fiction that the informant was Richard J. Wershe who was born in 1943. In truth, the information was coming from Richard J. Wershe, Junior who was born in 1969. Exactly how many in the Detroit FBI knew the truth about the informant named Richard Wershe and how high up the chain of command that knowledge extended is a subject of conflicting accounts to this day.

Title 18 § 1519 of the U.S. Criminal Code makes it a felony to destroy, alter or falsify records in a federal investigation. The maximum penalty is 20 years in prison. But it's a moot point. The statute of limitations expired long ago on the deliberate falsification of the FBI investigative files related to the informant code-named Gem.

The FBI informant relationship with the Wershes began slowly. Young Wershe was a street kid through and through. He was able to provide useful information right away.

"Source has the potential to provide a considerable amount of information regarding illegal activity in both hard and prescription drugs," one July, 1984 memo states.

Rick Wershe, Jr. began paying close attention to the drug-dealing activities in the neighborhood. He and his father would meet Special Agent Dixon on the west side, at a fast food restaurant or perhaps in an empty church parking lot.

The culture of Detroit is such that east siders and west siders tend to stay on their side of town.

Thus, it was sensible for the Wershes, who lived on the east side to meet with FBI agents at locations on the west side. The chances an east side doper would spot them were negligible.

Dixon's memory from over 30 years ago is a bit spotty, but he remembers some of the debriefing sessions with the Wershes. "He (the younger Wershe) was always eager to talk," Dixon said. "Especially after they started getting some money. He would come in with all kinds of information." Dixon says the kid was serious about his task. He seldom smiled during their meetings.

"He would do most of the talking at those meetings," Dixon recalled. The young man had an impressive memory for people, places and things that were said, things he had seen.

To this day, former agent Dixon marvels at Richard Wershe, Jr.'s depth of knowledge of the criminal underworld. "It was unbelievable what he had been involved in at that particular time," Dixon said. "He started rattling off stuff and you'd go, 'how does this 14-year old kid know all this'? But he was a street guy. He knew all these guys. He ran with them. He talked like a black street guy. He was hip."

Dixon, now retired, remembers Richard Wershe, Sr. didn't contribute much at the informant debrief meetings. "Whatever information he had was provided by his son," Dixon said. The informant-of-record wasn't much of an informant. "He might say something, but he would indicate Junior told him this," Dixon recalled. "He really didn't have any information."

The boy was the one with all the knowledge the Bureau was willing to pay for. "His dad was pushing him to provide that information," Dixon said. "To get information."

Q: For the money?

"Yeah, for the money. His dad was interested in the money. It always came down to the money where Senior was involved," Dixon recalled. "He was more interested in the (informant) money. I don't think he was looking at the safety of his son."

I wondered if the agents of the FBI gave any thought to the safety of a 14-year old white kid spying on a gang of adult black men involved in the often-deadly drug trade.

"We didn't push it because, I guess, we wanted the information," Dixon said.

Q: So, you were not going to question it?

"We were not going to question it."

Early on it was decided the Curry investigation would be an OCDETF Task Force case. The DEA wasn't involved, but the Detroit Police were. About two months after the Wershes were recruited as informants, Agent Dixon wrote a memo to the file indicating the Detroit Police narcs assigned to the Task Force wanted to work with the informant known as Gem.

"DPD has shown an interest in investigating alleged drug activity reported by source and requested that writer continue to provide information from source and coordinate contacts," Dixon wrote in a memo dated 9/20/84.

The knowledgeable teen informant was introduced to several Detroit Police narcotics officers assigned to work with the FBI in the OCDETF Task Force. Young Wershe's primary informant work was with Officers Kevin Greene and William "Billy" Jasper.

By December, 1984, Richard Wershe, Jr. had proven his value as an informant. "Source was contacted frequently from the date of opening providing significant information concerning various criminal activities, primarily drug activities, in the Detroit area," one FBI report stated. "Beginning in December, 1984, subject began to provide information concerning the Currie (sic) Brothers drug organization…Likewise, at this time, source provided information concerning one Kathy Volson (sic) (Cathy Volsan), niece of Detroit Mayor Coleman Young," the report said. "Source advised that Volson (sic) was dating Johnny Currie (sic) (Curry)," the report noted. There was one more informant nugget: "Likewise, source furnished other third hand information concerning (Detroit Mayor Coleman) Young's involvement in drug activity."

This was the heart of it. The tip that Young was somehow involved with illegal drugs was raw meat for major-case hungry FBI agents. But the key words were "third hand information." Coleman Young's "involvement in drug activity" was never substantiated. No one, including Rick Wershe, Jr., ever produced credible evidence linking Detroit's mayor to the city's drug trade. The younger Wershe passed along what he had heard as the FBI wanted him to do. If it panned out, it would be a political scandal of national proportions. It didn't.

As 1984 gave way to 1985, the FBI had put their young informant to work on the big case they wanted to pursue—an indictment of the Curry Brothers drug gang, with possible links to the mayor of the city of Detroit.

By his own admission Johnny Curry was peddling dope from around age 16. He began with marijuana, moved to heroin, then switched to cocaine when the crack craze hit in the mid-1980s. He lasted longer than many other dealers before he was busted. In a YouTube interview years later Curry cryptically explained, "My thing was so, like, covered up 'cuz of the police officers that was around me." It was not an idle boast.

The FBI was developing a conspiracy case against the Currys. Such investigations often involve wiretaps in an effort to nab as many participants in a criminal enterprise as possible. The longer the list of names of defendants on the cover page of a federal grand jury indictment, the better.

The Detroit Police were more interested in what is known as buy/bust. Their main mission was to rid the city of dope houses and the people running them. In a legitimate buy/bust scenario, an undercover operative makes a drug buy in a dope house or on a street corner and that becomes the predicate for a court-authorized search warrant. The narcs, the search warrant in hand, go kick in the door at the crack house and make arrests and seize any drugs and cash they find.

It was this kind of work the Detroit Police Task Force cops wanted Rick Wershe, Jr. to do at Curry Brothers dope houses. In numerous interviews, conversations, letters and emails, Wershe made it clear to me he didn't like it.

The narcs taught him the drug trade. Agent Groman recalls Rick Wershe, Jr., the street-savvy adolescent, was an enthusiastic student. For Groman, Wershe's portrayal of himself as a reluctant recruit should be taken with a block of salt.

This much is certain: 14-year old Richard Wershe, Jr. was involved in a life of dangerous secret adventure other kids his age couldn't even imagine.

"We started off driving around in a van, and I would point out people and houses to them," Wershe said.

"Summertime was always the best, and the most dangerous, because everyone was outside. So, I was always worried about being seen. They always told me not to worry."

At 14, Wershe was savvy enough not to buy the police reassurance. "Yeah. Right," he said, regarding the hollow words of comfort about his dangerous task.

While Wershe was a federal informant, most of his risky street work was for the Detroit narcs. "We would meet up and talk and then it was off to make some buys," Wershe said.

"I remember being very paranoid. Here I am a 14, 15-year-old kid, paranoid about who might see me and what might happen. Of course, the narcs were very reassuring.

Vince Wade

But even as a kid I knew they were blowing smoke up my ass because they weren't always around."

What Wershe meant was this: the narcs would bring him to a neighborhood that had a suspected crack house. They would have him exit their van and go to the crack house and make a hand-to-hand drug buy while they waited at the end of the block. They told Wershe they would be "right there" if something happened. That, of course, was a ridiculous lie. If the pushers in a crack house ever suspected Wershe was a police snitch and they shot him, it was cold comfort to know some cops would come charging in the door a minute or two after Wershe hit the floor, bleeding to death.

"Billy (narcotics officer William Jasper) was always the most vocal. 'We're there for you. Don't worry. We have your back.'" Wershe suspected it was a pack of lies. "Just little pep talks that I look back on now and realize, they were total BS!"

Wershe remains bitter about Billy Jasper.

"Billy practically burned my pager up," is the way Wershe described the volume of his clandestine work for Officer Jasper. In Wershe's view, he enabled Jasper to do a substantial amount of work as a narc, but when the chips were down, when Jasper's fellow narcs in the Detroit Police Department were ready to send Wershe to prison for mandatory life, Jasper didn't step forward to help.

Indeed, I could find nothing in the paper trail from the Wershe drug case to indicate Office Jasper did anything to help his teen informant. Robert Healy, the Wershe case prosecutor told me he doesn't recall anyone in law enforcement trying to intercede in Wershe's behalf in the drug case.

116

Kevin Greene, Jasper's Detroit Police narc partner, wrote a letter in 2010 urging that Wershe be given clemency or a pardon. Greene made a point of writing that witness statements that Rick Wershe was a major supplier of drugs to the Curry organization and that he was involved in acts of violence are untrue. Noting Wershe's role in the Curry case, Greene wrote, "His efforts were instrumental in our success."

I could find no evidence that Bill Jasper wrote a similar letter. My request to Jasper for an interview went unanswered.

Jasper is now a church youth minister in northern Michigan.

"At one point I really looked up to Billy," Wershe said. "I was this kid and here was this cool cop I thought was my friend. Boy, I couldn't have been more wrong about that!"

Wershe was indeed just a kid, and he was white, but in the grubby world of big city police narcotics work, he was just another expendable snitch.

"They wanted me to feel safe but that (my safety) didn't matter to them," Wershe said. "Hell, it didn't matter to them if I was killed. They never would have said anything about me working for them or being sent to the (crack) house to buy for them. I can see it now: '15-year old gunned down buying drugs.' And they wouldn't have said shit!"

There's another side of this picture of Rick Wershe, the teen snitch. The Detroit police narcs largely took over the use of Wershe as an informant and gave him wide latitude as an informant, including allowing him to keep drugs he purchased with police funds.

Vince Wade

These are drugs Wershe turned around and sold—and kept the profit. "They knew I was selling drugs," Wershe testified in 2017. "They let me keep the drugs." Wershe had a wink-and-a-nod discussion with his police handlers about his drug dealing. "Don't cross 8 Mile," Wershe testified that he was warned, meaning the city limits of Detroit. "We can't help you," Wershe said he was told.

In October, 1984, a few months after "Richard Wershe" was recruited as a paid informant by the FBI, the *Detroit Free Press* published a story stating, "Detroit is a city held captive by drugs, a city with a $2.5 million-a-day drug habit..."

In Washington, the Comprehensive Crime Control Bill of 1984 was passed and signed in to law by President Reagan. This wide-ranging revision of federal criminal law fit Reagan's conservative belief that federal criminal law should be about punishment. To Reagan and his admirers, punishment and justice were synonyms. Many Congressional Democrats, eager to appear tough on crime, participated in drafting the Crime Control Bill. It toughened the conditions of bail, imposed sentencing guidelines on federal judges and made sentencing harsher.

Another feature of the crime legislation was a change in asset seizure laws to allow the federal government to share confiscated assets with local governments. Cash, jewelry, luxury cars and yachts seized as part of federal law enforcement now had dollar value for the locals.

Asset forfeiture became a cash cow for many police departments. Suddenly, local cops were on the prowl for asset seizure opportunities. The law encouraged local police to find ways to seize property as drug or crime

118

proceeds and reap financial benefits for doing so. Under the forfeiture law, a person's seized assets were held under an upside-down system of guilty until proven innocent—by the owner.

Under the tough new law, the number of persons being held in custody surged. Mass incarceration was the new tactic in the War on Drugs and it would continue for a very long time.

Richard Wershe, Jr.'s career as a clandestine FBI informant almost ended just as it was getting started. In November, 1984 he was shot in the stomach with a .357 magnum by John Walker, a young school acquaintance. Walker stood there after the shooting, looking at Wershe, while his girlfriend called 911. Wershe was rushed to a hospital where he almost died. FBI agents and Detroit Police narcs from the federal drug task force raced to the hospital. They arranged to have Wershe admitted under a John Doe alias. To the outside world, young Wershe had vanished. Richard Wershe, Sr. was angry and vented his explosive temper at the lawmen gathered at his son's bedside.

Walker claimed it was an accident. The cops weren't so sure. Walker was also an associate of the Curry Brothers. Was the shooting an attempted hit? The question was never resolved. But there was a perverse upside to the incident. "Being shot gave me street cred," Wershe said. In the culture of the street, being shot and surviving meant young Wershe was the real deal.

Richard Wershe, Sr. told *Detroit Monthly* magazine he hired a tutor to help Rick during his recovery but the tutor quit when he learned his student was a shooting victim. While Wershe's father was upset about the shooting, there is no indication he demanded that the feds quit using his son for dangerous informant work—work for which the father was getting paid.

As the 1984 holiday season approached, many Detroiters were excited about a movie called *Beverly Hills Cop*. It starred comedian Eddie Murphy as Detroit Police Officer Axel Foley, a wisecracking, street-smart, out-of-the-hood cop who winds up solving a crime in posh Beverly Hills.

The film begins in gritty Detroit. Murphy's on-screen boss was, in real-life, a ranking Detroit Police officer. Gilbert "Gil" Hill, the head of the police Homicide Section, was cast to play Murphy's foul-mouthed superior with a low tolerance for Axel Foley's antics. Detroit was portrayed as a down-at-the-heels factory town but many residents were thrilled to see their city on the big screen, even if it was in stark contrast to Beverly Hills, one of the nation's communities famous for conspicuous consumption.

About five months after Richard Wershe was "opened" and Wershe Junior became the government's youngest informant, FBI investigative files indicate he was not only learning the ways of the drug trade, he was learning how to play the law enforcement informant game. Young Wershe and his father were demanding more money.

"Source has continued to provide reliable information since opening in June of 1984 and has indicated a willingness to continue," the FBI memo states. "Source recently indicates he/she has information on another large cocaine dealer in the Detroit area, but is reluctant to provide information without some type of considerable compensation. It is therefore requested that $750.00 be paid to source as payment."

Richard J. Wershe, Jr.was about to go deeper in the drug underworld. He was about to learn about payoffs to cops. He was about to find out that Gil Hill, a real-life homicide detective and minor movie star, was corrupt.

After he recovered from his gunshot wound, Rick Wershe, Jr. continued his informant work and continued to get paid. Wershe, now 15, would provide information about the Curry Brothers and other Detroit drug dealers and criminals and his father would receive FBI informant money as the source known as "Gem."

For example, the younger Wershe provided the agents with information about a major drug dealer who wanted the kid to sell drugs for him. The dealer tried to entice Wershe by showing him two punch bowls, each allegedly filled with a kilo of cocaine. There was a bedroom full of stolen merchandise, including TVs, stereos, video recorders and numerous guns. There was a filing cabinet containing a large sum of cash.

Wershe shared this information with his FBI handlers, who shared it with the Detroit Police. Wershe was cited, anonymously, as a reliable confidential informant in a Detroit police request for a search warrant. In the raid that followed 583 grams of high quality cocaine was confiscated, along with a dozen firearms, 61 pieces of silver, gold and diamond jewelry, 64 pieces of assorted electronic equipment and $192,075 in cash.

It was actionable intelligence like this that led retired FBI Special Agent John Anthony, the Detroit FBI legal adviser at the time, to say Wershe was "arguably the most productive drug informant of the Detroit FBI during that era."

In late March of 1985, Rick Wershe provided the FBI with information that changed everything. He told Agent Dixon the Curry gang was planning to fly as a group to Las Vegas the next month for a world middleweight championship fight between "Marvelous" Marvin Hagler and Detroit's Thomas "Hitman" Hearns. Many of Detroit's big dogs and high rollers would be there. For dope dealers, it was a see and be seen event.

"Source has further advised that (Curry) will meet with other narcotic suppliers from throughout the United States to arrange future shipment of heroin/cocaine/marijuana into Detroit, Michigan," Dixon wrote in a memo.

The Curry plan, Wershe told Dixon, was to connect during the Vegas junket with some Detroit city officials for the purpose of improving drug smuggling logistics in the city.

Wershe's tip was corroborated by intel from FBI agent Don Tisaby who heard a similar story.

Tisaby recalls being in a west side after-hours club where Willie Volsan, the mayor's drug-dealing brother-in-law, was mingling with the likes of David Ruffin, a cocaine addict and the lead singer of the popular Temptations vocal group, and Emmanuel Steward, the manager of boxer Tommy Hearns. Tisaby says Steward, now deceased, was fond of cocaine and young girls.

Tisaby learned Volsan and the Currys intended to meet in Las Vegas with a least one Detroit city official. It was believed the official might help move large quantities of drugs into and around the city.

Volsan had been a heroin supplier for the Curry drug organization and he wanted to improve the pipeline for moving drugs without arousing police suspicion or risking a rip-off by other criminals. Detroit City Airport, now known as the Coleman A. Young International airport, figured in the plan.

For the FBI, the Wershe tip about the planned meeting with city officials in Las Vegas, combined with the intel Tisaby picked up in the nightclub amounted to red-flag information.

Dixon made a point of relaying this informant info in person to Bob Reutter, one of the Detroit FBI Assistant Special Agents in Charge. Dixon remembers Reutter sat up and took notice. This intel suggested the Curry investigation might expand to include public corruption, as well as narcotics.

"We were constantly doing Title IIIs (Justice Department jargon for the federal law related to court-authorized wiretaps) on city officials at that time, 'cause we were always trying to connect Coleman Young in to this stuff," Dixon said. Dixon says Reutter instructed him to immediately put the information about the Las Vegas trip in a 302, the FBI's official form for interview summaries and case intel.

Dixon recalls that within a day or two, Reutter took him off the case and assigned the Curry investigation to Special Agent Herman Groman. Retired black agents say in those days white street agents and many white Bureau managers didn't trust black agents to handle public corruption investigations involving a black city administration.

After Dixon was replaced, Al Finch eventually bowed out of the case, too. He left Groman with the impression he didn't like working in a task force environment. Was the real reason because Finch didn't like the fact the Curry case was taken away from a black agent and given to a white agent? Dixon and Finch are black. Groman is white. Finch refused to comment.

Retired agent John Anthony, who is white, was the Principal Legal Advisor (PLA) for the Detroit FBI in that era. He offers a different interpretation of the removal of Dixon from the case.

"I think what Reutter saw was a narcotics case, which there are millions of those," Anthony said. "And (with the information about the Currys perhaps meeting a city official in Las Vegas) here's a public corruption case, which is a big deal for him and for the office. I think that's why Bob cut Dixon out."

Anthony doesn't think it was a racial issue. He thinks the decision was about agent expertise. "Dixon and Finch were drug investigators and they were very good at what they did, Anthony said, adding, "They were not public corruption investigators."

I spoke to several retired black agents who worked in the FBI's Detroit Division in that era. Their collective view is that in cases of suspected black political corruption, white managers worried that, in the end, racial solidarity would prevail if black agents worked the case. They agreed racial tension was part of FBI office politics in those days. FBI headquarters was making a concerted effort to recruit blacks and other minorities and it didn't always sit well in an agency that had been almost all-white.

A black FBI agent named Donald Rochon made national news when he sued the Bureau, claiming racial harassment while he was assigned to the FBI's Omaha and Chicago offices.

Agent Rochon alleged that fellow agents in Omaha taped photos of apes over pictures of his children on his desk. Rochon's then-wife was white. She, too, was a target of harassment, he said. There were threats to mutilate his genitals and rape his wife, Rochon said.

Eventually, several white FBI agents admitted to racially harassing Rochon. The case was settled out of court and Rochon left the Bureau.

Following Rochon's trailblazing lawsuit, 311 Hispanic FBI agents filed similar charges of discrimination against the Bureau. They represented most of the FBI's 439 Hispanic agents at the time. They claimed they were regularly assigned to demeaning duties they called "the taco circuit."

It was amid rancorous complaints of racism and bigotry by black and Hispanic agents that the FBI, with a house clearly divided, set out in the 1980s to help Ronald Reagan and his law-and-order supporters win the War on Drugs.

For Rick Wershe, Jr. the information about a possible important drug dealer meeting with Detroit officials in Las Vegas moved him from mere drug snitch to a confidential informant with potentially high-value intelligence about public corruption.

In the FBI, it is not unheard of for a case to be initiated by one agent and taken over by another agent for any number of reasons. Eventually, Agent Groman was taken off the Curry case and it was assigned to yet another agent, Gregg Schwarz.

As part of the case re-assignment Agent Dixon introduced Agent Groman to the Wershes—Senior and

Junior—at a McDonald's on Detroit's west side. "Herm and I walked in," Dixon recalled. "They were already there in a booth and I introduced them at that time."

Groman says he was stunned when he saw the young, freckly, baby-faced star drug informant.

"I thought I was meeting Howdy Doody," Groman said, chuckling. "He struck me as Howdy Doody, the old (children's TV show) puppet character." Groman's shock didn't end with Rick Wershe's face.

"When he talked, he had this definitive black dialect," Groman said. "To me it just seemed unusual coming out of his mouth, the way he talked." For the Ohio-born white FBI agent, ghetto slang and black street dialect coming out of a white kid's mouth took some getting used to.

The Currys had told Rick Wershe he could accompany them on the trip. The young man had never been to Las Vegas. The FBI gave Rick Wershe, Jr. $1,500 to cover his travel expenses. They also gave him something else.

The federal agents procured a very realistic-looking but fake Michigan identification card stating Richard Wershe, Jr. was 21 years old. The kid didn't look anywhere close to age 21, but the FBI's counterfeit state ID card was so realistic that anyone "carding" him would have to accept it.

Chapter 8—A Child is Slain; A Cop is Bribed

"I never bought a man who wasn't for sale."
—William A. Clark - 19th Century Montana politician and mining magnate

In war, combatants refer to "collateral damage." It is a bland term for the slaughter of innocent civilians and the destruction of property, of communities.

In the War on Drugs, Damion Lucas was collateral damage. The 13-year old Detroit boy who showed promise as an artist was inadvertently shot to death in a money dispute between drug dealers.

Key command officers of the Detroit Police Department obstructed justice in the investigation of the Damion Lucas killing to protect the niece of Detroit Mayor Coleman Young because she would have been a witness. They compounded the miscarriage of justice by falsely charging an innocent man to cover up the cover up. One of them accepted a bribe to make the investigation go awry.

FBI street agents and Detroit police officers assigned to a federal drug task force tried repeatedly to force Detroit investigators and prosecutors to charge the true killers.

Management of the Detroit FBI, the Wayne County Prosecutor, the Detroit U.S. Attorney's Office and top officials at FBI headquarters and the Justice Department turned a blind eye to the travesty of justice that engulfed the investigation of the Damion Lucas killing.

The trouble began with a dispute over the quality of some heroin. The Curry group had sold a batch of heroin to Leon Lucas, a small-time drug dealer. Lucas had met the Currys through Cathy Volsan, the mayor's niece.

The Currys were impressed with Lucas' skill with mixed jive, a concoction of heroin and a diluting agent. Lucas complained about the poor quality of the of the latest batch of heroin. His customers didn't like it. He was told he owed the Currys for the drugs, anyway. He said he'd need time to accumulate the money since he couldn't sell the drugs.

Meanwhile, Leo Curry and Wyman Jenkins of the Curry gang made their travel arrangements to Las Vegas through a cousin of Leon Lucas, a Detroit hustler named Robert Walton.

Walton, functioning as a gofer, made airline and hotel arrangements for Leo Curry and Wyman Jenkins and their girlfriends. Walton later told federal investigators that Curry and Jenkins changed their travel dates and didn't tell him. When the Curry group arrived in Las Vegas, the hotel rooms for Leo and Wyman had been sold because they didn't update their reservation dates. Walton told investigators Leo Curry and Wyman Jenkins called him from Las Vegas to vent their anger. Walton quoted Jenkins as threatening, "I'm gonna send someone to your house."

It's not clear if the Currys connected with a Detroit city official or officials in Las Vegas, but they attended a party thrown by Art Derrick, a white suburbanite who was one of their key cocaine suppliers. Derrick was what they call a weight man, a wholesaler. He had Miami connections and his owned several aircraft.

When the Curry group returned to Detroit, they were still angry. On Monday, April 29, 1985 Leo Curry, known on the streets as Big Man, called Leon Lucas who said Curry made threats, warning they wanted their money.

"We don't wanna hear no shit about you giving us our money," Lucas recalls being told. He replied that he didn't have it. The threat that followed was quite clear: "Yeah, well some niggers will be out to your house tonight and then you will wish you have gave it to us."

That night, Leon Lucas went out to with some friends and left his nephews, 13-year-old Damion Lucas and 11-year-old Frankie Robert Lucas, known as Little Robert, at home watching television. Lucas had custody of the boys after his sister, their mother, died from an illness. Life in Detroit in that era was such that Lucas had conducted drills on what the boys should do if there was shooting in the neighborhood. They were to run to the basement where Leon Lucas had prepared a place for them to hide.

It was near midnight when several shots were fired into a car in the driveway of Robert Walton. Walton lived three blocks from his cousin, Leon Lucas.

A few minutes later, automatic weapons fire peppered the front of the home of Leon Lucas. At least 20 shots were fired. The bullets tore through the walls. One went through a bedroom wall and landed above a stuffed toy monkey named Curious George. Another slug hit the chest of Damion Lucas, about an inch above his heart.

Damion said, "Little Robert, I've been shot." Damion told his little brother they should run to the basement and hide. They didn't make it. Damion staggered in to the kitchen and fell on the floor in front of the stove.

Terrified and sobbing as his older brother lay dying on the floor before him, Frankie Lucas frantically called 911, the police/fire/medical emergency number. This is a verbatim of that call:

Frankie: Could you send the police to 19965 Marlowe? Somebody just shot at my house. (Crying) Please...

911 Operator: Wait a minute. What's the address? Calm down. Give me the address...

Frankie Lucas (speaking urgently): 19965 Marlowe. My brother on the floor dyin'. Please!! I don't know what...

911 Operator: Somebody just shot your brother?

Frankie: Yes! I don't know what to do. (Unintelligible) Please!

911 Operator: Wait a minute now. Settle down. Did he come in the house shot? Or did someone shoot in to the house? What happened?

Frankie: Yes. Someone shot in to the house. (Urgently) Please hurry! Please!

911 Operator: OK. Wait. Calm down. Where are your parents?

Frankie: They're gone.

911 Operator: What's the street at the corner? I'm requesting the police and EMS. What's the corner cross street?

Frankie: Between Pembroke and Chippewa. (Pleading) Please tell them to hurry...

911 Operator: OK. As soon as they can they'll be there. OK?

Frankie: Yes. (After a brief pause Frankie wails frantically) He's not movin'! Please!

911 Operator: OK, OK, OK. They're coming. Wait for them. They're coming. Keep your doors locked until they get there...

Frankie: OK...

The fear in the young boy's voice was unmistakable.

911 Operator: Bye bye.

Frankie: He ain't movin'! Please!!!

911 Operator: OK. OK. Don't bother your brother. Don't touch him. Just wait for the police and EMS...

Frankie: (Pleading with fear and despair in his voice) Please hurry, please...

911 Operator: OK. Bye bye. As soon as they can. They're coming.

Damion Lucas was dead on arrival at Detroit's Mt. Carmel Hospital.

I interviewed Leon Lucas in 1988 for a series of investigative reports about the homicide that I produced and reported for WXYZ-TV, the ABC affiliate in Detroit.

Leon Lucas said he spoke with Frankie Lucas after the horrific incident:

"Frankie said, 'Uncle Leon I tried to pick him up, but he was too heavy.' "Then he said, 'I tried to wake him up but he wouldn't wake up no more.' And then he just bust out into tears."

❖

Early the next morning Homicide Inspector Gil Hill was reviewing the reports of overnight killings, a daily task in Detroit.

The Damion Lucas case must have made him sit up and take notice. Leon Lucas, the guardian of Damion Lucas, had told police detectives he suspected the killing was the work of Leo Curry and Wyman Jenkins, members of the Curry drug organization. The uncle of the dead boy told the police Leo Curry had called him earlier in the day and threatened there would be trouble that night if Lucas didn't pay them the money he owed them.

Hill's detectives had canvassed the neighborhood for witnesses, which was standard procedure. Several neighbors told the police Leon Lucas had been in a loud argument a few days earlier with LeKeas Davis, another neighborhood resident, and Davis had threatened to kill Lucas.

The morning after the shooting, the squad working the Damion Lucas case focused on learning more about the confrontation between Leon Lucas and LeKeas Davis. In addition to telling the police about the Curry threats, Lucas noted he and Davis had settled their dispute. The detectives working the Damion Lucas slaying ignored the information from the dead boy's uncle about the threats from the Currys. They focused on Davis, instead.

Apparently, Inspector Hill was concerned about the Lucas interview, and his belief that the Currys were responsible. Hill knew that Johnny Curry was a drug dealer who was engaged to Cathy Volsan, the mayor's niece. If the homicide investigation led to the Currys, the mayor's niece would be in the media spotlight amid sensational headlines. As a command-level officer in the Detroit Police

Department and as a savvy and ambitious player in city politics, Hill had to know this was a crisis in the making and it had landed on his desk.

Hill picked up the phone and called Sgt. James Harris, one of his homicide detectives. Harris was off that day, doing some painting at his home.

Harris wore two hats at the department. His primary assignment was detective work for Homicide Squad 7, which handled murders committed during the course of other felonies. His other role was as a sometime member of the mayor's security detail. Harris had known the mayor's sister, Juanita Clark Volsan, for many years. She apparently asked that Harris be assigned to look out for the family in police matters. Harris enjoyed detective work and he was good at it, so he kept his main assignment in the Homicide section, but Inspector Hill and the Squad 7 team understood that Harris would occasionally have to take care of any issues that may arise involving the mayor's family.

Hill told Harris he needed to talk with Cathy Volsan right away regarding the Damion Lucas killing. Harris called another police officer, Martrice Hurrah, and asked her to find Cathy Volsan. Harris went back to his painting chores.

Cathy Volsan was at Johnny Curry's house that morning. The FBI had what is called a pen register on Johnny Curry's home phone. A pen register is a court-authorized mechanical device that records telephone calls dialed or received. It does not record voices. It creates a log showing phone calls to or from the target line and the date, time and duration of a call.

Federal investigators obtain court orders authorizing the use of the devices. The court order is served on the local telephone company which enables the pen register to monitor a designated phone line remotely. Agents monitor pen registers and full-fledged wiretaps from their offices. Telephone companies comply with court wiretap orders by creating what amounts to a silent off-premises extension of the target telephone. They adjust the signal strength on the line so the tap cannot be detected. The idea that agents sit in a van in an alley next to a telephone pole with wires and alligator clips attached to a phone line is pure Hollywood fiction.

The Detroit FBI has a designated and secure Title III (the federal wiretap law) room where agents sit at carrels with audio recorders and headsets and notepads. When a targeted phone is active, they listen in. If the conversation is purely personal, they stop the recording and wait to see if the parties begin a discussion that might be relevant to the criminal investigation. This is called minimization and it is part of the protocol of court-authorized wiretaps.

Pen registers are used to show criminal conspiracy connections. This person knows this person who knows this person. Pen register data is analyzed and used with other investigative information to persuade a federal judge that the FBI should be authorized to initiate a full wiretap on a certain phone line. The pen register on Johnny Curry's phone was authorized partly because of Richard Wershe, Jr.'s informant work.

The FBI's pen register data from the Curry phone was not evaluated right away. When it was reviewed, it showed a short phone call from Johnny Curry's home phone to the unlisted home phone of Sgt. Harris. This was followed by a longer call from the Curry home phone to an unlisted number at Detroit Police Headquarters. That phone was on the desk of Inspector Gil Hill.

Years later, in a letter to a Detroit FBI agent, Harris's attorney addressed the phone calls that went back and forth the morning after Damion Lucas was shot to death. "Hill asked Jim to contact Johnny Curry's wife, Cathy Volsan Curry, ASAP and tell her the homicide detectives were looking at Johnny," attorney James Craven wrote.

Why would the head of the Detroit Police Homicide section urgently warn the mayor's niece that his detectives were looking at her husband, Johnny Curry, in a shooting death? Such a tip to the leader of a gang suspected in the shooting was improper, to say the least.

Timing is critical in homicide investigations. Witnesses often are shaken by the death and they tend to be more candid when interviewed by detectives as soon as possible after the event. Memories get jumbled quickly. The element of surprise—an unexpected knock on the door—works in favor of the police.

A police officer warning potential suspects they may be targets of the investigation violates the protocols and procedures of homicide case work. Yet, that is exactly what Gil Hill, the head of Detroit Police Homicide and an experienced detective, did the morning after Damion Lucas was killed. It was a step by Hill down the road to criminal behavior that could be prosecuted under several federal laws but for these purposes it will be described generally as obstruction of justice.

Criminal investigations are not immune to coincidences and the FBI's Curry case was no exception. On May 3, 1985, four days after the Damion Lucas killing, a federal judge authorized a full wiretap on Johnny Curry's telephone. One of the first calls the FBI recorded was between Johnny Curry and Charles Dillard, also known as

Fuzzy, on May 4, 1985. They are discussing the Damion Lucas incident and whether Leo Curry and Wyman Jenkins are suspects in the investigation. What follows is from an FBI transcription of the conversation and a review of the audio of the wiretapped call.

Fuzzy: "…Dig, what Wyman know what's suppose' to be on him?"

Johnny: "Huh?"

Fuzzy: "Or he'd just say he's the number one."

Johnny: "He, OK, from my contacts I got that he's a number one suspect…"

Who were Johnny Curry's "contacts" and how did they know Wyman Jenkins was a "number one suspect"?

The conversation between Johnny Curry and Fuzzy continued with Johnny affirming in a telephone conversation what Leon Lucas had told the homicide investigators. That is, his brother Leo and Wyman Jenkins had called and made threats the morning before the boy was killed.

Johnny: "…you know, like Wyman fucked up when he called over there and threatened them people, you know?"

Fuzzy: "Yeah."

Johnny: "And then, see, they done got the ah, DEA in that shit now, Drug Enforcement Administration."

Fuzzy: "Oh yeah."

Johnny: "And they tryin' ta see if it's drug related."

Curry had it wrong. The FBI was investigating, not the DEA. The real issue, though, was how did Johnny Curry know federal agents were involved?

Johnny: "That's why, you know, I'm just layin' low until this shit kinda weather down a bit."

Fuzzy: "Yeah."

Johnny: "So, you know…"

Fuzzy: "Best move."

Johnny: Mm hmm. That's why I'm in the house right now, just layin' low. And I told Wyman, you know, ah, he, right now he got ta stroke hisself this one."

Fuzzy: "Yep."

Johnny: "Shit. He got ta weather hisself outta this one, 'cause they went and done a dumb-ass move by killin' that little boy. Man, that's a little boy. Shit."

Fuzzy: "Yep. Boy. Twelve years?"

Johnny: "Eleven or thirteen. Somethin' like that. Thirteen. Shit."

This conversation is revealing beyond the verbatim exchange. First, Curry states, "…from my contacts I got that he's a number one suspect…"

His contacts? Who were his contacts and how did they know inside information about the homicide investigation? Second, this wiretapped conversation occurred just a few days after the murder. Curry's "contacts" had provided fresh, timely intelligence about what the police were doing in the investigation of the shooting death of Damion Lucas.

In other wiretapped phone conversations, Johnny Curry and Wyman Jenkins are heard discussing the Damion

Lucas killing. Curry said he is "weathering this storm." The two men discussed Jenkins making threats. Jenkins told Curry just because he had called someone doesn't mean he was involved in anything. Jenkins may have believed his logic was sound, but in fact, he admitted in a taped telephone conversation that he had threatened the victim's guardian the day of the killing.

Jenkins dug his hole deeper by talking about the death of the youngster in front of Rick Wershe. About a month after the killing Wershe told the FBI he was at Jenkins' residence when Jenkins and Sidney Dwayne Goodwin, known on the street as "Wac", discussed the Damion Lucas killing.

According to an FBI write-up of Wershe's informant report: "they (Jenkins and Goodwin) were the ones that had killed that little boy on Marlowe (Damion Lucas) approximately one month prior. According to source (Wershe) Jenkins and "Wac" did not mean to kill the boy but his (Damion's) uncle owed them some money, and they only meant to 'shoot up the house' and scare him into paying."

Meanwhile, the Police Homicide unit remained focused on LeKeas Davis, the neighborhood man who had argued loudly with Leon Lucas shortly before the shooting occurred. He had threatened to kill Lucas. There were neighborhood witnesses. Someone picked Davis out of a police lineup. His friends were vague when asked if he was with them when the house was shot up.

The police investigators ignored the opinions of Leon Lucas and his cousin that the Curry gang was responsible for the shooting, even though Lucas and his cousin, Robert Walton, were the targets. Detectives didn't seem to give credence to the fact Lucas told them he and Davis had patched up their differences. They seemed to be going out of their way to avoid questioning Johnny Curry, the drug dealer fiancé of Mayor Young's niece, and his associates.

The firing of Police Chief Philip G. Tannian for failing to tell Mayor Young about a secret DEA investigation of his brother-in-law and the sacking of Commander Anthony Fiermonti in 1980 over an arrest incident with the Mayor's female relatives and the Mayor's demand for undated letters of resignation from all command personnel must have been on the minds of the "brass hats" at Detroit Police Headquarters in the aftermath of the Damion Lucas killing. But career preservation is no excuse for failing to pursue credible leads in a homicide investigation, for filing false charges and for a series of obstruction of justice actions.

The police certainly understood the political ramifications of the Curry gang involvement in a homicide. Records show the day after the shooting death, which was the day of the phone calls from Curry's home to Sgt. Harris and Inspector Hill, Deputy Police Chief Richard Dungy ordered Inspector Joel Gilliam of Narcotics to prepare a report on the drug dealing background of Wyman Jenkins, one of the suspected shooters.

It was highly unusual for a deputy chief to ask for a backgrounder on one possible homicide suspect. Amid the hundreds of criminal investigations going on in the Detroit Police Department that day, Richard Dungy, the deputy chief in charge of all investigations, wanted to know about just one suspect in just one case—Wyman Jenkins of the Curry gang and his possible involvement in killing little Damion Lucas.

Dungy was told that Jenkins and Leo Curry, Johnny's brother, were, indeed, suspects in the case because of the threats they had made to Leon Lucas the morning of the fatal shooting. Their close association with Johnny Curry and Cathy Volsan, the Mayor's niece, guaranteed the case would be treated as a sensitive investigation.

While the Homicide squad assigned to the Damion Lucas case pursued LeKeas Davis, the top brass of the police department worried about the Curry gang and the political and career repercussions if the mayor's niece was linked to the killers of a little boy.

There's no evidence Coleman Young intervened in the Damion Lucas investigation. He didn't have to. The entire command structure of the police department understood the career risks of a police investigation that brought the mayor's family in to a homicide case in the town known as the Murder City. The other option was to frame and convict LeKeas Davis—an innocent man. The Homicide Section remained focused on Davis.

All of this was a source of serious concern at the FBI's Detroit office. The agency was very reluctant to tip its hand about the secret wiretaps in the Curry case, but a killing was involved and they had evidence and informant information indicating who was responsible. What's more, they saw that the police department was building a case against an innocent man.

It was decided that the Detroit police narcs assigned to work with the FBI on the OCDETF Task Force would discreetly approach their police superiors with the information the FBI had obtained about the Damion Lucas killing.

In early June, a little over a month after Damion Lucas died, there was a meeting between Deputy Chief Dungy, Inspector Gilliam and Lieutenant Bill Gray and Sgt. Jack Tynan. Gray and Tynan worked with the FBI on the OCDETF Task Force, FBI records show. Gray and Tynan confirmed the Las Vegas prize fight tickets dispute and revealed to Dungy that the FBI had confidential source information that Johnny Curry had been discussing with associates the involvement of Wyman Jenkins in the Damion Lucas killing. It's not known if they told Dungy that the FBI had wiretap evidence, too.

In the weeks and months after Damion Lucas was killed, the Detroit Homicide Unit did not interrogate Johnny Curry or any of his associates about the fatal shooting, even though the victim's uncle said he thought the Curry group did the shooting and two Detroit police officers assigned to a federal task force told a Deputy Chief that the FBI had informant information that two members of the Curry drug organization were responsible. Instead, the Detroit Police falsely charged LeKeas Davis with the death of 13-year old Damion Lucas.

One possible reason Detroit's seasoned and skilled homicide investigators looked the other way regarding Johnny Curry and his gang in the Damion Lucas investigation is because Curry paid their boss, Gil Hill, the inspector in charge Homicide, $10-thousand dollars to make the investigation focus elsewhere. Curry later admitted the bribe paid to Hill to FBI investigators—twice—while he was in prison.

Hill had been a cop a long time. He knew many ways to make life miserable for any of his investigators who crossed him in an important case.

Curry admitted the bribe publicly in a Sunday, December 13, 1992 front-page story in the *Detroit News*. What's more, reporters Norman Sinclair and Allan Lengel quoted Cathy Volsan Curry, the mayor's niece, confirming her husband's tale of bribery in exchange for obstruction of justice in the death of Damion Lucas.

Johnny and Cathy Volsan Curry separately said they paid Hill in his fifth-floor Detroit Police Headquarters office a few weeks after the Damion Lucas killing. The $10-thousand, Johnny Curry said, was in a leather bag he left with Hill.

"Gilbert was greedy," the reporters quoted Cathy Volsan Curry as stating. She and Hill met several times, according to Volsan Curry. She would tell him the information she wanted and then give him money. "I remember paying him several times," Volsan Curry said.

Rick Wershe said he was present for a revealing phone conversation between Johnny Curry and Gil Hill. Wershe said he and Johnny were cruising around in Johnny's car when a call came in from Gil Hill. Curry had a radio telephone, the precursor to cell phones.

Wershe recalls Johnny Curry put the phone in speaker mode and the young informant heard Inspector Hill tell Curry to be cool, not to worry about the homicide investigation, that everything would be handled. Wershe says he shared this information with the FBI.

Hill, now deceased, repeatedly denied being bribed to keep the homicide investigation away from the Curry drug gang. Yet, Hill's homicide investigators ignored the leads about Wyman Jenkins and Leo Curry and continued to try to frame LeKeas Davis for the Damion Lucas killing.

It was police injustice times two; a deliberately botched homicide investigation and a frame-up, which enabled the recently bribed Inspector Hill to "solve" the Damion Lucas case.

The police criminality went deeper than the obstruction of justice in the homicide investigation. Despite Hill's denials, someone was leaking critical federal investigative information to the Curry organization.

For one thing, the FBI noticed the Curry phones went quiet shortly after the wiretap was authorized. Agents are required to give an authorizing federal judge what are called Seven-Day Reports on activity in a court-approved wiretap. An FBI Seven-Day Report on the Curry wiretap showed between May 3, 1985 and May 9, 1985, "approximately 32 were related to drug trafficking." On May 4, 1985, Johnny Curry received a phone call from Cathy Volsan asking him to meet her in person to discuss "trouble." After that, the drug-related phone calls on Johnny Curry's phones ceased. On several monitored calls after the warning from Cathy Volsan, Johnny Curry told callers his phones were tapped. The access of Johnny Curry and Cathy Volsan Curry to what the feds were doing was so complete they even knew when raids were planned and when the FBI was going to seize a car or some other property as part of the investigation.

Significantly, Narcotics Inspector Joel Gilliam told me in an interview in 1988 that he turned over federal task force investigative information from the Curry investigation, including sensitive wiretap details, to Deputy Chief Richard Dungy "in early May" of 1985.

By May 5, 1985, Johnny Curry started talking guardedly on his telephones and warned callers to be careful because his phones were tapped.

By all indications, investigative secrecy in the Curry investigation, including the use of covert wiretaps, was maintained until the information landed on the desk of Deputy Chief Dungy. The Deputy Chief didn't have a background in investigations, he didn't have a lot of criminal contacts, but people under his command did. People like Inspector Gil Hill.

Did Dungy tell Hill about the wiretaps and did Hill warn Johnny Curry?

Cathy Volsan Curry says he did. At the 1992 trial of her father, Willie Volsan, and Sgt. James Harris as a result of an FBI sting operation, Volsan Curry testified that it was Inspector Hill who told her Johnny Curry's phones were tapped by the FBI. In November of 1987, she told FBI Agent Gregg Schwarz the tip came from Sgt. Harris, an accusation he vehemently denies.

Clearly, there was a leak from *someone*. It underscores one of the fundamental flaws of the Organized Crime Drug Enforcement Task Force concept. Too many people have access to too much information.

Drug dealers are always secretive about their operations and to be successful, police investigations of drug rings must operate in secret, as well. In a police task force, operational secrecy is often an oxymoron. As Benjamin Franklin observed: "Three can keep a secret, if two of them are dead."

Like police officers assigned to any task force operation, the Detroit cops working the Curry investigation had an obligation to keep their commanding officers apprised of what they were doing. What their superiors in the police department did with that information was out of their control.

In the normal chain of command and flow of information, Inspector Hill, the leader of the Homicide unit would not be privy to reports of covert investigations in the Narcotics section. But in an autocratic city administration like the one Coleman Young established during his reign in Detroit, any police matter involving anyone in the mayor's family was to be treated with the utmost delicacy. The Detroit Police Department command ranks of that era were thoroughly compromised by politics. The normal rules and command channels didn't apply, even if the investigation involved drug trafficking and a killing. The Damion Lucas matter was a homicide case and a drug case. It's plausible that in Coleman Young's police department, Hill was given detailed sensitive narcotics reports about the Curry investigation, possibly by Deputy Chief Dungy, to "assist" the homicide investigation.

Another possible source of the leak was the Chief of Police.

William Hart was a quiet, up-through-the-ranks cop. As noted in Chapter 5, Hart had arrested Mayor Coleman Young in the late 1940s as part of an investigation of illegal gambling in the black community. Hart kept advancing until he was named police chief in September 1976. replacing Philip G. Tannian who, as noted in Chapter 5, was fired by Mayor Young for failing to tell him about a DEA investigation of possible narcotics corruption involving Executive Deputy Chief Frank Blount and Willie Volsan, the mayor's brother-in-law. Mayor Young had promised Tannian autonomy in all investigative matters. Apparently that agreement did not extend to investigations involving Coleman Young's family.

The point was not lost on Hart that Tannian was fired because he didn't keep Coleman Young informed about a major drug investigation that involved one of his in-laws. Thus, it is not surprising that Hart demanded briefings from his command officers on any case that might involve Cathy Volsan Curry, the mayor's drug-addicted niece.

Joel Gilliam was the kind of subordinate to comply with a demand by the chief to tell him everything about the Curry investigation. Hart was the kind of cop who could rationalize compromising an important investigation to shield one of the mayor's relatives. In Detroit there was law enforcement and then there was the political power of Coleman Young.

Gilliam and Hill were not alone in mastering the art of palace intrigue in the police department. They were equaled, perhaps, by a mysterious police officer named Sylvester Chapman, code-named Banjo.

Chapman was unique. He was recruited directly out of the police academy to work deep undercover, doing work supposedly so secretive that he wasn't even officially listed on the police department payroll. No one except Chief Hart and a few select command officers knew Chapman was a police officer.

Chief Hart was eventually indicted and convicted on charges he and a civilian deputy chief named Kenneth Weiner looted $2.6 million from the police department's Secret Service fund for covert drug operations—the War on Drugs. Hart claimed as part of his defense that much of the money went to Officer Chapman for super-secret operations and to pay a network of unnamed street informants. Chapman was thrown in prison briefly for defying a federal grand jury demand that he provide the names of the informants who allegedly received the cash payments.

The so-called Secret Service fund was looted so thoroughly and regularly that one month, an account to maintain the unmarked cars used for narcotics and organized crime surveillance work, fell to less than ten dollars.

William Dwyer was the Commander in charge of the Chief's office when the Secret Service fund was formed. Dwyer had been the head of narcotics before that. He left the department in 1985, the year of the Damion Lucas murder, to become the police chief in Farmington Hills, an upscale suburb. Dwyer has a theory about the massive embezzlement from the Secret Service fund and he emphasizes it's only a theory. But it is based on daily observations as Hart's chief of staff for several years.

Dwyer thinks Mayor Young may have ordered Chief Hart to withdraw cash from the secret service fund for unknown reasons, perhaps to pay hush money to someone. Dwyer theorizes Hart saw an opportunity to skim. "If the mayor asked him for five-thousand or ten-thousand, Hart would ask for double what the mayor wanted," Dwyer said. In Dwyer's theory, Chief Hart would give the mayor whatever cash he requested, and then keep a like amount for himself to make improvements on a vacation cottage or provide money and gifts for his mistress.

Government prosecutors never raised the possibility that the mayor might be receiving some of the cash meant for the War on Drugs. That would take the case to a much more explosive level, so the investigation didn't explore that. Government prosecutors narrowly focused their argument by stating Hart stole the money to support several mistresses and for his personal use, too. In Hart's federal court trial, the government sought to portray Sylvester Chapman as Chief Hart's personal bag man in the long-running theft scheme. Chapman would show up at the chief's office after business hours, shabbily dressed, presumably as part of his undercover role. Chapman would be given thousands of dollars in cash, no questions asked, no accountability given.

Dwyer doesn't believe Chapman kept any of the money for himself. Rather, the former Commander of the Chief's staff believes Chapman was a fall guy for Hart.

Yet, at Hart's federal trial, none of the police department's leaders could point to a single criminal case that was investigated or prosecuted as a result of Chapman's secret activities and frequent requests for significant cash from the Secret Service fund.

One Chapman assignment that did come to light was his development of a 24/7 bodyguard unit to protect Cathy Volsan Curry and her mother, Juanita Volsan, the mayor's late sister. How Chapman, who was supposedly so secretive and so deep undercover that no one knew he was a police officer, could recruit and organize a personal protection detail of other police officers was never explained.

At Hart's trial, it was said that Chapman and the surveillance team were assigned to this task of bottomless overtime because of death threats—from Richard Wershe, Jr. This isn't supported by the facts.

At the time Chapman and his watchdogs were supposedly "protecting" Cathy Volsan Curry and her mother from Rick Wershe, Wershe was having an affair with the mayor's niece, and occasionally spending the night with her at her mother's home in northwest Detroit—while Chapman's protective detail kept watch from a rented house across the street.

It should be remembered that on the court-authorized wiretaps, FBI agents heard Johnny Curry bragging shortly after the 1985 Damion Lucas killing, that he knew what was happening in the investigation because "my contacts control the police department."

What is clear is that Johnny Curry, one of the city's major narcotics dealers, had astonishing access to what was happening in the secret FBI/Detroit Police joint investigation of his drug empire, and he was seemingly fully informed on the police investigation of the death of 13-year old Damion Lucas. It appears multiple high-ranking members of the Detroit Police Department may have engaged in obstruction of justice and dereliction of duty in order to please Mayor Coleman Young. After the sacking of Chief Tannian and the destruction of

Commander Fiermonti's career over incidents involving Coleman Young's family, the Detroit Police top brass proved through the Damion Lucas case that the integrity of criminal investigations didn't apply to the above-the-law relatives of the mighty Mayor of Detroit.

Chapter 9—Rick gets Washington's attention

If you are going to sin, sin against God, not the bureaucracy. God will forgive you but the bureaucracy won't.
—Admiral Hyman Rickover

Through the summer of 1985, the FBI agents working the Curry Brothers drug case worried that members of the gang were going to get away with murder.

What's more, the agents and the Detroit Police narcs working with them on the anti-drug task force were alarmed that the Homicide Unit seemed hell-bent on convicting an innocent man.

This compound miscarriage of justice in the making was topped off with a growing realization within the FBI that Gil Hill, the Inspector in charge of Homicide, was corrupt.

Hill was a celebrity cop, at least in Detroit, thanks to his minor recurring role in the *Beverly Hills Cop* movies as Eddie Murphy's foul-talking, perpetually miffed boss. Hill was high profile and well-connected in his own department and with other area law enforcement before he made it to the big screen.

Paul Lindsay, a veteran Detroit FBI agent who worked many fugitive cases, spent a lot of time at Detroit Police Headquarters, perhaps more than any other G-man. (He went on to second career as the writer of half a dozen crime thrillers.) Lindsay was buddy-buddy with Gil Hill, which was a cause for concern among the Detroit FBI agents who suspected Hill was a crooked cop. There was no evidence that Lindsay, now deceased, did anything improper. Still, there was a recognition that Inspector Hill had his own intelligence network within the law enforcement community.

As Detroit Homicide and the Wayne County Prosecutor's office moved forward with charges against LeKeas Davis in the Damion Lucas death, the agents and cops in the federal/local task force decided they should take more aggressive action to let it be known that an innocent man—Davis—was facing charges. "I firmly believed he didn't do it," FBI Special Agent Herman Groman said when I interviewed him. For Groman, the killing of an innocent 13-year old boy and police efforts to shield the Johnny Curry gang from prosecution because of the leader's relationship with the mayor's niece, took this investigation beyond just another drug case.

This was potentially obstruction of justice, deprivation of rights under the color of law and public corruption at its worst. Why the FBI, the Detroit U.S. Attorney and the Justice Department didn't open an investigation of what they found in the Detroit Police handling of the Damion Lucas-LeKeas Davis matter is a troublesome question that lingers to this day. Since it involved possible top police command protection of a major drug gang in a homicide investigation, it goes to the issue of the conduct of the War on Drugs, too.

In mid-May of 1985, two of the Detroit Police narcs assigned to the federal task force alerted Deputy Detroit Police Chief Richard Dungy, the head of criminal investigations, that they had solid reasons to believe members of the Curry gang, and not LeKeas Davis, were responsible for the death of Damion Lucas. This was followed by a second meeting with Dungy in early June regarding information that LeKeas Davis was an innocent man.

The efforts in June by the task force investigators to get Detroit Deputy Police Chief Richard Dungy to order the Homicide detectives to take a look at the Currys as suspects went nowhere. The Homicide Section was under Dungy's command. The fact that the false prosecution of LeKeas Davis was moving forward was proof Dungy had done nothing with the FBI information or was powerless to shift the investigation to the Curry drug gang in the Damion Lucas killing.

In early August, Agent Groman and Sgt. Jack Tynan, one of the Detroit narcs assigned to the federal drug task force who is now deceased, met face to face with Sgt. Tom Dunn, the homicide investigator assigned to the Damion Lucas case. They told Dunn they had information from a reliable informant that Wyman Jenkins and Dwayne Goodwin of the Curry drug gang were responsible for the death of Damion Lucas, not LeKeas Davis. Furthermore, they told Dunn the FBI had wiretap recordings supporting the case against Jenkins and Goodwin. An FBI report says Dunn assured them he understood the confidentiality of the wiretap information and the need for discretion.

Sgt. Dunn, also deceased, apparently did nothing with the information.

The Detroit Police couldn't proceed with their frame-up of LeKeas Davis without the acquiescence of the Wayne County Prosecutor. The police investigate but the prosecutor files charges and takes cases to court.

On August 13, 1985, FBI Special Agent Gregg Schwarz showed the Bureau's evidence in the Damion Lucas killing to Assistant Wayne County Prosecutor Augustus "Augie" Hutting, who was prosecuting the

153

LeKeas Davis case. Schwarz and his colleagues figured
Hutting would demand a more thorough investigation.

Did Hutting raise hell with the Homicide detectives?
Did he demand to know why they were framing an
innocent man? Did he demand to know why they hadn't
pursued the leads about the Curry gang? There is no
evidence he did. Assistant Prosecutor Hutting, now
deceased, apparently did nothing with the information.

After all of this, the FBI, for its part, did nothing to
open an investigation of the obstruction by the top
command of the Detroit Police Department and possibly
the Wayne County Prosecutor's Office. This didn't involve
a questionable tip from a civilian. FBI agents had
witnessed the odd and unusual police and prosecution
behavior first hand.

The clock and calendar were moving forward on the
frame-up of LeKeas Davis. The FBI obtained an August
21, 1985 Detroit Police interoffice memo from Inspector
Gilliam of the Narcotics Section to Deputy Chief Dungy
noting that as of August 8, 1985, Homicide investigators
had not interviewed Wyman Jenkins, Dwayne Goodwin
and Leo Curry about the April 29th Damion Lucas slaying,
despite the axiom that it is vital in such investigations to
move quickly to interview witnesses and suspects.

The federal team decided to go to the top. The Detroit
narcs on the Task Force asked their boss, Inspector
Gilliam, to arrange a meeting with Police Chief William
Hart so they could play the wiretap tapes for him. They
hoped this dramatic and highly unusual presentation would
persuade Hart to demand that the Damion Lucas homicide
investigation include interrogation of the Curry gang.

Hart balked at having an FBI agent present at such a
meeting. He was told the FBI wasn't going to release the

wiretap tapes to anyone, but an agent would come to a
meeting and play them for the chief. Hart relented.

On August 20, 1985, FBI Special Agent Gregg
Schwarz, accompanied by the Detroit Police Task Force
narcs and Inspector Gilliam, met with Chief Hart and
several wiretap tapes were played. Schwarz kept custody of
the tapes but he gave the Chief a copy of the telephone pen
register data showing calls from Johnny Curry's home to
the unlisted home phone of Sgt. James Harris, followed by
a longer call to the private, unlisted phone in Inspector
Hill's office in the Homicide Unit. The tapes Schwarz
played for Hart left no doubt Johnny Curry knew his
phones were being tapped and that his "contacts" within
the police department were keeping him informed
regarding the homicide investigation.

Chief Hart, deceased, apparently did nothing with the
information.

Nationally, that same month, U.S. Attorney General
Edwin Meese and the DEA were taking a bold step in the
War on Drugs, or so the public was told. They launched
"Operation Delta-9."

It was supposed to be an all-states effort to eradicate
marijuana cultivation and harvesting. The nation was abuzz
about crack cocaine, but the Reagan Administration
remained fixated on marijuana.

Meese flew to the steep hills and valleys of the Ozark
National Forest in northwestern Arkansas. Reporters from
major newspapers and wire services were invited to join
him on a helicopter tour to watch marijuana plants being
chopped out of the ground by federal agents. It was
reminiscent of Prohibition-era police raids that culminated

in axe-wielding cops splitting open barrels of booze for the benefit of news photographers.

Unfortunately, the Ozark Mountain mist was so thick the Meese aerial crime-fighting dog-and-pony show had to be cancelled. His helicopter was grounded. That didn't stop Meese from declaring a few days later that Operation Delta-9 was a big success. The Justice Department said they had targeted a quarter of a million marijuana plants at hundreds of crop sites in all 50 states.

No one asked why, in the face of the endless War on Drugs, marijuana cultivation was so plentiful in every state of the nation. Reporters knew the answer: it was a matter of supply and demand, and demand was voracious.

The following year, Meese announced Operation Delta-9 might expand to include the National Guard. Meese also suggested that National Guard troops might be deployed along the 2,000-mile U.S. border with Mexico to interdict marijuana smugglers and to deter illegal immigration. This time, there was no helicopter show-boating in the Ozark Mountains or anywhere else. Operation Delta-9 quietly faded away as marijuana cultivation and harvesting continued unabated coast to coast. Years later, a California company selling marijuana-related products went in to business as Delta 9, "manufacturer of the finest cannabis-based products on the market." Today there are medical marijuana clinics and services in various locations in the U.S. and Canada that are named Delta-9.

In Detroit, in a last-ditch FBI effort to move the Damion Lucas investigation in the right direction, wiretap and informant intelligence was taken to Inspector Clint Donaldson, the head of the Internal Controls Bureau, commonly called Internal Affairs. Unlike his peers in the command ranks of the police department, Donaldson took action, up to a point. He ordered Sgt. Harris and Inspector Hill to come to the Internal Controls office for formal questioning regarding the FBI wiretap information.

Hill and Harris apparently weren't concerned. They showed up at Internal Controls as ordered, without attorneys, and submitted to interviews. Both men acknowledged they knew Cathy Volsan Curry and admitted they had frequent contact with her. Both Hill and Harris apparently said 'Yep. We know her,' and 'Nope, we didn't do anything wrong.' That was that. The Internal Controls inquiry ended without any action.

By the fall of 1985 the *New York Times* had discovered crack cocaine. "A New, Purified Form of Cocaine Causes Alarm As Abuse Increases," was the headline. In the herd journalism mentality that drives American media coverage, this was an important signal. Many editors and reporters don't think an issue is newsworthy unless it has been in the *New York Times*. For many editors and reporters with unsteady news judgment, the *Times* tells them what's news and what isn't. A new "crisis", a new "epidemic" was about to unfold. It was time for local reporters to spring into action to produce alarm stories about this new crack cocaine stuff.

In December, the case against LeKeas Davis moved to the trial stage and Agent Groman decided the time had come to contact Davis's defense attorney and tell him about the FBI's information that cast doubt on the case against his client. "I'm all about justice," Groman said. "An innocent man being convicted of something he didn't do;

To me, that just didn't sit well and I wanted to make sure that was rectified."

The attorney did what any criminal defense lawyer would do. He issued a subpoena for Groman to appear in front of Davis's trial judge and to have the FBI's confidential informant with him. The issue was no longer under the radar. The United States Attorney for Detroit was notified because the trial subpoena affected an on-going grand jury investigation. To make matters worse, the informant on the books, Richard Wershe, Sr. wasn't the real informant. The true informant was Richard Wershe, Jr.

FBI Headquarters was notified because a local court was demanding that one of its agents divulge the identity of one of its informants.

The FBI knows it would quickly go out of business as a law enforcement agency if it couldn't reassure a snitch that his or her identity would be protected. Snitches are so important to the Bureau's work that informant development is one of the ways management evaluates the performance of street agents.

"The informant files were always something closely guarded and protected," according to retired agent John Anthony, the Detroit FBI's legal adviser at the time. Richard Wershe Jr. wasn't just any run-of-the-mill snitch, either. "The information that White Boy provided was significant," Anthony said. "It wasn't little petty-ass stuff. It was significant information on drug trafficking in Detroit."

Anthony remembers the subpoena ordering Special Agent Groman to appear at the LeKeas Davis trial and to bring his confidential informant with him. This prompted a top-level meeting with Roy C. "Call me Joe" Hayes, the U.S. Attorney for Detroit, and top aides from Hayes's office and the local FBI. When the issue of the informant's identity rose to the level of a court debate, U.S. Attorney Hayes, now deceased, was in favor of revealing the FBI's source of information.

Hayes was a former Wayne County assistant prosecutor. He had directed the Organized Crime unit. Wayne County Prosecutor John O'Hair and his prosecutors were his old teammates, his pals.

Ken Walton, the head of the Detroit FBI, on the other hand, was a Hayes adversary. The two did not get along and the hostility between them was unmistakable. Hayes was accustomed to prosecutors giving police officers directives. Walton wasn't about to take orders from Hayes. Walton saw the FBI as the nation's premier law enforcement agency and U.S. Attorneys were political appointees, there to prosecute the Bureau's investigations. In Walton's view, the FBI did not answer to the U.S. Attorney. Ever.

John Anthony was not surprised to be attending a crisis meeting over a Herm Groman case. Also attending was Bob Reutter, the FBI Assistant Special Agent in Charge (ASAC) who oversaw the drug squad and meted out agent discipline, if necessary. "If he (Groman) wasn't in Reutter's office once a week, he wasn't workin'" Anthony said of Groman. "But he produced."

This time, however, Groman's investigative adventures had gone beyond the confines of the federal system. This was a what-to-do-about-Herm-and-his-informant meeting.

"We're all over there," Anthony recalls. "They're talking legalese, what to do and what not to do. Bob Reutter said 'It's the policy of the FBI that we don't give up informants.' I piped up and said, 'If push comes to shove Herm is going to jail.'"

Anthony said Hayes and his assistant attorneys were dumbfounded. "Their reaction was, 'You gotta be crazy.' I said, 'No. We're not giving him up. Herm is going to jail.'"

Hayes took the problem to the Justice Department. The issue landed on the desk of Deputy Attorney General Arnold Burns, who had a better understanding than Hayes of the FBI's role in the federal criminal justice system. Burns conferred with Floyd Clarke, his counterpart at the FBI. Clarke apparently said the FBI wasn't going to divulge the informant's identity.

The day Agent Groman was due in court, Anthony recalls needling him by asking if he had his toothbrush. The joke occurred to others, too. Groman said on the ride to court he chatted with an assistant United States attorney who would represent him in the local trial court.

Groman recalls: "I said, 'Well, how ya doing? Are you all set? Are you ready to defend me vigorously?' She said, 'Well, I was thinking about that when I was getting ready and I brought you a present.' She gave me a toothbrush. She said, 'I think you might need this.'"

Groman was called before Judge James Roberts, the presiding judge at the LeKeas Davis trial. Roberts was an older, well-regarded black lawyer with decades of experience as a prosecutor, public defender and judge. He ordered Groman to identify his informant and to explain the case surrounding the wiretap recordings. Groman refused. The judge told Groman if he didn't respond he would be held in contempt of court and sent to jail.

Judge Roberts wanted the matter resolved without the drama of sending an FBI agent to jail for contempt of court. He adjourned the trial until after the holidays to give the parties time to work out a compromise.

The postponed confrontation in Judge Roberts' court
prompted another crisis meeting at the U.S. Attorney's
office. A decision was made to appeal to the Wayne
County Prosecutor to act on the FBI's information by
empaneling a state grand jury to investigate the handling of
the Damion Lucas homicide. The LeKeas Davis trial was
adjourned until February. The Wayne County Prosecutor
convened a grand jury to explore the matter but nothing
came of the inquiry.

In the meantime, the top brass of the U.S. Justice
Department and the FBI were now involved in the
informant storm brewing in Detroit. In late January of
1986, U.S. Attorney Hayes was called to Washington to
discuss the situation.

The federal law enforcement big guns were present at
the Justice Department to discuss what to do about the
local court demand in Detroit that the FBI give up one of
its informants. Deputy Attorney General Lowell Jensen
was there. So was Oliver "Buck" Revell, the Executive
Assistant Director of the FBI. The Department of Justice
decided it would not compel the FBI to disclose the
identity of the informant. Throughout the discussions in
Washington, the fiction was maintained that informant
"Richard Wershe" was the father, not the son. Memos and
notes refer to Informant Wershe's "business interests."
Young Wershe's business interest was limited to his FBI
informant payments and occasional drug sales he was
doing on the side to generate money for his lifestyle. There
is no indication in available documents that the top
leadership of the Justice Department and FBI took any
interest in the ramifications of the top commanders of the
Detroit Police Department repeatedly resisting FBI efforts
to help them solve a homicide and avoid prosecuting an
innocent man.

That same week, Hayes met with Richard Padzieski, the chief of operations for the Wayne County Prosecutor's office. Padzieski, now deceased, must have been in a conciliatory mood. He told Hayes he didn't think the FBI should have to disclose the identity of its informant and equally important, he thought charges against LeKeas Davis should be dropped. He said he could recommend both positions to Prosecutor John O'Hair.

The standoff was defused by all sides agreeing to a confidential, off-the-record meeting in the judge's chambers. The attorneys for the prosecution and defense and the assistant United States attorney were called in to the closed session where Agent Groman explained the situation to the judge by describing the Curry drug investigation, the authorized wiretap and the informant intelligence that indicated members of the Curry group were responsible for the death of Damion Lucas, not LeKeas Davis. Groman said the court-authorized wiretaps seemed to corroborate what the informant told them. He did not reveal the informant's name.

As part of a compromise, the FBI agreed to allow two assistant county prosecutors to come to the FBI offices for a telephone interview with the secret informant. The prosecutors wanted to tape record the interview. The FBI said no. The prosecutors had to go to the FBI offices for the interview to ensure there was no recording of the telephone conversation. They did the interview, took notes, and left.

On February 19, 1986, Judge Roberts dismissed the charges against LeKeas Davis on a motion from the Wayne County Prosecutor. The issue of the identity of the FBI informant was now moot.

After charges were dropped against LeKeas Davis, the Damion Lucas homicide was dropped, too. Members of the Curry gang were interviewed months after the killing, with defense lawyers present. On September 19, 1988, some two-and-a-half years after the death of Damion Lucas, Assistant Prosecutor Hutting wrote a memo for the file stating there were too many problems and complications with the case, that too many people would have to be granted immunity to testify. Therefore, Hutting concluded the Damion Lucas killing should not be prosecuted "in the best interest of justice."

There was another, sharper memo about the Damion Lucas/LaKeas Davis investigation written in November, 1988, by David Ries, a supervisor in the Detroit FBI office. It was a summary of the case from an FBI perspective.

"It appears that DPD Homicide was not really too concerned with the obtention of the investigative information concerning the Damian (sic) Lucas murder produced by the FBI," Ries wrote. "...it appears, from review of the files, that DPD Homicide, never made any active effort to obtain further information the FBI may have produced, nor does it appear that DPD Homicide actively pursued leads generated by the FBI in a timely manner."

The Ries memo contains what should have been a red flag for his own office, which was forever looking for a case that might lead them to a prosecution of Mayor Coleman Young. Squeezing top leaders of the Detroit Police Department in a federal grand jury-based investigation of serious police misconduct in the investigation of the killing of a little boy and the attempted railroading of an innocent man may have been their ticket to an investigation of Coleman Young.

Vince Wade

The Ries FBI memo on the Damion Lucas case
concluded: "It is the writer's opinion, based on all available
information, that the involvement of Kathy Volson (sic)
(Cathy Volsan), the niece of Mayor Coleman Young, as
well as the involvement of two DPD officers in this entire
matter has had an effect on the DPD Homicide
investigation," Ries summarized the double injustice this
way: "From a review of this file…it appears as if the
termination of the prosecution of LeKeas Davis was done
in spite of the DPD and Wayne County Prosecutor's Office
rather than at their behest. That is, it appears as if the FBI
was forced to convince both of these state prosecutive
agencies that LeKeas Davis was not involved in this
murder."

The Curry investigation did not stop while the court
confrontation played out. Groman, Schwarz and the Detroit
Police narcs working with them continued to build their
case against the Currys.

Groman received information that Johnny Curry might
have some real estate investments in Florida. He decided to
investigate.

Groman had just dodged a visit to the county jail. It
was winter in Detroit and the Task Force narcs wanted to
get out of town, too. But Groman couldn't get
authorization for travel for the Detroit OCDETF Task
Force cops. They decided to go, anyway. They put in for
leave from the Police Department and paid their own way
to sunny Florida.

The vagaries of airline travel were such that the local
narcs wound up leaving Detroit a day ahead of Groman.
On the flight to Miami, one of the Detroit narcs got in to a
conversation with another passenger, who turned out to be

164

a drug dealer. They made a deal in the air. When the plane landed, the Detroit cops arrested the luckless doper. They called the FBI Miami office and said they needed help with an arrest at the airport. They explained they were working with Special Agent Herman Groman of the FBI's Detroit Division, who would be arriving the next day.

The Miami FBI didn't know what they were talking about. Groman had neglected to contact the Miami office and tell them he would be in their territory doing some case work. That is a major no-no in the FBI way of doing things.

A bureaucratic fault line erupted between the Miami and Detroit FBI offices. FBI-Miami wanted to know why no one told them an agent from Detroit would be doing Bureau work in their jurisdiction. FBI-Detroit thought Groman had followed protocol and notified Miami. FBI-Miami wanted to know who the hell these narcs were from the Detroit Police Department and who authorized them to contact the Miami FBI for assistance with an arrest made aboard a flight. FBI-Detroit knew nothing about the Detroit police narcs or what they were doing in Miami. It went downhill from there.

David Vlasak, Groman's squad supervisor, apparently wanted his head. Groman and Vlasak didn't get along, even on good days. Groman clearly had casual regard for the two ponderous volumes of FBI Rules and Regulations. If this were kindergarten, Groman would be marked down for not keeping his crayon work inside the lines of his coloring book.

Vlasak wanted Groman transferred to another division, maybe even fired. John Anthony, the office legal adviser, was in on the discussions. "Herm Groman was too valuable to the Division, even though he's a little wacky and unorthodox," Anthony said. "He was too valuable to transfer him out of the Division."

Groman had something else going for him and it was a big something. The SAC—Special Agent in Charge—liked his style. The SAC of the Detroit office during this time was Kenneth P. Walton, a flamboyant G-man fond of pompadour hairstyles and double-breasted suits. Walton was known to wear a real cape on occasion. Walton had had his own problems in the FBI for not following the rules and proper procedure. But like Groman, Walton produced excellent work, so he advanced through the ranks in spite of himself. Walton was known in the Bureau as an agent's agent.

"Herm Groman was the type of agent that Ken Walton liked," John Anthony said. "He (Groman) was aggressive. He was not a rules guy. I think Ken liked Herm from that standpoint." "Walton was never going to fire him or transfer him or anything like that. He was too valuable," Anthony added.

There was a compromise. Groman would be transferred off the drug squad. He was re-assigned to the public corruption squad—immediately. On March 27, 1986, the Curry case was re-assigned to Special Agent Gregg Schwarz who had been working on the wiretap and electronic surveillance components of the investigation. Schwarz was fully up to speed on the elements of the case. And he was fully up to speed on why he was now the case agent.

As for Rick Wershe, Jr., all communications with Groman and the Detroit narcs on the OCDETF Task Force came to an abrupt halt. "They quit taking my calls," Wershe said.

Anthony tried to put the situation in perspective. He said the Miami dust-up probably prompted Walton, now deceased, to sit down with Bob Reutter, the Assistant Special Agent in Charge responsible for the drug squad, to review what was going on. "Hey, there's much more going on here," Anthony imagines Walton probably said. "This thing is a like a comet spinning out of its orbit. It's going to crash and kill all of us. Let's cut our losses and make some changes here."

Exactly what the Detroit FBI managers and supervisors knew about the informant known as "Gem" continues to elicit vague answers and evasions. Before he died Walton told me he didn't remember Rick Wershe. Walton was ill when we spoke so I didn't challenge him. But the Ken Walton I knew was a details freak. He took pride in knowing everything going on in the squads under his command. It defies belief and his own work ethic to accept that he couldn't remember an informant case under his command that went up the FBI chain of command to the Number Two honcho of the Bureau and the top level of the Justice Department. It defies belief that he didn't find out who "Richard Wershe" really was.

Did Walton, his two Assistant Special Agents in Charge and the squad supervisors know Rick Wershe was a juvenile? John Anthony says no. But retired agent Mike Castro, who worked with Groman on another big case explored in another chapter, says it was no secret in the squad areas that the informant named Richard Wershe was a juvenile. Castro recalls it being discussed openly. Managers of the Detroit Division of the FBI would have had to go out of their way to NOT know that their most productive drug informant of that era was a white kid.

To this day, there is nothing in the FBI files indicating a juvenile was working as a paid informant on the Curry investigation. "You can't find any documentation," John

Anthony said with certainty. "Everything on paper and everything that was documented was perfect." Everything on paper implies the valuable drug intelligence was coming from Richard Wershe, Senior., since he was the informant-of-record. Yet, all of the agents directly involved with the case say the info was coming from Richard Wershe, Junior, a teen. Rick Wershe, Jr., agrees.

When Rick Wershe, Jr. complains the FBI was illegally using him as a juvenile informant, he's technically wrong on two counts. First, according to Walton, there was no rule, regulation or law in those days prohibiting the use of juvenile informants, although there was an unwritten rule that it simply was not done. Second, there is nothing whatsoever on paper to support Wershe, Jr.'s claim that he was working for the FBI as a teen snitch. "You couldn't find a piece of paper anywhere that documented him as a 'FBI informant'" Anthony states. There's no "evidence" the Detroit FBI used a juvenile in the War on Drugs in the 80s.

Nevertheless, even though he wasn't an informant on paper "Rick became a liability," John Anthony said, confirming the truth about the teen informant. "No doubt about it."

By the spring of 1986 the FBI and U.S. Attorney were well on their way to wrapping up the Curry investigation and securing a grand jury indictment. Wershe's intel about the activities of the Currys was no longer necessary. The evidence was in, the case was made.

"We didn't need him anymore," Anthony says flatly. "So why risk the problems associated with information from a juvenile?" A juvenile who didn't exist anywhere in FBI paperwork.

Since age 14, Richard Wershe, Jr. had been living the jet-setting life of a secret agent and getting paid by the FBI and Detroit Police to do it. He was a street-savvy kid who wound up partying and hanging out with the biggest drug dealers of Detroit. Suddenly, without warning, it was all over.

Chapter 10—CIA Justice in Detroit

"Now we know what CIA really stands for: Crack in America."
—Quip on a Florida radio show during a discussion of the Iran/Contra affair.

While FBI agents Groman, Schwarz, Dixon, Tisaby, Finch and others were building a case against the Curry Brothers with the help of Richard Wershe, Jr., one of their colleagues in the Detroit office was pursuing a drug smuggling conspiracy that made the Currys look like minnows swimming amid sharks. The Currys were trafficking in kilos. This drug case was measured in tons.

Ned Timmons was a former local cop who joined the FBI and brought street smarts with him. Timmons was working undercover against biker gangs, many of them naturals at smuggling and drug peddling. They were rough and violent. Killings were not uncommon. Unlike the Curry case where a confidential informant was doing the dangerous dirty work, Agent Timmons was the one who was undercover. He looked the part, too, muscular with long strawberry blonde hair and a droopy moustache. He rode a government-supplied big Harley, the kind bikers would admire and envy. His cover story was that he had easy access to the chemicals needed to make crystal meth.

The bikers Timmons was pursuing were enthusiastic drug peddlers but most of them weren't any higher up the narcotics food chain than the Curry Brothers. The big break for Timmons happened in the classic method law enforcement uses to make narcotics cases. He made multiple buys of crystal meth from a Detroit biker named

Buck, then busted him. Timmons reminded Buck he had been dealing within a thousand yards of a school. The out-of-luck biker could be facing fifty years in prison—in effect a life sentence.

Timmons told Buck his only chance was to do a different kind of deal, this time to trade underworld intelligence for lighter charges—to become a snitch. Buck was told he had to give up someone of real value in the biker underworld. The biker/meth dealer decided to give up a fellow criminal known as Shine.

Shine was described to Timmons as a big shot in a national and international dope smuggling operation; an organization that raked in millions of dollars on a regular basis. Timmons listened, but there wasn't any proof that Shine was part of a major drug ring.

Clinton Anderson, aka Shine, was a deadly joker. Like many bikers, Anderson was overweight but physically powerful. His eyes were dark slits in a big, round face, yet somehow, they were expressive. He was quick with a joke and he could yuk it up in a crowd, but he could be violent, too. He once killed a man in a bar fight. Anderson is deceased, a victim of cancer.

The late Ken Walton, Timmons' top FBI boss, was fond of saying he would rather be lucky than good. With Clinton Anderson, Timmons was both lucky and good. Buck, the meth-dealing biker/dope peddler Timmons busted, brought the undercover agent to meet Anderson, who was at home and in great pain. He was recovering from a .12-guage shotgun blast. Anderson nearly bled to death before he could be rushed to a hospital. Anderson had been shot during a drunken fight with a fellow drug smuggler who Anderson suspected was trying to take his place in a massive drug trafficking enterprise.

Timmons and Buck brought a case of Jack Daniels whiskey to Anderson's house. Buck, the new informant, introduced Ned as "Ed", a fellow biker. Buck said he and "Ed" just happened to be in the area and they decided to stop by and see how Anderson was doing during his recuperation. The street-savvy Anderson was skeptical of this story, so they told him they were looking for work in the smuggling business, perhaps driving a load or helping with offloading. Buck told Shine his meth sales business was getting a little too hot due to police attention, so he needed to find another source of income. Illegal, of course.

The whiskey started flowing and Anderson started bragging, as he was prone to do. Timmons paced his drinking while the other two men drank freely. Timmons was undercover, working—and wearing a wire.

Shine boasted that he was a key player in a massive international smuggling ring. He handled security. He operated his own version of a lie detector. Prospective smugglers for the organization were screened by Anderson to ensure they were not an undercover cop or police informant. Anderson talked about how he worked for Mike Vogel, a Detroit-area guy in marijuana sales and distribution who was partners with two other smugglers; Leigh Ritch, who had homes in the Cayman Islands and Tampa, Florida and Steve Kalish, a Texan who also had a home in Tampa. The trio, Shine bragged, had made over a hundred million dollars smuggling tons of marijuana into the United States from Colombia, and they were getting better at it and expanding their smuggling operations.

Anderson said the man who shot him did it because Vogel was angry with him for not delaying a massive shipment of marijuana his partners had smuggled by ocean-going barge in to a bayou near Lafayette, Louisiana. Vogel, the sales guy for the smuggling ring, had not been able to sell all of the marijuana from a previous smuggling venture and he was upset that the so-called "Bulldog" load was going to drive prices down. Anderson had no control over the Bulldog load, but he believed Vogel blamed him, anyway. Anderson figured his assailant saw killing him as a way to replace him in Vogel's end of the operation. Now Anderson was furious with Vogel. Getting even is one of the time-tested motivations for becoming a police informant.

What Anderson didn't know was that Timmons was recording everything that was said during the drinking session. Anderson incriminated himself many times over. Timmons had him on the first try.

Timmons broke the news to Anderson that he was an undercover FBI agent and he was wired and Shine had screwed himself with his bragging about the smuggling ring and his part in it. He said Anderson had a choice: he could become an FBI informant and his wife and kids would be protected by the federal government, or he could refuse to cooperate and take his chances that his enemies wouldn't botch the job the second time they came to kill him.

After pondering his options Anderson agreed to roll over, but only on the condition that he would not do any time and his family would be safe. In exchange he would offer up the truck drivers, the off-loaders, the aircraft pilots and the boat captains of perhaps the largest smuggling operation of its kind in U.S. history. And he'd offer up the leaders, too. In reviewing what Anderson had revealed, Timmons and federal prosecutors estimated it was a billion-dollar operation.

The recruitment of Clinton "Shine" Anderson put Special Agent Ned Timmons in a situation most narcs can only dream about. Unknown to Timmons, FBI agents in Florida and North Carolina were after the same smuggling ring. So were DEA and U.S. Customs agents. In each case, the investigators had leads on a different piece of the multi-state smuggling operation. Early on, no one in federal law enforcement had any idea how vast this drug organization truly was.

Anderson introduced Timmons to Leigh Ritch on Grand Cayman Island. Anderson said Ned was Ed. Ed Thomas, his cousin, who was a security expert and international arms dealer who had recently been in Saudi Arabia selling gunboats. Timmons told Ritch he was an expert at electronic surveillance, wiretapping and sophisticated security measures. Timmons was amazed when Ritch bought his story and hired him on the spot to handle security for the entire smuggling operation. Anderson and Timmons would work together to ensure "security" for the smugglers. Timmons would get to know all the players.

One of the first things Ritch had Timmons do is check his Grand Cayman Island home and office for bugs. Timmons did a sweep and proclaimed everything was clean.

Michael Paul Vogel began dealing marijuana in the early 1970s while he was in college at the University of Miami. Marijuana was viewed as the modern version of bootleg booze. Vogel's friends in Detroit, knowing he was in drug-infested Miami, asked if he knew anyone who could score some marijuana. Of course he did. As he later put it in testimony before a U.S. Senate Committee, "I talked to some people, put a few people together, and I made a couple of thousand dollars." Vogel very quickly turned from college student to drug dealer. He never looked back.

Connections lead to connections. Many people in the drug underworld know one another or at least have heard of each other. A girlfriend introduced Vogel to Leigh Ritch who was dealing large amounts of marijuana through his association with Jerry Carroll, a well-established drug smuggler based in Michigan, Vogel's home state. Carroll and Ritch needed someone to sell and move the product. Vogel had warehouse and trucking connections, and he was a pretty good salesman. Vogel got in deeper and started making serious money.

Leigh Ritch was using sailboats and commercial fishing boats to smuggle marijuana into the United Sates. Carroll was smuggling marijuana by air. He had a group of pilots using two types of aircraft. One was the Piper Navajo Chieftain, a twin-engine small cargo plane with powerful engines. It could haul about 7 thousand pounds of cargo, in this case, marijuana. The other was the much larger Douglas DC-6, designed as a military transport near the end of World War Two. It was a long-range transport plane with a cargo capacity of about 28 thousand pounds of cargo, or about 14 tons of marijuana.

One of the pilots was Michael B. Palmer, a veteran flyer for El Salvador's TACA Airlines. Flying for TACA, Palmer got to know Central America.

Palmer left TACA for Delta Airlines.

But he found the smuggling business paid much better. Palmer wasn't just any shady flyboy wearing pointed-toe cowboy boots in case he had to make an escape over a chain-link fence. FBI agent Timmons would later liken Palmer to a near-genius and a master at reading people and telling them what they wanted to hear. "He had an IQ of about 10,000," Timmons recently estimated, with a wee bit of exaggeration.

Palmer sometimes functioned as the coordinator of air operations for the Carroll-Vogel smuggling group. He would arrange the aircraft and the flight crews and on occasion, Vogel said, Palmer would act as an air traffic controller for the covert landings. The planes would land in the middle of the night at remote, rural airports. The group went to considerable lengths to avoid detection by law enforcement.

They favored rural landing strips to keep their clandestine flights clandestine. Smuggling trips were carefully planned. Sites, while rural, were selected for good access to Interstate highways. Young women associated with the smugglers would be sent to the area weeks in advance to take jobs as waitresses at coffee shops favored by the local police. Their job was to listen as much as possible to casual cop conversation, to learn what they could about day to day operations of local law enforcement.

Weeks in advance of a shipment, a team of smugglers would arrive in the area claiming to be buddies on an extended hunting or fishing trip. They would rent cottages or cabins and make a point of getting to know the locals. The smugglers knew that in rural America strangers attract nosy attention, so they made a point of becoming casually familiar faces. They also made a point of doing counter-surveillance. They discreetly took note of police patrol patterns. Cops, like most people, are creatures of habit.

The drug smugglers had state-of-the-art electronic equipment, including top-of-the-line police scanners. They made it their business to learn the frequencies used by local, state and federal law enforcement in the landing area.

Those frequencies were monitored diligently before a shipment so the team would know the radio chatter of routine patrol work. The police radios were monitored until a load had been successfully offloaded. The smugglers also noted large parking lots in the area such as those at high schools and churches. They knew police raid teams always stage in places where a number of people can congregate. When a flight was inbound, potential police staging areas were watched.

Preparations included emergency escape plans. In the event of a surprise raid, the team knew to scatter and run to designated pick-up locations and hide and wait for a pick-up vehicle cruising at designated times.

Shortly before a smuggling flight was due to arrive, makeshift landing lights were placed along the landing strip. The lights were shrouded so they were only visible from the air. When the plane landed, experienced off-loading teams would get to work transferring the marijuana or cocaine to waiting trucks. The entire operation was quick and quiet. Tons of drugs could be traveling down the highway and the plane could be back in the sky without law enforcement being aware of what had happened in the middle of the night in the tranquil countryside.

After the operation fell apart as a result of the investigation by FBI Agent Timmons and others, Mike Vogel eventually told a Senate committee that on rare occasions, when the police slipped through all the careful pre-planning, he had to pay bribes. Vogel said 50 thousand or 60 thousand dollars would typically do the trick to avoid getting busted.

"Usually, all we requested is that they do nothing," Vogel testified. "Look the other way?" Senator John Kerry asked. "Look the other way, yes sir," Vogel said. Air smuggling earned the group hundreds of millions of dollars through the 1970s and up to the mid-1980s.

Jerry Carroll went his own way and formed new alliances. A preppy-looking Texan with a head for business named Steve Kalish took his place in the Vogel-Ritch group.

Kalish eventually appeared before the Senate Permanent Subcommittee on Investigations of Governmental Affairs, where he said he and Ritch and Vogel didn't invest in drug smuggling by themselves. "There was an individual in the Detroit, Michigan area associated with the Teamsters' Union that provided us with the vehicles we used in the transporting of marijuana," Kalish testified. The Teamsters provided more than transportation. FBI agent Timmons learned several Teamsters with access to the union's Central States Pension Fund would help themselves to the union cookie jar, investing two or three million dollars at a time in air smuggling loads organized by the group, and turn a handsome profit, making four dollars for each dollar invested. According to Timmons, Teamster money and transportation resources were invested in large-scale drug smuggling on several occasions.

Working undercover on Grand Cayman Island and in Florida, Timmons learned the smuggling ring Clinton Anderson had introduced him to had considerable skill and connections that extended offshore.

This group had printouts of Coast Guard cutter locations and they had obtained military and law enforcement communications frequencies, including the radio frequency for Air Force One. They had figured out Coast Guard and military resources would be tasked with assisting with Space Shuttle launches, so ocean-going smuggling shipments often occurred when federal air and sea resources were on Shuttle duty.

Kalish helped the group increase their profits, which caused a problem—what to do with all the money?

The group had houses in Tampa, Florida and Farmington Hills, Michigan used for storing drug profits. Every room was filled with money. Floor to ceiling. At first, the group tried counting the money but they burned up several money-counting machines because they had so much cash. "...at one point, we had in excess of thirty-five million dollars in Tampa," Kalish told the Senate Permanent Subcommittee on Investigations. "The sheer volume of cash generated in 1983 soon overwhelmed our organization."

Leigh Ritch also testified before the Kerry subcommittee on narcotics trafficking. Senator Kerry asked Ritch how much money he estimated the group players he was involved with—Jerry Carroll, Mike Vogel, Steve Kalish and Michael Palmer—grossed in about 15 years of drug smuggling. "It was in the hundreds of millions. I'd say you could go into the billions," Ritch testified.

In 1982, President Reagan had declared a "new" War on Drugs, claiming the tsunami of illegal dope flooding the nation was a matter of national security. "We've taken down the surrender flag and run up the battle flag," Reagan said. In 1986, he signed the Anti-Drug Abuse Act, appropriating an additional $1.7 billion to fight the drug war.

Kalish, Ritch and Vogel were waging their own War *Of* Drugs, a constant battle against the rising flood of cash that was pouring in from illegal drug sales. They flew their drug money to banks in the Cayman Islands, but eventually the banks complained it was too much cash for them to handle. "At one particular bank, we delivered twelve million dollars in twenty-dollar bills. The head office in Nassau (Bahamas) refused to accept any more small bills from us," Kalish testified.

Steve Kalish considered laundering their drug profits in Europe, but he decided they needed to take their business to Panama, the banking center of the global drug trade. Kalish put over two million dollars in a suitcase and boarded a private jet for Panama. It didn't take long for Kalish to meet a Panamanian banker with "connections."

Those connections were in the person of General Manuel Noriega, the military ruler of Panama. Kalish was soon invited to Noriega's home for a meeting. He brought his stunning, shapely, beauty-pageant-gorgeous girlfriend and soon-to-be wife Denise, with him. Noriega was smitten. It was lust at first sight. Panama's leader told Kalish Denise was always welcome to accompany him on visits to Panama.

Kalish also brought a briefcase stuffed with three-hundred-thousand dollars in cash, which he left with a smiling Noriega. The door was now open to move drug profits in to Panamanian banks and to move shipments of drugs through Panama on their way to the United States. Manual Noriega went into business with Steve Kalish and his smuggling group.

Noriega was also in business with the CIA. He was the Agency's Numero Uno asset is keeping tabs on Cuba and various pro-Communist movements in Central and South America. The CIA knew Noriega was on the take big-time in the drug-smuggling racket. But they didn't care. Throughout most the 1980s, Noriega's value as an

Vince Wade

intelligence asset outweighed his key position as one of the enemies in the War on Drugs.

FBI Agent Timmons continued to infiltrate the Ritch-Kalish-Vogel group and continued to build a solid drug smuggling case against the operation, including the pilot Michael Palmer.

For his part, the wily Palmer had finagled his way in to the heart of the secret Reagan Administration effort to help the Nicaraguan Contras battle the Leftist Sandinistas. Palmer got involved with a Miami aircraft leasing company called Vortex. Vortex was hired by the U.S. State Department's Nicaraguan Humanitarian Assistance Office (NHAO) to fly "humanitarian" aid to the Contras. This was widely regarded as a CIA operation under the direction of Lt. Col. Oliver North of the White House National Security Council—the NSC. Vortex had two cargo planes and Palmer had used both of them to smuggle drugs. Ollie North and the CIA were aware that Palmer had been a long-time drug smuggler. This fight-the-Commies-at-all-costs band of CIA and White House covert operators also knew Palmer was under investigation by the FBI in three jurisdictions and that a federal grand jury in Detroit, working from evidence compiled by Timmons, was preparing to indict Palmer. A February 10, 1986 memo from NSC staff member Robert Owen to North complained that one of the planes "...was used at one time to run drugs and part of the crew had criminal records. Nice group the Boys choose (sic)." Media reports later described Owen variously as North's "courier" to the Contras, an "off-the-books intermediary" and Ollie North's "bagman" for cash payments to the Contras.

At about the time Ollie North was told some of his patriotic Contra-aid pilots were a bunch of drug smugglers,

182

his attractive secretary, Fawn Hall, was snorting cocaine on
the Washington, D.C. party circuit. Hall, who had a big
mane of blonde hair, admitted to DEA agents that she was
a regular user of cocaine between 1985 and 1987 when she
worked in sensitive national security positions in an
Administration that had redoubled the War on Drugs as a
matter of national security. Several years later she admitted
in TV and press interviews that she had become addicted to
cocaine. She entered rehab for her addiction.

Michael Palmer's long history as a drug smuggler
apparently didn't trouble Ollie North or anyone in the
White House.

Agent Timmons says he clearly remembers being in
Palmer's office in Florida on one occasion when he spotted
a framed photo of Mike Palmer in a group picture. Palmer,
a veteran drug smuggler responsible for the importation of
tons of drugs in to the United States, was at the White
House, shaking hands with President Reagan, accompanied
by his wife, "Just Say No" Nancy. Rex, the Reagan's
Cavalier King Charles Spaniel, was in the photo with
Palmer, too.

Did the CIA know about Palmer's history of big-
league drug smuggling when he was hired to covertly fly
supplies to the Nicaraguan Contras in direct violation of
the Congressional Boland Amendment that forbade U.S.
aid to the Central American rebel group? Various
Congressional hearings in 1988 and an internal
investigation by the CIA's own Inspector General show the
answer is, yes. But, apparently, they didn't give a damn.
Fighting Communism was more important than the War on
Drugs.

One of Michael Palmer's talents, in the view of the FBI's Ned Timmons, was an understanding of the bureaucratic rivalries of federal law enforcement. Palmer understood that the fight for splashy headlines about this week's drug bust of the century was a fight for a bigger slice of the federal budget pie. The FBI, DEA, and U.S. Customs were/are in a never-ending struggle to win appropriations dollars in Congress and the White House. One way to do that is through drug bust stats. "We did X-many busts and interdicted Y-tons of drugs and arrested Z-number of drug peddlers." Timmons says Palmer knew all of the top brass cheerleading for inter-agency cooperation and joint task forces to fight the War on Drugs was just so much bullshit for public consumption. If one federal agency could pull the rug out from under a rival agency, they'd do it.

As Timmons and FBI agents in Florida and North Carolina closed in on Palmer and the Ritch-Kalish-Vogel organization, the shrewd smuggler-turned-CIA Contra contract pilot scampered to U.S. Customs and the DEA and offered himself as a veteran drug smuggler-turned-good citizen willing to work undercover to help them score some big drug busts. On one of his drug runs to Colombia, Palmer and a Michigan pilot named Ken Jayson were arrested by the Colombians and thrown in jail for several months until Palmer's partners paid a ransom. Palmer testified his time in a Colombian jail gave him time to reflect on the error of his ways. That, and knowing the FBI was close to getting him indicted, apparently inspired Palmer to become a big-time snitch.

Palmer was busy cooking up airborne smuggling deals for the DEA and Customs when he was indicted by a Detroit federal grand jury for drug trafficking. He was arrested in Florida on the Detroit indictment and spent about a week and half in jail before making bail. He went back to work for DEA and Customs, devising smuggling stings that were sure to generate splashy headlines.

Palmer came up with a sting operation where he would fly to Colombia, take on a load of 17 thousand pounds of marijuana and fly it to an airstrip on an island in the Detroit river so the DEA could seize it. DEA said it was an international operation, therefore the FBI had no jurisdiction. Palmer, recognizing Timmons had lots of evidence against him, and understanding the inter-agency rivalries, insisted Timmons be part of this sting operation or he wouldn't do it.

Timmons says it amounted to a double-sting. "What I *suspect* is, Palmer bought the fucking dope," Timmons told me. "I think he bought 17-thousand pounds of pot. He put a crew together that used to fly for Ollie North. He got an old, beat-up DC-6 and flew out in to the Guajira (Colombia's Guajira Peninsula) with the people he used to smuggle with." Timmons admits he has no proof of this. It's an educated guess based on how Palmer operated.

When Palmer landed in Colombia another plane had crashed and burned at the landing strip shortly before his arrival. That plane was carrying a thousand kilos of cocaine to the U.S. Several hundred kilos burned, but 573 kilos were salvaged. The Colombians, brandishing guns, told Palmer he was going to take their load of cocaine along with his 17-thousand pounds of marijuana and fly all of it to the United States with several of the Colombians on board as passengers. Palmer's staged drug sting suddenly became more significant for law enforcement show-and-tell purposes.

Palmer, his crew and three Colombians flew to the Grosse Ile Airport in the Detroit River where they were met by narcs from the DEA, FBI, U.S. Customs, State Police and Wayne County Sheriff's Department. It was important for appearances that all the agencies had representatives in on the act.

The bust was front-page news. William Coonce, the head of the DEA's Detroit office, was in the morning paper posing with one foot atop kilos of cocaine spread out in a conference room.

The real story was what happened next.

Suddenly, there was pressure from Washington on the U. S. Attorney's Office in Detroit to drop the FBI case against Palmer. This was not about allowing Palmer to cop a plea and get a reduced sentence. This was about totally dropping *all* charges against Palmer. No criminal record. Timmons says the pressure to let Palmer walk away came from the DEA, the CIA and the White House.

"Palmer knew too much," Timmons told me. Palmer knew, and still knows, the truth about the Nicaraguan Contras, Ollie North, the CIA, Contra drug-dealing, drug flights to the U.S. under CIA-cover—all of it.

If Palmer was a big-time drug smuggler, shouldn't the CIA, which is in the business of gathering intelligence about people, have discussed situation with the DEA, FBI and Justice Department, regardless of his work for Ollie North?

Not exactly. When the Iran-Contra scandal surfaced, two letters surfaced which proved what was truly important and what wasn't in the Reagan Administration. Attorney General William French Smith and CIA Director William Casey exchanged letters in the winter of 1982 about whether the CIA was obligated, under the law, to inform the Justice Department when the agency became aware of criminal activity, including drug trafficking in Central America. This included CIA "assets" who might be smuggling dope.

Attorney General Smith wrote to Casey on February 11, 1982, saying it wasn't necessary to make it official policy, "…in view of the fine cooperation the Drug Enforcement Administration has received from CIA."

CIA boss Casey wrote back on March 2, 1082, stating these "procedures" "…strike the proper balance between enforcement of the law and protection of intelligence sources and methods."

In other words, it was totally optional for the CIA to alert the DEA that some of its secret intelligence operatives in foreign countries were major drug smugglers. If they were near the top of the pyramid in the War on Drugs, so what? If prosecuting them might mess with CIA covert operations, don't tell. That official policy was at work when it was time to decide what to do about the FBI case against Mike Palmer, one of Ollie North's Contra-supply pilots.

For his work on a drug smuggling empire that measured its illicit product in tons and its profits in the tens of millions of dollars—so much money that banks couldn't handle the volume of cash—Timmons was given an FBI "incentive" award—totaling two-hundred dollars.

Timmons, who had spent three years working undercover, traveling thousands of miles, building a case against 300 defendants in 25 states, threw in the towel and agreed to let Palmer get off scot-free. Timmons left the FBI not long after that. The Detroit U.S. Attorney's Office approached the judge on Palmer's case and said the U.S. government was dropping all charges, "in the interest of justice."

In June of 2017, Richard J. Wershe Jr. spent over four hours before a panel of the Michigan Parole Board, baring his soul, admitting his guilt in *trying* to become a major dope figure and pleading to be released from prison after serving over 29 years for possession of eight kilos of cocaine when he was a teen.

Michael Palmer, who admitted he was a drug pilot involved in importing tons of marijuana and cocaine in to the United States in over a decade of smuggling during the ballyhooed War on Drugs, but who had White House and CIA connections, spent less than two weeks in jail and ultimately, with pressure from Washington, had all drug charges against him dropped.

Chapter 11—Business as usual, until one day...

"I'm not addicted to cocaine. I just like the way it smells."
—The late Richard Pryor, comedian

Rims were a big deal to the dopers Rick Wershe, Jr. ran with when he was working as a secret informant for the FBI. Rims are wheel rims, the sometimes-fancy, outward-facing design of wheels on a car, costing as much as five-thousand dollars or more. In the inner cities, costly rims are evidence you have money. You are somebody. At least, by ghetto reckoning.

Comedian Chris Rock used rims in one of his stand-up routines to explain the difference between being rich and wealthy. Real wealth is empowering, Rock said, and most blacks are new to having money so they don't understand the difference between rich and wealthy. He cited highly-paid NBA star Shaquille O'Neill as rich, versus the white man who signed O'Neill's paychecks, as wealthy.

Rock said black people love wheel rims. "We'll put shiny-ass rims on any piece of shit car in the world," Rock said. He suggested black men might even try to put wheel rims on a toaster. Rock was saying car wheel rims are a poor man's idea of appearing rich. But they aren't evidence of being wealthy.

For inner city dope dealers, it's important to have and show "bling." Fur coats, gaudy gold jewelry, designer sun glasses and luxury cars with fancy rims are symbols of success among ghetto dope slingers.

Rims were a "Check it out—I've arrived" symbol when Rick Wershe, Jr. went clubbing with Johnny Curry. Pulling up to a club in a luxury car with gaudy rims was part of the see-and-be-seen ritual.

"The Lady" on Detroit's lower east side was a favored night spot. "It was like they had taken a scene out of *Scarface* (the Al Pacino gangster movie)," Wershe said. Tuesday nights were dope dealer nights, Wershe said. He described a milieu that evoked the social cliques in high school. "Everyone would have their own little section," Wershe recalled. "Everything was excess. Everyone wanted to be seen. Everyone wanted the best table. Everyone wanted to spend the most money."

Johnny Curry was treated like a god at the nightclub and he liked the shock value of making an entrance with a white boy as his sidekick, or perhaps he was a mascot. As a teen, Wershe looked every bit his age. His wimpy moustache didn't make him look any older. According to Wershe, Curry had the kind of clout that allowed him to bring a kid in to a nightclub, no questions asked: "I remember the first time I went with him to The Lady on Jefferson, and they were like, 'Who's this kid? You can't come in.' And Johnny was like, 'He's with me.' And they were like, 'Oh, go ahead.' It was like nothing else mattered once they knew I was with him," Wershe said.

Participants in the club scene say Johnny Curry didn't like to stay long at the night spots. It was part of his effort to keep a low profile. Still, as Johnny Curry's novelty sidekick Rick Wershe got to meet most of the top low-lifes of the Detroit drug trade in the mid-1980s. The task force narcs may have severed their relationship with Wershe in 1986, but he didn't sever his relationships with Detroit's drug dealers.

Prisoner of War:
The Story of White Boy Rick and The War on Drugs

"Maserati Rick (Carter) was always there," Wershe recalls. "He never missed a night." "Big" Ed Hanserd and Clifford Jones were among the major dopers Wershe encountered in the drug underworld social scene. Nightclubbing enabled the FBI's teen informant to meet Larry and Leroy Buttrom, the leaders of the Pony Down drug gang, which succeeded Young Boys, Incorporated as the top purveyors of heroin in Detroit—for a time. The Pony Down crew was flying high until the feds busted them. But others quickly took their place. The drug pushers knew and understood the street saying, don't-do-the-crime-if-you-can't-do-the-time. The lure of easy money and lots of it and the reality that consumer demand was always there had strong risk/reward appeal for many young men in the inner cities.

Anyone who takes the time to search newspaper archives since 1971 regarding narcotics enforcement will be struck by the hamster wheel nature of this kind of police work. Law enforcement is endlessly "dealing a blow" to some city's drug trafficking by arresting "Mr. Big." But the Mr. Bigs Rick Wershe met strutting in nightclubs, the ones who wear fur coats while driving around in luxury cars with garish wheel rims are ultimately the bottom feeders in the drug trade. They are—temporarily—a notch or two above nobodies. They are big fish only for the purposes of the police and prosecutors telling the public that *this* time, with *these* arrests, they've made a *real* difference in the drug racket.

Seldom, if ever, are the Big Dogs—the narcotics wholesalers, the importers, the money launderers or international bankers—featured in perp walks for the TV cameras. In the War on Drugs, law enforcement wins an occasional battle, but never the war. The war never ends.

Rudy Thomas can attest to that. He's a retired Detroit Deputy Police Chief who is both proud and ashamed of what he accomplished in his law enforcement career.

Crack cocaine became the "it" drug in the nation's ghettos about the time the FBI recruited Rick Wershe to become an informant. Crack houses suddenly proliferated in many inner-city neighborhoods. Unlike heroin "shooting galleries" where junkies would shoot-up a syringe of smack, crack houses were cocaine convenience stores. Addicts were in and out of them all hours of the day and night and residents got fed up.

Thomas, who had a reputation as a can-do honest cop, was summoned in January, 1986 by Police Chief William Hart and given an assignment to clean up the crack house problem. "'Rudy, the community is all over me,'" Thomas recalls Hart telling him. 'I have around 800 corners with young kids slinging drugs,' the Chief said. 'I want you to eliminate that. Solve the problem. Create (request) new laws if you have to. Do whatever you have to do so I can satisfy the citizens of Detroit.'"

Thomas, a lieutenant at the time, said he assembled a hand-picked crew of police officers to do the job. They had a list of addresses where the neighbors had complained about the crack traffic. Thomas and his team went after them relentlessly. He would send a surveillance team in to a target neighborhood, identify the pushers and where they kept their dope, where they kept their money. Unmarked vans would roll in and the narcs would jump out. "We'd go running after the drug dealers," Thomas said. "Identify them, arrest them, confiscate their drugs and the monies and anything else they may lead us to at that point." Thomas says his crew was tenacious.

"We were conducting these types of operations seven days a week," Thomas said. "We were averaging 5 to 10 thousand arrests a year. We led the Narcotics division in monies forfeited."

The results were noticed by Detroit's older, mostly black, citizens. "We made the senior citizens and those that were engulfed with drug houses on both sides of them, love us," Thomas said. "They wanted to cook meals for us. They thought we were the only ones (police officers) doing work at the time."

This was in 1986. It wasn't until years later that Rudy Thomas, who is black, had deep regrets and second thoughts about all that work busting thousands and thousands of young drug dealers. Thomas now realizes he was helping incarcerate an entire generation of young black men. It doesn't seem to matter to a new generation of black activists that in the mid-1980s *black people* were the ones demanding tougher police enforcement on the streets. It's easier for people to blame the police—rather than themselves—for law enforcement that later proved to corrosive to the community's long-term social health. It's easy to overlook the Law of Unintended Consequences.

Former Deputy Chief Thomas is a man who has given a lot of thought to crime, policing, mass incarceration and the War on Drugs. His father, Porter Thomas, who ran a Detroit auto collision repair shop, was killed in a robbery. Thomas says his mother thinks that, as a police officer, he should have somehow been able to stop the killing of his father, a random act of crime.

Thomas struggles with what he knew then and what he knows now. In his heart, he knows he and his crew tried to do the right thing for decent people who were victims of drug trafficking. "Especially the senior citizens," Thomas said. "They were literally locked in their houses. Imagine: some of them had crack houses on one side and on the other. They were taunted. They were robbed. They were afraid. They couldn't leave their house. They couldn't live."

Thomas says his team would shut down a neighborhood crack house and another would pop up. "The crack houses would reappear like roaches," Thomas said.

Several years later a Rand Corporation study quantified what Thomas and his narcs and the citizens saw on the streets. Detroit emergency room data on drug abuse showed that between 1983 and 1989, smoking drugs, meaning crack, had quadrupled, and "...the proportion of patients who ingested the drug by smoking had soared to 76 percent." The Rand study noted in 1987 "half the homicide victims in Wayne County tested positive for cocaine."

Former Deputy Chief Thomas doesn't have a magic answer to the nation's illegal drug problem. But he knows what he and his officers did, didn't work.

"What I think about it now, Vince, is we put tens of thousands of minorities, blacks, in jail, for life and now they have no life, they have no family. I feel bad about that. I know it was state and federal law that was imposed. We enforced it. But we didn't accomplish anything."

Thomas, a veteran police executive who personally spent considerable time on the urban battlefield, summed up his view of his part in the War on Drugs: "I feel bad. I was doing my job. We were doing our jobs, we were helping the community and at the same time we helped destroy the community."

A drug overdose in Baltimore, Maryland in the summer of 1986 sent shock waves through the War on

Drugs like no other event. It was one single death that changed the nation's history.

College basketball star and highly anticipated NBA crowd-pleaser Len Bias died of a cocaine overdose, two nights after he had been selected by the Boston Celtics as a first-round draft pick. Basketball fans were sure Bias would be the next Michael Jordan. Bookies from coast to coast were drooling over the prospect of a boost in illegal sports betting centered around Bias. His University of Maryland basketball coach said, with a straight face, that Bias's worst personal indulgence was eating ice cream. Gullible, besotted sports fans swallowed such talk whole. When news broke that Bias died from a cocaine overdose, the sports world, Congress and many in the nation went in to shock. The public, the politicians, the news media—all demanded action. How could this happen to our next sports superstar? Somebody DO something!

For Washington's politicians, Bias was the hometown college basketball hero. It was about a thirty-minute drive from the Capitol to watch Bias play at the University of Maryland. For all of its supposed worldly sophistication, Washington, D.C. is a very parochial town. Tragedies elsewhere are an abstraction. Tragedies that affect the District are *real* tragedies. The death of Len Bias was BIG news in the nation's capital city.

The Bias autopsy was controversial. There was a dispute over how the basketball star ingested the fatal dose of cocaine. Did he snort it? Did he swallow it in a drink? There was evidence to suggest he had free-based a massive amount of nearly pure cocaine while partying with friends. His buddies admitted they had been on a three-hour cocaine binge just before Bias died. The public wanted to believe he was an innocent young celebrity who had made a bad choice one night. The facts suggested otherwise. A packet of cocaine was found hidden in his leased sports car. Witnesses said the supposedly clean-living Bias spent a considerable amount of time nightclubbing. often four nights a week. Regulars at Chapter III, a popular D.C. nightclub, said Bias was often there when they arrived and he rarely left before closing.

Later, at the trial of Brian Tribble, the man who was alleged to have supplied cocaine to Len Bias, prosecutors said the basketball star was more than a one-time cocaine user. They claimed he had been an occasional dealer, selling Tribble's cocaine to some of his close friends. Prosecutors called Bias a "courtesy middleman." Tribble was acquitted in the Bias case but he was convicted on a separate cocaine charge and sentenced to ten years in prison.

None of this mattered in the public indignation stampede that followed the death of Bias in June, 1986.

Various media outlets, including ESPN, NPR, Salon and the Washington Post, among others, quoted Eric Sterling, chief counsel of the House Judiciary Committee as saying House Speaker Thomas P. "Tip" O'Neill came back from the Congressional Fourth of July break demanding legislation in the wake of the Bias death. Bias, as noted, had been drafted by the Boston Celtics. Sterling says O'Neill told colleagues all he heard while home in Boston was outrage over the Len Bias cocaine death.

In his book, *Smoke and Mirrors*, Dan Baum recounts how O'Neill, a powerful Democrat who always knew which way the wind of public opinion was blowing, called a meeting of all of his committee chairmen who had any role in crime legislation. "Write me some goddamned legislation," he thundered. "We need to get out front on this now. This week. Today."

The Republicans had dominated the crime issue in 1984, a Presidential election year, with the Comprehensive Crime Control Act. Ronald Reagan easily won re-election over Walter Mondale.

O'Neill told his colleagues he didn't want the Democrats outmaneuvered on crime again.

Thus, the overdose death of Len Bias became the catalyst for a Congressional stampede to write the toughest, most draconian, punishment-oriented legislation imaginable regarding cocaine.

Eric Sterling, the chief counsel of the House Judiciary Committee was tasked with crafting legislation to deal with crack cocaine and other drug abuse.

In an interview with *Salon* in 2011, Sterling said committee chairmen were scrambling to get a piece of the action. Cocaine became the evil of the year on both sides of the aisle in Congress. "Literally every committee, from the Committee on Agriculture to the Committee on Merchant Marine and Fisheries were somehow getting involved."

There were no hearings. The stampede wouldn't allow it. Ordinarily, legislation is circulated for wide-ranging review and hearings are the foundation for what is supposed to be a deliberative process. Not this time. Not after the drug death of a sports hero. There was no effort to evaluate the human consequences of using different forms and strengths of cocaine. In the hysteria that followed the death of Len Bias Sterling said, "It was hyperbole piled on top of exaggeration.".

With just days to go before Congress adjourned, Sterling faced a big problem. Republicans were demanding to know where the get-tough provisions were in the Democrat-driven legislation. Where's the punishment, they asked. No thought was given to the long-term consequences of mass incarceration and long prison sentences.

Sterling scrambled to fill the penalty void in the legislation. "I consulted with a D.C. local narc who was assigned to the House Narcotics Committee, and he suggested numbers," Sterling told NPR host Neil Conan on *Talk of the Nation.*

The D.C. Metropolitan Police narc was named Johnny St. Valentine Brown, also known as "Jehru." It was this lone local narc who dreamed up the mandatory minimums to be imposed in drug trafficking cases without any consultation with police chiefs, sheriffs, judges, prosecutors, defense attorneys, law professors or any crime and punishment experts, Brown was involved with the so-called 100 to 1 rule. The new federal legislation mandated a 10-year minimum sentence for anyone caught with 50 grams of crack cocaine. For a dealer of powdered cocaine, the form of coke favored in white suburbia, the dealer would have to possess five *thousand* grams of cocaine to receive a similar sentence.

Clearly, the law was getting "tough" mostly on blacks and Latinos, not white sellers and users of cocaine. The *New York Times* described it as the equivalent of imposing the same sentence for a candy bar-sized amount of crack cocaine versus a briefcase-sized amount of powdered cocaine.

It turns out Johnny St. Valentine Brown was a poor choice of advisor on momentous drug legislation. Brown held himself out as having a Howard University degree in pharmacology and that he was a "board certified" pharmacist. Some of Brown's fellow D.C. police narcs suspected he was a bullshitter, that he was not who he claimed to be. They were right.

In 1999, a lawyer in a civil suit, who suspected Brown
was a faker, posed a trick question while deposing the self-
proclaimed expert cop. He asked if Brown was familiar
with the Marijuana Reagent Test. Brown said, of course,
that he had administered it to suspects hundreds of times.
In fact, there is no Marijuana Reagent Test. The lawyer had
made it up. It was a trick question to test Brown's
credibility. The lawyer learned Brown had no degree from
Howard University.

Brown was later convicted of perjury. At his trial, he
submitted letters from judges and others recommending
clemency. It turns out Brown had forged some of those
letters. Thus, a lying, disgraced cop played a key role in
sending millions of American minorities to prison in a
hysteria-driven phase of the War on Drugs.

In the rush to enact tougher drug laws, "Both sides
were trying to be quicker and tougher than the other,"
Sterling said. The result of the minimum-sentencing in the
Anti-Drug Abuse Act of 1986 was a soaring increase in the
nation's prison population with an untold cost in money
and human misery. But the War on Drugs didn't stop the
flow of illegal narcotics. Not even a little bit.

While Tip O'Neill was leading the charge in the House
of Representatives, the politically ambitious presidential
hopeful Joe Biden of Delaware was not about to let this
opportunity pass. Biden became an ardent advocate of
mandatory minimum sentencing. Biden pushed for the
naming of a national drug "czar" to have all power and
authority over the War on Drugs. Biden was a champion of
guilty-until-proven innocent asset forfeiture laws, too.

Radley Balko, a long-time observer of the criminal
justice system and a blogger for the *Washington Post*, is

not a fan of kindly Uncle Joe. "Biden has sponsored more damaging drug war legislation than any Democrat in Congress," Balko wrote.

In recent years Biden may have realized, belatedly, all of the damage he has done in the War on Drugs. His attitude on drugs seems to have softened, aided perhaps, by the fact his son, Hunter Biden, was discharged from the Navy in 2014 after he tested positive—for cocaine.

Chapter 12—Killing the Competition

"Competition is a sin."
—John D. Rockefeller – Industrialist, monopolist

Endowment-grubbing business schools, sycophant business columnists and numerous motivational hucksters pay lip service to the glories of free markets and entrepreneurship, but American business managers hate competition, so they buy it out or destroy it.

Large, predatory law firms often have platoons of M&A lawyers; legal eagles toiling away on Mergers and Acquisitions, helping big companies get bigger by buying competitors to put them out of business and stifle competition.

In the narcotics trade, dopers do the same thing but without a veneer of legitimacy. They kill the competition—literally. Instead of legal Mergers and Acquisitions vultures, the drug world has predators called hitmen. Assassins. Paid executioners.

Hitmen are cold-blooded criminals who will whack someone for a price. They are usually hired by up-and-coming drug dealers who understand mergers and acquisitions from a mean streets perspective. Ego plays a role, too. In this world, "dissing" (disrespecting) an ego-tripping dealer, or even bumping up against him in a crowd is sometimes enough to merit a "contract" to kill you. Human life is cheap in the ghetto.

In Detroit in the latter half of the 1980s, a team of for-hire killers who called themselves Best Friends murdered their way to street fame for a time, leaving a trail of blood and an estimated 80 dead bodies in their wake. They were remorseless hitmen and Nate "Boone" Craft was one of them. The Boone nickname stood for frontiersman Daniel Boone, although it's doubtful the historic Boone did any of the things Nate Craft has done. Associates called Craft "Boone" for his willingness to get up close and split a victim's head with a hand-axe—he calls it a baby axe— rather than using a gun.

Nate Craft is a big bear of a man. He looks remarkably like the late Michael Clarke Duncan, the actor who starred in movies such as *The Green Mile*. Craft went to Vietnam in the Army and learned how to kill. He returned to Detroit, entered "tough man" contests, and won. This got him noticed by dope dealers who are always on the lookout for hired muscle.

I spent an afternoon with Craft in his modest Detroit home. We sat at his kitchen table and talked for several hours. It was hard not to look at his left forearm. Scar tissue covers a sizeable hole there. He noticed I was staring, so he lifted his shirt to show me another large hole in his abdomen. Bullet holes from an AK-47 assault rifle, he explained.

Craft said he killed "about" 30 people in his career as a hitman with the Best Friends organization. Maybe a few more. He lost count.

Craft said he took pains to keep his real name off the street. In addition to "Boone" he was also known as The Grim Reaper, because he favored wearing hooded sweatshirts and dark sunglasses.

"I was huge and people was always intimidated by just lookin' at me, like 'Whoa! Who the fuck that nigger down with?'" Craft said. "I was never claimin' to be down with no one. I just claimed, 'You got money, I'm there. Have

Gun, Will Travel.'" Craft laughs a big, deep belly laugh at this reference to an old TV western about a for-hire killer.

Craft said killing people wasn't personal. It was just business. He told me he was not one to take sides. "You got money, I'm witcha," Craft said. "You ain't got no money I'm not witcha. Somebody hire me to hit somebody, man it's who got the top dollar? I'm down wit whoever got the money."

Craft tried to instill some discipline in the Best Friends about the business of murdering people. He told them to avoid using their real names. People, including associates, should only know them by their street names. If someone gets busted and turns snitch, the police only know you by your street name, Craft counseled. They will have to search for you by street name and physical description.

He also showed them you don't need a gun to be a hitman. Attacking an imaginary target, Craft demonstrated how to kill a man with your bare hands.

"I was showing Reg and Boo how to fight, how to handle guns, even how to do hand-to-hand combat," Craft told me. "Reg" and "Boo" were Reginald and Terrance Brown, two brothers who were the leaders of the Best Friends murder-for-hire gang. "'Dude, it's easy!" Craft told them. "Hit that nigger in his throat.'" He made a fist using the three middle fingers of his right hand so the knuckles protruded and formed a weapon. He gave the air a fast, powerful punch. "Wham!" Craft said. "Once he go down, kick him in the mouth, then reach down and snap his neck."

Craft continued his description of how to murder a man without a weapon. "Kicking him in the mouth was just my way of people knowin' this nigger ain't gonna do no talkin', even if he survive. But he won't survive because we gon snap his neck."

"You can get away with that shit," Craft said. He said a contrived confrontation in a public place, like a shopping mall, is a good place to kill someone in this manner.

"Self-defense," Craft said. "You got all these people that gonna say we witnesses. It was a legal fight. Dude seen you, bumped you, you bumped him back and blows started blowin'. You just happened to get the best of 'im. And when you grabbed him by the head, tell 'em you wuz tryin' to stop him from bitin' you. He didn't get a chance to bite you, but you turned and his neck snapped." Craft laughed another big belly laugh at the thought of it.

He said there was a legal reason for killing a target hand-to-hand. "An accident murder!" Craft seemed to relish his oxymoron. "But they will call it manslaughter. You might do some probation on that. You can do probation."

Craft did some years in prison, but he got a reduced sentence because he rolled over and testified against his former associates in the Best Friends organization after they killed his brother. He was charged with one murder but not the other 29 he admits he committed.

During his debriefing, as he turned on his old friends, Craft said he told the DEA that on occasion he and his fellow killers wanted their victim to disappear after a hit. Craft told me that's how they came to use a large tree shredder in a vacant lot at Mack and Holcomb on Detroit's east side.

"Hey, we butchered a lot of people and you might not even find 'em cause they done met the tree shredder," Craft said. "And that's why I don't eat pork. We fed 'em to the pigs."

Prisoner of War:
The Story of White Boy Rick and The War on Drugs

Disposing of a human body with a tree shredder isn't as simple as it may seem. "The head was the hardest part to crush down," Craft explained. "Sometimes we had to take a sledgehammer. Whump! Hummp! Put a pole up in it so it would hold still so we could smash it up and then put it in the tree shredder with the wood."

Another Best Friend, Charles Wilkes, was good for about a dozen murders but he got a "Rule 35" sentence reduction for "substantial assistance." In federal cases, prosecutors will give away the store in plea deals to get a conviction of an individual or individuals they have targeted. U.S. Attorneys will agree to eye-popping plea deals for assistance prosecuting someone they want to convict. That's how hitmen like Charles Wilkes can do a dozen murders and still get a sentence reduction or Nate Craft can admit 30 murders and still get a reduced plea. Such plea deals may mean a decade in prison, as opposed to a life sentence.

In the Best Friends case, the Detroit U.S. Attorney's office wanted to "get" the key leaders of the gang and criminal defense attorney Paul Curtis. They were convinced Curtis was stashing money for the Best Friends group and Wilkes alleged Curtis had helped the Best Friends figure out who in their circle were the federal informants. Two informants against the Best Friends were in fact, killed, but Curtis was never charged or indicted.

The Best Friends weren't just killers. They peddled dope, too. Murder was a specialty service. The money was in selling drugs. Craft remembers the transition from heroin to crack cocaine in the ghetto. "We was giving away a whole lot of it free, just to get people hooked," Craft said. "We would give out 'tests.' 'Here, go test this, man. This is new shit. Go test this.' Once you hit it, you hooked. If you tried it, you was hooked on it." Craft said they warned their underlings to not use crack personally. If the leaders discovered one of their street peddlers was also a user, he was kicked out of the group.

"We was still pushin' heroin (he pronounces it hair-o-wahn) at the time, too, because heroin was still movin', too," Craft said. "But when the crack came out, that took over."

Craft doesn't drink or do drugs. He says it's rare to see him in a bar, and if he's there he's not drinking and he's eager to leave. He does smoke, however. Craft says it eases the pain from his gunshot wounds.

Best Friends had an interesting business model. They would accept a contract for a hit from some big dope dealer, complete the murder, collect their money, then kill the doper who hired them and take over his portion of the drug underworld. The city's drug dealers quickly took a dim view of this practice. Craft says the dealers had a meeting at which it was agreed the Best Friends had to be eliminated. The Best Friends got wind of the plan and a street war began.

The group's leaders, Reginald "Rockin' Reg" and Terrance "Boogaloo" Brown, had two brothers and both of them were among the first to be killed. After that, Craft says, Rockin' Reg snapped. "Reg was on the nut," Craft said. "He was poppin' acid and shit and he was ready to go. Every day that nigger wanted to go kill somebody."

Craft recalled a time when Rockin' Reg was at his place and they were cooking food. "We do some cheese and broccoli and shit and then after that he like, 'C'mon man, let's go see if we can find somebody,' Craft recalled Reg saying. 'We go over to the west side. We know we'll find people over there.'"

One night, Craft and Brown were cruising Detroit's northwest side when Reg spotted a supposed enemy at a service station pumping gas. He told Craft to pull in. "Reg stepped out of my car and just start blastin' up this car. Woo! Woo! Woo! Woo!" is how Craft described the volley of shots. He was horrified, because there were plenty of witnesses at the gas station. "Man, you better get your bitch ass in this car!" Craft said. Brown improbably replied no one was looking while he was shooting. Craft zigged and zagged through side streets, hoping to hide their getaway.

It happened again at another gas station on the east side. This time, they were in separate cars. "I was gettin' gas when the guy pulled up," Craft said. "He got gas (and then) Reg shot his motherfuckin' ass. I took off when Reg pulled that trigger. I jumped in my car and got the fuck outta there."

Craft explained Reginald Brown's propensity to shoot people was how he got the street name Rockin' Reg. "That nigger be rockin' niggers anywhere he seen them," Craft said. "He's gonna wanna shoot 'em dead—in there rockin'. That's why they call him Rockin' Reg. That bitch wanna rock a nigger right then and there."

Before Best Friends, Craft failed at one job he was hired to do. He was getting paid to "hang with", that is, be a bodyguard for, Maserati Rick Carter, one of the major drug men on Detroit's east side. Carter had a need to showboat, to be seen, and it was a fatal flaw. Carter was feuding with another doper named "Big" Ed Hanserd, who was short in stature but had the nickname "Big" for his alleged penis size.

Craft said Maserati Rick came up with the bright idea to ambush Hanserd outside his home, but blew the hit by jumping from behind some bushes too soon and shooting as Big Ed was walking out of his front door. Carter missed and Hanserd ducked back inside. "After that, it was just crazy," Craft said, "because Big Ed was always running around, trying to find Rick. They was always shootin' up each other's cars when they see each other." What started the deadly feud? "I ain't quite sure what started the two fools at war with each other," Craft said.

Craft said he and Carter were in an apartment, trying to lay low and avoid Hanserd. Carter was not supposed to leave without Craft by his side. Craft said one day he went to the bathroom and Maserati Rick left the apartment without him. Craft said he didn't know it immediately. Carter had been in the living room and Craft went straight from the bathroom and flopped on a bed. He didn't know Carter had left the apartment until he got a phone call that Maserati Rick had been shot.

Carter was blasted at a car wash popular with dope dealers. He was hospitalized with multiple gunshot wounds. As he lay in Detroit's Mt. Carmel Hospital recovering from the shooting, a hitman visited him in his hospital room and finished the job, putting a bullet in Maserati Rick's head. Carter was buried in a sixteen thousand-dollar casket customized to resemble a luxury Mercedes-Benz with fancy tire rims, and an authentic front-end grille with the three-point star logo featured prominently.

Nate Craft's massive size prompted a crime innovation. The cars favored by the dope crowd were too small for Craft to get in and out easily when it was time to shoot someone. 'These little bitty cars y'all gettin', I can't get out most of 'em'" Craft told his fellow hitmen. "'I'm too damned big.'"

On one murder mission Craft was left struggling to get out of the car while his fellow hitman did all the shooting alone. This prompted Craft to suggest they buy a full-sized van. The other Best Friends told him it was too expensive to buy a van each time they want to kill someone. "I said 'No, let me show you how to do dis,'" Craft said he told the Best Friends. Craft came up with the idea of re-painting the van after each hit. "We did one (execution murder) and we took it up to Earl Scheib," Craft said. "A whole new paint job!"

A few weeks later, there was another hit and another paint job. Craft said the paint shop staff was perplexed because the van had been painted recently. Craft told them they decided they didn't like the color and he paid them to paint it a different color.

The van was orange the night they tried to kill Rick Wershe, Jr. The Best Friends had decided Wershe needed to be hit because he was behaving like a police snitch. The police, who like to think the dopers are the only ones who behave stupidly, had Wershe making buys from dealers who were competitors. One of the first to eye Wershe suspiciously was Maserati Rick, when he was still alive.

"Maserati Rick was tellin' me, 'Yeah, man. I'm kinda skeptical of sellin' to this white boy." I said, 'Don't he get down with the Curry Brothers?' He said, 'Yeah, but every now and then he sneak to one of them other houses and be tryin' to cop.'

Craft said when he heard this, it aroused his suspicion, too. "Why would he come to you when he could get all his shit from the Curry Brothers?" Craft asked Carter. "He tryin' to buy from other people," Carter replied. Craft says another member of the Best Friends gang thought a hit was the best way to resolve the White Boy Rick dilemma. "Man, I don't trust that white boy, man. I think we should kill him," Craft recalls his fellow hitman telling him.

The police were having Wershe make lots of drug buys from lots of drug houses, regardless of who ran them. That's a red flag in the drug world. That's the way to get a productive informant killed. But cops view informants as the lowest life-form on the planet.

Mark Patrick, another Best Friend, didn't like this white kid "tryin' to act like he a brother" Craft said. Craft recalls Patrick was blunt in his assessment of Wershe who, in Patrick's opinion, was "tryin' to get down. He ain't doin' shit but runnin' his mouth," Patrick told Craft. "I believe that boy is tellin' for somebody, man. We been suspicious of that boy for a whole year. We just didn't take him out because he ain't nobody, he ain't nobody big." Patrick was later killed in a drug-related murder in suburban Inkster.

The wariness about Wershe lingered until one night, in the spring of 1987, the Best Friends decided it was time to kill him. Three of them piled in the now-orange van and went hunting. They found Rick Wershe at a large east side street intersection, riding as a passenger in a sports car driven by his friend, Roy Grisson.

The van pulled up alongside the sports car at a stop light. Craft was driving the van. Terrance "Boogaloo" Brown was in the passenger seat. Craft said Boo had organized the hit. Rockin' Reg Brown was in the back with an assault rifle. Craft says Reg slid the van side door open and tried to open fire. The gun jammed. Wershe realized what was happening and reacted swiftly, stomping his left foot on the accelerator. He floored it through the red light.

Grisson, caught by surprise, tried to steer while trying to figure out what was going on. By the time Brown was able to begin firing, Wershe and Grisson had escaped.

When Craft got home he caught hell. His wife was Roy Grisson's sister and she was beyond upset. "You tried to kill my brother?!" Craft remembers her saying. Craft denied it. "No!" "They said you was drivin' an orange van," his wife said. "I ain't got no orange van," Craft replied. "My van is red."

As the family discussion raged in the days after the episode, Grisson was adamant. "It was the Best Friends! We saw Boo and Reg!" Grisson said. "You ain't seen me!" Craft replied. He asked Grisson what he was wearing. Grisson couldn't say. "See there, man, you got all them gunfires comin' at ya and you assumed it was me," Craft told his brother-in-law. "But man, you part of Best Friends," Grisson replied. "I said to Roy, 'What that got to do wit it?" Craft said. "They probably tried to kill White Boy Rick. The word is out that he's snitchin'." Craft weathered the family storm because his van was red and the hit team was in an orange van, courtesy of a local auto paint shop.

Craft claims the Best Friends weren't the only ones who wanted Rick Wershe eliminated. He says Detroit police officers wanted him dead, too. "When Rick got arrested, the Detroit cops got scared," Craft said. "He knew stuff."

Killing Rick came up on Nate Craft's radar one more time. He got word that someone had put a "contract" on the kid. That someone was Detroit Police Homicide Inspector Gil Hill. The federal indictment of the Curry Brothers in a major drug case and the top-level machinations between the police brass and FBI over revealing the informant in the Damion Lucas murder case were more than enough to show veteran investigator Hill that Rick Wershe, Jr. was the snitch. It was Wershe, Hill realized, who put the FBI on his tail for obstruction of justice in the Damion Lucas murder. But Craft said there was a problem with the "contract" on Wershe. The money was too puny. As Craft understood it, Hill didn't want to pay top dollar for killing Rick Wershe even though it would be a hot, high-profile murder because at the time, Wershe was front-page news.

"Nobody wanted that bullshit money, five-thousand, ten-thousand," Craft said. "Man, that ain't enough to kill that boy." Craft suggests he could have used a sniper rifle to kill Wershe as he was entering or leaving the courthouse during his drug trial. "But that didn't come about because they didn't want to up the price," Craft said. Eventually, he said, the contract price was increased to one hundred thousand dollars, an amount more in line with a hit that was sure to be high profile.

Q: Who was offering the money?

A: "The main man behind it was Gil.

Q: Gil Hill?

A: "Yeah. Him and Young. They was runnin' buddies."

The reference to Young meant Detroit's mayor, Coleman Young. There is no evidence, beyond the tale Craft has told, that Young, or for that matter, Hill, was willing to pay to have Richard Wershe, Jr. killed. Hill and Young had a relationship, but it's a stretch to call them 'runnin' buddies.' Craft admits the information about the alleged murder contract from Hill and Young to kill Wershe was second-hand. He heard about it from Terrance "Boo" Brown of Best Friends.

I asked Craft why he wouldn't be involved personally in discussions of a contract murder worth this kind of money and involving what was sure to be sensational headlines and police heat.

"Boo knew to keep me back," Craft said. "I don't like meetin' people, cuz they could give me up later."

There's no way to substantiate this story, which has been the subject of some media coverage. What can be said is this: Coleman Young, Gilbert Hill and Terrance "Boogaloo" Brown are all dead. Richard J. Wershe, Jr. is still alive.

Chapter 13—Playing with Fire

*"She's the kind of girl who climbed the ladder of
success wrong by wrong."*
—Mae West

Back in the day, Cathy Volsan was a looker. She was
attractive enough to do some occasional professional
modeling locally. She kept her hair done, her nails
manicured and her wardrobe was always in fashion.

Unlike most inner city black women, Cathy Volsan
seemed to have it all. She certainly wanted it all, to the
point of living recklessly. She was the favored niece of the
most powerful politician in Detroit—Mayor Coleman A.
Young—and she behaved accordingly. Some called her a
ghetto princess due to her perceived arrogance. Traffic
tickets for speeding or reckless driving meant nothing to
her. Sgt. James Harris, a Homicide detective who
eventually got caught up in an FBI sting operation, had the
unofficial task of running police interference for Mayor
Young's family, including Cathy. Harris admitted to me
that one of those chores was fixing Cathy's tickets.

Cathy Volsan had a weakness that led to a lot of
trouble. She was a drug addict. She was good at keeping
her habit hidden. Sgt. Harris was dismayed to see this
young woman trashing her life because of drugs. He told
me Cathy Volsan's family called him one New Year's Day
and asked him to go immediately to a drug rehab center on
Woodward Avenue, Detroit's biggest thoroughfare. At the
rehab center, he linked up with Cathy Volsan's half-sister
who was there to intervene, too. Cathy was in rehab,
supposedly trying to get straight. Harris said he found her
dressed in a nightie, threatening to leave the facility. Harris

said he told her she was upsetting her family. This seemed to provoke her. "The next thing I know she's busted out the door," Harris said. "I tried to grab her. Her gown came off. She's running down Woodward Avenue nekked as a jay bird. I'm chasing her. Her sister is with me. Finally, I grabbed her, took off my coat, put it around her. She's kicking and screaming as I brought her back there."

Harris seemed a bit sad when he told me about Cathy Volsan's long battle with drug addiction and the times her family asked him to save her from herself.

Harris said Cathy's family called him one time in the middle of the night and wanted him to rescue her from yet another drug house. They told Harris to make sure he got her fur coat, too. He shook his head and had a can-you-believe-it? look on his face when he told me of her family's concern about retrieving the fur coat, too.

Harris found her in a drug den on Detroit's northwest side. The operator of the joint was James "Red" Freeman, a longtime Detroit doper with a nasty reputation. Freeman had been a figure in an infamous drug-related shooting and multiple beheading incident in the city in 1979. Freeman was tried for his part in the episode but he was acquitted because the jury didn't believe the police informant's story of what happened.

"I knocked on the door," Harris recalled. "He (Freeman) came to the door. I showed him my badge. I said 'I'm Sgt. Harris of Homicide. I want to talk to you.'" Freeman let him in.

"I said, 'You have Cathy Volsan.' Freeman replied, 'How do you know that?' I said, 'Let's cut the bullshit out. The only thing I want is to get her out of here and bring her home. No police are going to mess with your operation."

Harris recalls Freeman seemed to be thinking about what he was saying, so Harris kept talking. "I said, 'You know who she is. You know who her uncle is. Can you imagine all the goddam heat that's going to come down on you for somethin' stupid?"

Harris says Cathy Volsan was there, surrounded by a group of men.

Harris reminded Freeman they had met in the past when Harris was assigned to the 10th police precinct. "Hey, Red. You know me from Number 10. Gimme her goddam coat. Okay?"

Years later, Harris can still recall Freeman's reply: "I'm gonna tell ya somethin', Harris. I'm gonna do dis for you." As Freeman was talking, Harris looked over and saw feet under a window curtain. "I know he had a shotgun," Harris said of the man behind the curtain. As Freeman retrieved Cathy's fur coat, Harris remembers the hard-bitten dope man gave him a warning: "This is the last time I'm gonna do dat. Don't come back here no more. And you tell that bitch if she comes around again, she's a dead bitch."

For a time, Cathy Volsan was mentioned as the romantic interest of one of the Detroit Pistons basketball stars, but that gave way to relationships with a string of drug dealers. Through the 1980s Cathy Volsan took up with various dopers; Timothy Peoples of Young Boys, Incorporated, Mario Winfrey, Demetrius Holloway, Johnny Curry, who became her husband, and later, Richard Wershe, Jr.

Cathy and Johnny got married in a small ceremony, consistent with his low-key style. They moved in to a nice condo on Navarre Place, in an upscale neighborhood close to downtown Detroit.

Roy Grisson, who was friends with the Curry Brothers and with Rick Wershe, Jr., moved in with Johnny and Cathy for a while. He said Johnny was seldom there.

Cathy apparently led her own life while Johnny tended to his growing drug operation. "Cathy always kept herself up," Grisson told me. "She would get her hair, her nails and her feets done to go shopping."

Her favored shopping destination was Somerset Mall in suburban Troy, an upscale retail center featuring Neiman-Marcus, Saks Fifth Avenue, Tiffany's and other luxury brand names. "With her," Grisson said, "it's about money."

As Grisson recalls, Cathy Volsan liked to hang out with a "little squad of girls" who enjoyed "talking shit"—gossiping about other people in derogatory terms.

It didn't take long for Johnny Curry to discover his wife's drug habit and he claims it led to a confrontation. In a provocative statement on YouTube, Curry said: "So me and Coleman put her in a clinic." The implication is that Johnny Curry, a major drug dealer, worked with Coleman Young, the Mayor of Detroit, to get his wife, Young's niece, in rehab. Young is deceased so there is no way to ask him if he and Curry cooperated to combat Cathy's drug habit.

When Rick Wershe was gathering intelligence on the Curry drug organization for the FBI, he began to play a second risky game. He started flirting with Cathy Volsan Curry, about seven years his senior. It was subtle at first. Wershe's interest in her surfaced when the Curry group went to the Michigan State Fair. Cathy wanted to ride the roller coasters. Johnny wasn't interested. Wershe rode the

roller coasters with her. Hands and knees touched. Looks
were exchanged. The fuse was lit.

The flirtation was warming up just as Wershe was
starting down the path to becoming a dope dealer. In April
of 1986 the agents and cops of the federal OCDETF task
force had dropped Wershe, suddenly, without warning, due
to the law enforcement bureaucratic intrigue swirling
around this juvenile informant. High-ranking muckety-
mucks in Washington were asking questions about this
informant named Wershe and the FBI Detroit office knew
that was dangerous, so all contact with him was severed.
Young Wershe didn't know what had happened.

He had grown fond of his high rolling life as a covert
paid drug informant. "I was blinded by the life," Wershe.
told me. What teen male wouldn't be? He had hot cars,
designer clothes, garish jewelry, including a belt made with
gold and he had plenty of hot women willing to hop in bed
with a rising star of the drug underworld. Wershe
remembers thinking, "Fuck, this is the best thing in the
world. I was a kid. I wanted the money." But in the spring
of 1986 the cash flow from the FBI and the Detroit police
narcs ended abruptly.

By then, Wershe was a school drop-out. He had no
trade, no marketable skill. The only business Rick knew is
the one the FBI and the DPD narcs had taught him. He
knew the dope racket. This combination of factors led to a
very bad choice. Richard Wershe, Jr. decided to become a
"weight man", a wholesaler in the cocaine underworld. As
a young white guy in a predominately black market, this
made sense. Wershe didn't have, and couldn't effectively
control, inner city crack houses. Nor did he have a gang
that could operate retail establishments in the

neighborhoods. Acting as a wholesaler to the city's black retail drug dealers was viable.

Wershe and one of his childhood friends, Todd Reliford, who later changed his last name to Scott, became partners in the dope biz. Reliford, according to Wershe, had been working for a major dealer named James Lamar, who was shot to death by Terrance "Boogaloo" Brown, one of the Best Friends murder-for-hire gang. Brown was eventually killed execution-style in Georgia.

As kids, Reliford and Wershe had cruised the neighborhood spotting the heroin dens and later, the crack houses. They knew this underground economy was alive and flourishing.

Rick and Todd pooled their cash and bought seven ounces from a dealer they had met through the Curry Brothers. The dealer wanted nine-thousand dollars. They told him they only had seven thousand. He sold them the dope, anyway.

"We started selling small amounts," Wershe said. "We worked our way up, saving our money, re-investing." They graduated to half-kilos, then a kilo from Demetrius Holloway, one of the biggest dealers in town.

After Wershe got rolling, he began to get his cocaine from Florida because it was much cheaper than buying it from sources locally. Cocaine sourced in Florida meant a hefty markup on the streets of Detroit. In late summer, 1986, the *New York Times* reported the Reagan administration's South Florida Task Force was a failure. "...the most ambitious and expensive drug enforcement operation in the nation's history," the *Times* reported, has "...barely dented the drug trade here. Far more cocaine is being smuggled through Florida today than before the task force was established in February 1982..." the *Times* reported.

Richard Wershe Jr. of Detroit could attest to that.

Business was good but Wershe was a novice and his inexperience manifested itself when he and some friends went to Miami in September of 1986 and scored two keys of coke, only to get busted with the drugs when they returned to Detroit's airport. Wershe told drug agents he had been to Florida for an uncle's funeral, but he had only swim trunks and casual clothes. The agents found the cocaine in the duffel bag of Robert Ward, one of Wershe's companions. Ward was arrested and received a six-year prison sentence. Wershe was noted as an associate.

Not long after the airport incident, a neighborhood street guy known as Cowboy introduced Todd Reliford to undercover DEA agent Hawthorne Hope. Reliford sold Hope two ounces of cocaine and got busted. Wershe and Reliford were broke. Reliford had been snared by the DEA. He received a short prison sentence, but it disrupted his partnership with Wershe.

Wershe looked for another partner and found one in Chuckie Lewis, one of the Curry Brothers' customers. Wershe had developed a relationship with Lewis through the Currys, but the new partnership needed help getting back in the game after the airport bust.

Art Derrick, Johnny Curry's white cocaine supplier from the suburbs, came to the rescue. Derrick was what Wershe hoped to be. Derrick had a nice house behind a security wall in a suburb. He had his initials inlaid at the bottom of his swimming pool. He had large-scale cocaine connections in Miami. He had airplanes, several of them, including an executive jet. Derrick would transport kilos of cocaine to Detroit in his private aircraft. He had a black partner who would distribute Derrick's wholesale quantities of cocaine to the city's biggest drug dealers. They were selling kilos of coke and making lots of money.

Derrick, who died in 2005 from complications related to drug abuse, took Wershe under his wing, to an extent. "Art helped me get back on my feet," Wershe said. "I was kinda like a son to him." Derrick had a son who was close to Rick Wershe in age.

Wershe flew with Derrick to Miami and Las Vegas. They went clubbing and cavorted with prostitutes. Before his death, Derrick prepared a signed and sworn affidavit attempting to help Wershe get a parole. Derrick says police and prosecution claims that Wershe was a drug lord or drug kingpin, were blatant lies. "Mr. Wershe was a kid when I met him," Derrick wrote, "and was nothing near a sophisticated trafficker. I referred to Mr. Wershe as a 'wannabe'."

Derrick claims credit for the street name White Boy Rick. In his affidavit about Wershe Derrick says he and his partner were supplying two "Ricks" in Detroit; one was white, the other black, and they kept stumbling over which was which in telephone discussions.

Derrick claims that's when he came up with the idea of calling young Richard Wershe, Jr. White Boy Rick and calling their other customer, a black dealer named Richard Carter, Maserati Rick after the luxury car. It was a way to identify which Rick was which. Derrick's claim is open to debate. Wershe's late father told the now-defunct *Detroit Monthly* magazine that in their increasingly-black neighborhood the black teens would call out to his son, "'Yo! White Boy! White Boy Rick!'"

Prisoner of War:
The Story of White Boy Rick and The War on Drugs

Whatever the origin of the White Boy Rick street name, by the fall of 1986 Richard J. Wershe, Jr. was trying to become one of the Big Dogs of the Detroit cocaine underworld. Chuckie Lewis had the inner-city connections for moving dope that Wershe lacked. Following a roadmap of sorts set out by Art Derrick, Wershe started buying kilos of cocaine in Miami, first from a relatively small-time source named Pedro Mantilla, then a bigger player named Edwin Scheer.

Wershe has testified under oath on two occasions that Edwin Scheer was responsible for a lot of the cocaine that found its way to the streets of Detroit. Unlike Mantilla, Scheer could provide volume, Wershe said. "I started dealing with Edwin instead of Pedro," Wershe testified at his June, 2017 parole hearing.

Scheer appears to be an example of one of the fundamental flaws in the War on Drugs. Prosecutors— federal and local—emphasize imprisoning "kingpins" who are visible in the community, the guys who ride around in pricey cars with garish wheel rims, the guys who have a "posse" or entourage to signify their street importance. In other words, the visible drug pushers at the bottom of the illegal drug food chain. In most instances, guys like Scheer are not named as co-conspirators in the heavy-duty racketeering and continuing criminal enterprise prosecutions. When the DEA, FBI or local narcs make cases for prosecution, they only go so far up the ladder of the drug trade and they stop. Importers who traffic in tons of cocaine and the bankers who enable their smuggling networks are seldom named as defendants in "major" drug prosecutions. This is explored in more detail in the last chapter.

Scheer apparently got a sweet deal from federal authorities in Miami. Even though Wershe testified he once bought 15 kilos—about 33 pounds—of cocaine from

Scheer in a single shipment, Scheer was never charged
with major drug trafficking. He never attracted attention
from the Miami news media. He pleaded guilty in a
marijuana case and did six months in prison. Edwin Scheer
is now a prosperous businessman in Miami.

As he worked toward his goal of becoming a "weight
man" in the cocaine business, young Wershe traveled the
same path as other youthful dope slingers in the inner city.
He adorned himself in flash-and-trash that told the street he
was rollin', he was somebody.

"I was stupid," Wershe says now. "I bought a lot of
stupid stuff." Wershe estimates he probably made, in total,
a quarter of a million dollars in the drug trade while he was
dealing. "It went quick," Wershe said. It's a notable
amount of money, but it hardly qualified him as a drug lord
or kingpin.

Wershe's luck went bad again in the spring of 1987.
His partner, Chuckie Lewis, caught a "650" life drug case
in suburban Macomb County. Wershe was on his own
again.

"I tried to do things on my own and it didn't work out
too well," Wershe said. "I was a little overwhelmed or out
of my league, I guess, to be on my own."

Wershe turned to Steve Rousell, another longtime
friend, for help.

The FBI was entering the homestretch in its drive to
indict and prosecute the Curry Brothers drug gang. The
evidence, including court-authorized wiretaps, was piling
up. Although Special Agent Groman was officially off the
case, he was concerned about the drug-dealing path being

taken by Rick Wershe, his former informant. Groman called Rick's father and asked for a meeting. The two men met in the parking garage of Cobo Hall, the city's convention center. Groman, in keeping with his habit of living on the edge of FBI rules, recalls sitting in a car playing a wiretap tape for the elder Wershe.

The intercepted call made it clear Richard J. Wershe, Jr was involved in selling drugs. Groman thought the tape might jolt the father's sense of paternal responsibility, that the father might intervene with the son before it was too late. Richard Wershe, Sr. appeared unfazed by the wiretap tape. Groman had stuck his neck out for young Wershe by playing a secret court-authorized wiretap tape for a civilian, but it was evident the elder Wershe wasn't interested in pulling his son off the path to prison.

For a time, Johnny Curry benefited from his wife's ready access to law enforcement intelligence, thanks to the fawning Detroit Police command officers who served at the pleasure of the mayor and who were eager to please the mayor by treating his family, including Cathy, like they were above the law.

For a time, Curry knew about secret FBI search warrants shortly after a federal judge signed them. The Detroit Police narcs assigned to the OCDETF task force were obligated to inform their bosses that a federal raid was in the works. The bosses in the Narcotics section shared that info with the Chief's office and the Major Crimes Section.

Once the information got to Detroit Police Headquarters, there was almost a straight line to Johnny Curry.

"I was married to the Mayor's niece! You know what I'm sayin'?" Curry recalled in a YouTube interview. "My wife was more vicious than me," Curry added.

Yet, the FBI, despite apparent top-level investigative sabotage in the Detroit Police Department, was able to build a strong criminal case against the Curry Brothers.

Unlike many other drug dealers, Johnny Curry was cautious. He didn't use his own product and it was said that he wouldn't be in the same room as drugs. But he ran an organization that could be violent when it was deemed necessary.

An indictment was returned in early April of 1987 and Johnny Curry was jailed as a flight risk. During the post-arrest detention hearings, FBI Special Agent Gregg Schwarz testified the Curry gang delegated enforcement to Lamont "Bummy Lou" Davis and Lee "Bull" Potts. On one occasion Johnny and Leo Curry were apparently upset that some upstarts were selling crack on a certain corner. Schwarz testified they dispatched Potts to order the group to quit selling on the corner. Later, one of the individuals, Eric Dunson, made the mistake of telling Potts he would sell drugs wherever he wanted to. Schwarz said Potts immediately pulled a gun and killed Dunson.

On another occasion, Schwarz testified, Lamont Davis confronted an individual who owed money to the Currys for narcotics. When the debtor didn't pay up, Schwarz said, Davis set the man's genitals on fire and later burned down the house where the incident occurred.

It wasn't long after Johnny Curry was locked up that his wife got involved in a torrid fling with Richard Wershe, Jr.

Prisoner of War:
The Story of White Boy Rick and The War on Drugs

Who pursued whom depends on who's retelling the story. Cathy Volsan Curry has kept her mouth shut for years about everything in her life, regardless of the storms of controversy that sometimes swirl around her.

If Rick Wershe is telling the story, Cathy Volsan Curry showed up unannounced at his door one evening and suggested they hook up. In his telling, Wershe says he was surprised but he readily agreed. "The sex was fantastic!" Wershe said.

Roy Grisson, who was friends with both of them, has a different recollection. Grisson says Wershe had the hots for Cathy and pestered him to act as a matchmaker of sorts. "Rick was always messing with older women," Grisson said. Cathy was about seven years older than Rick. Grisson remembers the relationship was hot but "rocky." "She wouldn't trust him out of her sight," Grisson recalled. "She knew other women wanted him." Arguments between Cathy and Rick over other women were frequent. One heated exchange ended with Rick locking himself in the bathroom while Cathy plunged a butcher knife through the door.

Grisson recalled a time when one of the arguments led to a high-speed chase. Grisson said he was driving, with Rick as his passenger, as the two of them fled in a car at high speed, with Cathy Volsan Curry giving chase and venting her rage as they raced through city streets. Cathy seemed to be trying to run them off the road.

Grisson isn't the only one who witnessed the volcanic eruptions between Cathy Volsan Curry and Rick Wershe, Jr.

The late Enid Lawlor was a neighbor of the Currys when they lived on Navarre Place. In 1988, Lawlor told me she saw Wershe's clothes strewn all over the lawn in front of the Navarre Place condo. It was obvious, she said, that Cathy had thrown Rick out in one of their many arguments.

Lawlor, who kept track of things she found odd or unusual in the neighborhood, told me there had been a shooting at the Curry condo late one night in September of 1987. She counted seven shots. Cathy wasn't home. She had departed minutes before the gunfire.

This woman with a penchant for neighborhood awareness also noted an incident in October, 1987, when a private ambulance took Cathy Volsan Curry away. "The boil broke," Lawlor said, referring to chronic drug abuse by the mayor's niece.

Lawlor said one time, Cathy Volsan Curry angrily confronted her because she had allowed the FBI to use her residence for surveillance of the Curry condo. There were three FBI/DEA police raids on the condo. In one raid, Rick Wershe was present with Cathy Volsan Curry. One of the raiders was the aforementioned FBI Special Agent Schwarz, who had taken over the Curry case when Herm Groman was transferred to the public corruption squad.

"That was my first contact with Rick," Schwarz said. When the raid team barged in to the condo Wershe asked Schwarz what he wanted him to do. "Sit down and shut up," Schwarz recalled telling Wershe. Wershe did as he was told.

The raid team didn't find any drugs but they found other items of investigative interest. There were various confidential Detroit police narcotics investigative reports and a laminated card in Cathy Volsan Curry's possession. The card contained the office, home and mobile phone numbers for Detroit Police Sgt. James Harris, Police Officer Martrice "Marty" Hurrah—and Gil Hill, the former

head of the Homicide Section who was now the
Commander of the Major Crimes Division.

Johnny Curry, out of prison since 1999, has said on
several occasions recently that he doesn't have a grudge
against Rick Wershe for having an affair with his wife
while he was locked up.

"She allowed him in, so I have no problem with that,"
Curry said in a YouTube interview. "If he didn't rape her
or force his hand, she played her own hand, so that was on
her."

Rick Wershe's tempestuous relationship with the
Mayor's niece was the least of his problems. As noted
earlier, he found his way onto the local DEA radar when
his traveling companion on a return trip from Miami was
busted at the airport with two kilos of cocaine. He surfaced
again when an undercover DEA agent bought two ounces
of coke from his partner, Todd Reliford. But his blip on the
DEA radar got much brighter when he did some occasional
business with the Chambers Brothers.

The four Chambers Brothers—Billy Joe ("BJ"), Larry,
Willie and Otis were, for a time, the retail kings of crack
cocaine in Detroit.

William Adler, author of *Land of Opportunity*, a book
about the Chambers Brothers, called them "the Lee
Iacoccas of the crack trade." It was a comparison to the
immensely successful chairman of Chrysler Corporation.

These dirt-poor brothers from the dirt roads of rural
Arkansas migrated to Detroit and ran their cocaine business
in a manner that would impress business school professors.
The Chambers Brothers had as many as 500 employees.
There were sales competitions between their various crack

houses. They offered their customers discount coupons and two-for-one sales. Supervisors would sometimes pose as customers, ensuring the quality of their crack wasn't being compromised. There were strict rules governing business in the crack houses and punishment was severe for infractions. Little kids were their lookouts. The street urchins were well-schooled in how to spot the kinds of unmarked vans used by narcs. The cocaine wholesale supplier for the Chambers Brothers was Art Derrick through an associate named Perry Coleman. Derrick was also supplying the Curry Brothers organization.

The up-from-nothing Chambers Brothers were brash and befuddled by their newfound wealth. They bought things just because they could. They had a fondness for shooting home videos. In one video confiscated in a raid and played repeatedly on TV after their fall, one associate, William Jackson, is seen running his hands through piles of cash as he says, "Money! Money! Money! We rich, goddammit!"

A team of DEA-led OCDETF task force narcs set their sights on the Chambers Brothers and began making buys and conducting surveillance. They called themselves the No Crack Crew. And what a crew it was.

One member of the No Crack Crew was Detroit police officer Gerard "Mick" Biernacki. He's the cop we met in Chapter 1 who confronted Rick Wershe years earlier over his son's missing bicycle. The incident happened outside Wershe's cousin's house in suburban St. Clair Shores. Biernacki's badge meant nothing there and Wershe told him that with all the street bravado and defiance he could muster. Now Biernacki was in pursuit of that smart-mouth white Detroit kid as part of a federal drug task force.

In addition to a severe drinking problem, Biernacki and the truth didn't get along. He had a reputation as a cop who routinely lied under oath in court—a felony. FBI Agent Groman told me Biernacki was known among other cops as Pinocchio, a reference to the children's tale puppet whose nose grew every time he told a lie. Biernacki, who was known to drink himself in to oblivion in a bar called J. Edgar's, died in 2007.

Another member of the No Crack Crew was Greg Woods—who once admitted to being a racist. In *Land of Opportunity*, author Adler quotes Woods as saying, "…I'm a racist. I'll be honest, I am. Fuck them niggers."

Woods' self-description is supported by retired Detroit Deputy Police Chief Rudy Thomas, who ran a real no crack crew as a lieutenant in the Narcotics Section as profiled in Chapter 11. Thomas is black.

Thomas had worked with Woods years earlier in the Detroit Police 11th Precinct. "He never disrespected me or anything like that," Thomas said. "But I knew he hated affirmative action. He hated it when I was at 11."

Thomas tells the story of how racist white cops would refer to black sergeants as "Willie." Thomas says sergeants drove police cars designated as the 700-series on the police radio. A "Seven-Oh" radio call was from a sergeant. When a black sergeant notified radio dispatch that he was in his police car and on the move, some anonymous white officer often would get on the radio and say, "Watch out. Willie Seven-Oh is on the street."

"When I got to Narcotics I saw a different Greg Woods," Thomas told me. "He had joined the No Crack Crew. You could tell they didn't like you as a minority or black officer. They had no respect for you. He probably thought, based on our affirmative action plan, that if you were a sergeant you were Willie Seven-Oh. They didn't respect a lot of the black supervisors."

Most officers assigned to Detroit Police Narcotics did their jobs and avoided controversy. Most, but not all.

Sgt. Ronald Ferguson was once hailed as the city's top narcotics investigator. But Ferguson was eventually prosecuted for framing a popular high school basketball coach in a cocaine case. A jury acquitted Ferguson, after prosecutors charged him with paying an informant to lie to create a phony case against Mumford High School basketball coach Larry Moore. The prosecution said fabricating a case was "just business" in Ferguson's determination to keep his narcotics crew ranked high in the number of arrests.

Ferguson, according to a trial subpoena in the Wershe case, was in charge of Rodney Grandison, the officer who arrested Rick Wershe in his life-changing 650 narcotics case.

The No Crack Crew was part of the federal anti-drug task force. In the federal system they operated under the direction of Richard Crock, a veteran DEA agent. The primary focus of the No Crack Crew was the Chambers Brothers drug gang, a worthy target to be sure. The team was able to make a case against the Chambers Brothers despite their primary informant—Terry Colbert.

Colbert grew up with the Chambers Brothers in Arkansas. Like the Chambers Brothers, Colbert migrated to Detroit in search of a way to make money. It didn't take long for him to join their growing drug empire. The problem was, Colbert became addicted to crack. He was unreliable for the Chambers Brothers operation, but he turned out to be a pliable informant against them.

Colbert admits he said whatever the No Crack Crew wanted him to say, as a way to get the police to pay for his crack habit. Author William Adler quotes Colbert as saying he was agreeing to whatever the No Crack Crew suggested, as long as they kept giving him money to buy more crack. "…whatever bullshit the cops asked me, I said yes this, no that—whatever they wanted." In recent years Colbert has been in prison in Kentucky—on drug charges.

The Chambers Brothers were so successful peddling crack they sometimes ran low on supplies. As Rick Wershe was working to establish himself as a cocaine wholesaler, he sold a kilo or two of cocaine to "B.J."—Billy Joe Chambers. "Every now and then, if he needed something, I would give it to B.J.," Wershe said. This was noticed by the DEA. They began to take a look at Rick Wershe, too. This white kid was cocky, arrogant and flaunting his role in the cocaine underworld. The No Crack Crew started doing raids aimed at young Wershe.

They arrested Wershe and his pal, Steve Rousell, in March, 1987 in a raid on a house on Hayes Street, confiscating about two grams of cocaine and roughly nine thousand dollars in cash.

A month later, the police got luckier. The gang squad arrested Rick Wershe in a case that would send him to prison for life.

Chapter 14—The Journalism Herd Stampedes

"Never let the truth get in the way of a good story."
—Mark Twain

Before the curse of 24/7 news on the Internet and on cable TV channels, savvy consumers of journalism knew a little secret. If you scanned the front pages of the *New York Times*, the *Washington Post* and *The Wall Street Journal* first thing each morning, you could confidently skip the first ten minutes of news on ABC, CBS and NBC that evening. Why? Because the TV networks slavishly repeated the coverage in that morning's Big Three newspapers. Network news executives invariably decided the most important stories of the day were the ones the *Times*, the *Post* and the *Journal* had put on Page One. This in turn convinced hundreds of newspaper editors nationwide that front-page news in the *Times, Post* and *Journal* and what they saw Walter Cronkite, Huntley-Brinkley and Howard K. Smith leading with in the first ten minutes of nightly network news must be the most important news in the nation. They edited their newspapers accordingly.

The national wire services; the Associated Press and United Press International (Reuters is based in the U.K.) knew they had to provide news their client newspapers wanted, so they gave priority to the same stories. For many years, news on any given day in the United States was decided by the editors of three newspapers. The mainstream news media was all about copycat thinking. Things haven't changed much in the Internet age.

Vince Wade

Some call it herd journalism. Some call it pack journalism. Whatever it is called, there is an often-mindless Me-Too factor in the pursuit of news and current events. In the highly competitive news racket, it is important for each media outlet to be able to say, 'Yeah, we had that story, too.'

"If it bleeds, it leads" is a cynical, but largely-true observation about the TV news business. Television news sanitizes violence, supposedly out of concern for the tender sensitivities of the audience. News videographers have become skilled at depicting carnage without showing severed limbs, pools of blood, splattered brain matter, lifeless eyes and other visual truths about violence. They give thanks for the body bag. The result is sanitized PG-rated news. TV journalism goes to great lengths to report violence without showing its true and ugly consequences. It can be argued that TV audiences and print readers are inured to violence because they don't have to confront the grotesque ugliness as a result of dishonest journalism.

Americans enjoy complaining about all of the "bad" and "negative" news, but truthfully, they love it. It feeds a deep need to feel safe from ain't-it-awful events. A TV station or newspaper reporting nothing but "good" news would quickly go out of business.

Humorist Dave Barry once wrote about newspapers having what he called a Bummer Desk to find and report depressing stories for the front page. Barry said such stories often involve catastrophes, and in the rush to beat the competition, the facts are often wrong, but the top priority of journalism isn't accuracy, it's to be first to report the bummer news.

Speed over accuracy can mislead with terrible consequences, yet reporters and editors are seldom held accountable.

Prisoner of War:
The Story of White Boy Rick and The War on Drugs

The media can be rightfully blamed for indoctrinating the public with so much fast-paced kinetic imagery that people have the attention span of a gnat on amphetamines.

The advent of 24/7 saturation news coverage on TV and the Internet has persuaded people that what they are seeing represents reality, rather than aberrations and unusual events.

As Matt Taibbi wrote in *Rolling Stone* magazine: "We learned long ago in this business that dumber and more alarmist always beats complex and nuanced. Big headlines, cartoonish morality, scary criminals at home and foreign menaces abroad, they all sell."

Taibbi noted the media's role in shrinking attention spans and in fostering "powerful addictions to conflict, vitriol, fear, self-righteousness, and race and gender resentment."

A shameful example of the cascade-effect of journalistic error is the story of Richard Jewell. He was a humble security guard at the 1996 Summer Olympics in Atlanta, Georgia.

One night, Jewell found a backpack filled with pipe bombs in the crowded Centennial Olympic Park. He alerted the police and began helping evacuate the area. The backpack exploded. One person was killed, over a hundred were injured. The injuries would have been worse if Jewell hadn't acted. The media herd rushed to cover the story, portraying Jewell as a hero.

That changed quickly when the *Atlanta Journal-Constitution* reported the FBI was looking at Jewell as a possible suspect based on a psychological "profile" of the bomber. The FBI suspected Jewell had planted the pipe bomb backpack so he could become a hero. No sources were named in the story.

The *Journal-Constitution* story was quickly picked up by the rest of the news media. In the stampede that followed, Richard Jewell was stomped by hundreds of frenzied journalistic hooves in print and on the air. He was mockingly compared to the infamous Unabomber who had killed three people and injured close to two dozen others. Jewell was ridiculed with names like Una-Doofus and Una-Bubba.

After reporters, anchors and talk-show hosts thoroughly trashed Richard Jewell coast to coast, the real bomber was identified as a domestic terrorist named Eric Rudolph.

Jewell had indeed been a hero, but his name and reputation were ruined by herd journalism and the desperate desire to "break" the news, to be "first" with an "exclusive", even if it's wrong. Jewell spent years suing—and winning—lawsuits against the news media in an effort to clear his name. He died of complications from heart disease and diabetes in 2007.

The hypocrisy of Americans who say they hate "bad" news is exposed every time there is an injury accident on a roadway. Traffic invariably grinds to a halt while drivers rubberneck, hoping to see blood and gore. This is why TV stations, in Los Angeles in particular, preempt regular programming to go live, sometimes for hours, with uninterrupted helicopter coverage of an unimportant police chase. While the news anchors gravely intone hopes that the car chase doesn't end in a horrific crash, in truth, that is precisely what they are hoping will happen. It's the money shot. There must be enough dimwit viewers who will watch this live "news" to make it worth scrapping regular commercial-carrying programs.

Many young TV reporters have the mistaken belief they are in the "news" business. Not true. They are in the eyeball-delivery business for advertisers. News is the hook to get the eyeballs to watch. In two and three-hour blocks of repetitive stories about car crashes, minor fires and dead bodies in dumpsters, the news coverage is video Styrofoam to keep the commercials from bumping in to one another.

Crime coverage is a reliable ratings-getter. Crime is near the top of the bad news that audiences love to hate. I was a news reporter in Detroit for over 25 years. For most of those years I was on the crime and mayhem beat. I spent much of my professional life participating in the coverage I'm criticizing here. As mentioned in Chapter 5, I did stories on hundreds of murders. I reported on countless drug raids, never stopping to wonder what, if anything, was being accomplished and how these stories truly informed the public. But cops in raid vests bashing in doors with battering rams and slamming people to the floor and slapping handcuffs on them while the camera is rolling makes good television. People watch this and think they are seeing law and order in action. For a minute and thirty seconds on TV, the good guys are seemingly winning in the War on Drugs.

My experience was hardly unique. The stations I worked at ground out daily news in the same way as TV newsrooms everywhere else.

Each morning, TV news assignment desks slice up the morning newspapers and hand story clippings to reporters who are assigned to produce a TV version of it. The drill is the same whether it's one of the networks or a local station. Shameless plagiarism and content theft are common in the TV news biz. This is harmless enough in human-interest features, but it's a serious flaw in what is known as hard news.

As the herd journalism in the Richard Jewell case demonstrated, errors in major stories get repeated exponentially in the echo chamber of Me Too news.

Left uncorrected, inaccurate reporting becomes accepted as truth in subsequent stories. A reporter may put a "new top" on an on-going story, but repeat what's been reported before, almost word for word, in the body of the piece. Decent, ethical reporters working under deadline pressure routinely read archive story clippings and repeat the "facts" they find there. If those "facts" are wrong, if an editor hasn't challenged the basis for the initial sensational claims and accusations, the factual errors get repeated again. And again. And again.

Richard Wershe, Jr. is painfully aware of lies posing as facts in fevered media coverage. He has been smeared as a "drug lord" and "kingpin" in countless TV reports and print articles for three decades. There isn't any evidence in the record—none—to support those labels, but that didn't stop the Detroit journalism herd from mindlessly repeating them over and over whenever Wershe would surface in the news. It was a factual failure of Me Too journalism writ large.

Overall, Detroit's two newspapers were reasonably good at covering the news. Talented journalists were employed there. But accuracy and fact-checking went out the window in the Rick Wershe case.

The false image of Wershe as a juvenile godfather of Detroit's crack cocaine underworld had its start with one reporter: Chris Hansen. We were colleagues at the time, at WXYZ-TV, Channel 7, the ABC affiliate for Detroit.

Hansen replaced me as the crime beat reporter when I moved to investigative reporting and special projects.

Hansen was good at his job. He was the station's crime reporter when the crack cocaine frenzy swept the nation. Hansen and the station's news bosses hit on the idea of having him become "embedded" with a narcotics team as a way of chronicling the battle against crack. He was paired with the No Crack Crew. The concept of "embedding" a reporter didn't come along until the Gulf Wars a few years later, so this was, to some degree, a reporting innovation.

For over a year Hansen and his cameraman went on raid after raid after raid. Afterward, Hansen bought round after round after round at the bars favored by the No Crack Crew. Hansen got great footage, but it came at a price far beyond the bar tab.

Did he allow himself to get too close to the narcs he was reporting on? In source-dependent reporting there's a danger of becoming a propaganda or public relations mouthpiece. It's tough to maintain a sense of balance and have the courage to tell the story in a way that's at variance with the spin of your sources.

In *Land of Opportunity*, William Adler wrote that Hansen got so close to the No Crack Crew he "virtually (traded) his press card for a deputy's badge."

Hansen, working with Bill Bonds, the station's bombastic, hyperbolic, over-the-top, news anchor, aired a ratings-grabbing you-are-there five-part series on the Chambers Brothers drug gang in July of 1987.

The final night's segment was a stunner. It left the impression that a white Detroit kid identified as White Boy Rick was riding atop Detroit's crack market, which was dominated at the street level by the Chambers Brothers.

White Boy Rick was much more memorable than the guy's real name; Richard Wershe, Jr. The White Boy Rick moniker became an albatross around Wershe's neck for decades. It was code for a young, cocky, ruthless top-level drug dealer. Over the years, people in Detroit and Michigan would respond with a blank look if you mentioned the name Richard Wershe, Jr. But often, there would be a flash of recognition if you mentioned White Boy Rick.

It took nearly 30 years, but Rick Wershe was able to call Hansen out about his role in creating and nurturing the corrosive White Boy Rick legend. It happened in the summer of 2016. Hansen had leveraged his coverage of White Boy Rick and other high-profile crime stories to win a job as a correspondent on NBC's *Dateline*, where he made a name for himself doing on-camera gotcha segments about sex offenders. NBC dropped him when he got caught up in a personal scandal, so Hansen transitioned to doing crime segments for syndicated television.

In 2016 the White Boy Rick story had faded from the headlines and newscasts. Wershe was forgotten, left to languish behind bars. But an article in *The Fix*, an obscure web site about addiction and recovery, turned things around in terms of media interest. The author, Seth Ferranti, was an inmate himself, doing time on a drug case unrelated to Wershe. Ferranti did a broad strokes explanation of the Wershe story and wrote, "White Boy Rick is a poster child for what is wrong with the War on Drugs."

People noticed, including Hollywood, which is always on the prowl for a good story. When Hollywood studios starting competing to tell the White Boy Rick story, media interest was aroused.

Hansen wound up doing an hour-long satellite radio show in July of 2016 featuring Rick Wershe and the retired FBI agents who knew him best; Herman Groman and Gregg Schwarz.

The program covered the basic story; teen drug informant is taught the dope trade by the police, gets kicked to the curb, decides to become a drug dealer himself, gets caught and thrown in jail for life, tells on the wrong people and they work hard to see that he never gets paroled.

Near the end of the program, Hansen asked Wershe his opinion on how much the nickname White Boy Rick—the epithet the media used with abandon for three decades—had to do with his imprisonment for nearly 30 years.

"I think it's pretty much everything to do with it," Wershe replied. "Chris, you made it a household name. You put it on the news every day for probably a year straight when you were in Detroit."

There was a long, awkward silence. Hansen was momentarily stunned, but defended himself by stating it was a "darn interesting story" and attributed the provocative nickname to "...something that was used on the street and by police investigators."

Wershe disagreed. Hansen may have been half-right. His cop pals may have latched on to the catchy street name, but in numerous interviews for this book, no one from the streets called Wershe "White Boy Rick." He was simply Rick or Ricky. But street names appeal to cops and reporters. They make it sound like they are in the know, which impresses the public. Alphonse Capone doesn't have the same cachet as "Scarface." Salvatore Gravano is not as evocative as "Sammy the Bull." Charles Arthur Floyd just doesn't have the same ring as "Pretty Boy Floyd."

In 2017 Rick told the Michigan Parole Board he's "not a fan" of Chris Hansen. "Chris Hansen did a lot of damage and reported a lot of inaccurate stuff over the years," Wershe testified.

"Like what?" he was asked.

"That I was a drug kingpin. That I supplied the Curry boys with drugs. Just a lot of stuff that he didn't know what he was talking about."

In answer to Shakespeare's famous question—"What's in a name?"—the answer in crime reporting is: quite a lot.

Calling Richard Wershe, Jr "White Boy Rick" was a quick and easy way to tell viewers and readers this news is about a young white underworld gangster. The story line was irresistible. The mostly-white editors of Detroit's newspapers, hyper-sensitive to accusations of racism, seemed thrilled to be able to report that someone white— not black—was calling the shots in the crack cocaine depravity coursing through the inner city. At last there was a white face to blame.

Not a single journalist in Detroit seemed to stop and ask how a charming but boyish white teen could be the godfather, the commanding general, of the illegal crack cocaine trade on the streets of Detroit.

It was a racket dominated by prison-hardened adult black men, some of them killers. He who ruled the roost controlled millions of dollars. As far as can be determined, no reporter asked the cops or prosecutors for proof, for evidence, to support the claim that this kid was atop this often-murderous racket.

Prisoner of War:
The Story of White Boy Rick and The War on Drugs

Hansen tarred Wershe with the first swipe of the brush, but the Detroit newspapers took over. They kept smearing Rick Wershe, claiming he was a "drug lord" and "kingpin" in story after story. Suddenly, Rick Wershe's pending trial for possession of about 17 pounds of cocaine became an important crime story.

The media coverage of Wershe was so sensational that a local judge got swept up in the hyperbole about him. During a Wershe court appearance, Judge William Hathaway, a white jurist, said without a shred of evidence behind his tirade: "Even though he's only 18-years-old and looking like Baby Face Nelson (a notorious Depression-era bank robber), he's worse than a mass murderer!"

Wershe was never charged with a violent crime, much less murder. Wershe was never charged with conspiring to commit or order a violent crime. Yet the media coverage of him was so over the top, it put a sitting judge over the top, too.

In her story about the judicial outburst, *Detroit News* reporter Denise Stinson included this line: *"Wershe, described by Detroit police as a local drug kingpin..."* There was no attribution, just a matter-of-fact line citing "Detroit police" as describing this kid who hadn't had a trial yet "a local drug kingpin."

In November, 1987, with Wershe due to go on trial in January, *Detroit Free Press* reporters Bill McGraw and Sandy McClure did a profile piece comparing what his family said about him with the public image. The judge's intemperate "Baby Face Nelson" and "mass murderer" line was featured prominently in the story. It's true that the judge said it, but in repeating the mass murderer line, unchallenged and unquestioned, as the third paragraph of the story, the *Free Press* helped shape the emerging legend of White Boy Rick.

Vince Wade

As Wershe's jury trial began, the *Detroit Free Press* published a story about a missing prosecution witness. The story by reporter Jocelyn Zablit began, *"A witness in the trial of reputed cocaine kingpin Richard Wershe, Jr. apparently has vanished."*

This story at least had a fig leaf—the term "reputed." As it turns out, the witness, David Golly, later said under oath that he disappeared because he feared the *police* who, he said, roughed him up and warned him he had better testify against Wershe because "Rick is going down."

When Wershe was convicted, the *Detroit Free Press* story by Joe Swickard began, *"Teenage drug kingpin Richard (White Boy Rick) Wershe Jr. faces spending the rest of his life in prison..."* Swickard didn't bother with the usual "reputed" qualifier.

The next day the same paper ran a story by Mark Lowery that began, *"The father of convicted drug kingpin Richard (White Boy Rick) Wershe..."* This was followed a few days later with a story by Bill McGraw that began, *"A federal magistrate denied bond to the father of teenage drug kingpin Richard (White Boy Rick) Wershe, Jr...."*

Each of these *Detroit Free Press* stories, by different reporters, reported as truth that Richard J. Wershe, Jr was a "drug kingpin." This description was factually based on—nothing.

That is, there never was, and never has been, any evidence in any indictment or documentation presented in any court that Wershe was a kingpin, drug lord, godfather, CEO or major figure in the drug business. He was convicted of "possession with intent to distribute cocaine in excess of 650 grams." That makes him a drug dealer, alright, but not a drug kingpin or drug lord. There are laws to prosecute people dealing drugs at drug lord and kingpin

246

levels, but Wershe wasn't charged under any of those statutes.

Yet, he was repeatedly smeared in the *Detroit Free Press* as a drug "kingpin" based upon…what? What evidence? What facts?

Multiple *Free Press* reporters failed to do their jobs. They failed to do basic reporting. If they had, they would have asked a fundamental question: what is the basis for calling this guy a kingpin? Like the Richard Jewell case, it was herd journalism on an endless loop. It was reliance on anonymous police and prosecution sources who lacked the balls to put their names behind the libel. These cops and prosecutors knew they didn't have "kingpin" or "drug lord" evidence against Wershe, so they had reporters, eager to suck up to cop sources to ensure a future supply of stories, make accusations law enforcement couldn't substantiate in court before a judge and jury.

The *Detroit Free Press* reporters weren't alone in the herd. A city magazine called *Detroit Monthly* did a profile piece on Wershe and quoted William Coonce, the head of the DEA in Detroit at that time, as saying in the War on Drugs, "Detroit is our Vietnam." That metaphor was popularized nationally among DEA Special Agents in Charge by Robert Stutman, the head of the DEA's New York office.

Reporters ate it up. It was a quotable quote. The *Detroit Monthly* article writer, playing off the Detroit-as-Vietnam imagery went on to write, "If that is true, then White Boy Rick could be considered a teenage Ho Chi Minh."

Not to be left out, the *Detroit News* ran articles by Mike Martindale and Rob Zeiger variously calling Wershe a "convicted east side drug kingpin" and "convicted east side drug lord."

This was false reporting. There was nothing in the charges, conviction or sentencing of Rick Wershe categorizing him as a "kingpin" or "drug lord." But it contributed to the smear of a young man's name.

Detroit TV and radio stations, as was and is their practice, shamelessly ripped off the White Boy Rick stories appearing in the papers and repeated them over the air, almost word for word, compounding the false legend.

The drug lord canard followed Wershe almost every time his name came up in a news story. *Detroit Free Press* reporters Margaret Trimer and Joe Swickard, wrote a piece in May of 1989 with photos and an organizational chart claiming White Boy Rick was a co-founder of the Best Friends murder-for-hire drug gang.

It wasn't true, but the paper's editors didn't do their job; they didn't challenge the story as written by the reporters. The *Free Press* chart mimicked one created by a DEA agent involved in investigating the Best Friends.

Nate Craft, the admitted Best Friends hitman profiled in Chapter 12, said he saw that chart in the DEA office when he decided to turn on his fellow killers and testify against them after they killed his brother. Craft said the information on the chart about Wershe being a co-founder of Best Friends was false.

As noted in Chapter 12, the Best Friends had tried to kill Wershe because they suspected he was a snitch. "He shouldn't have been on that chart, period," Craft told me. "He wasn't no big-time drug dealer. He wasn't no big-time anything."

Prisoner of War:
The Story of White Boy Rick and The War on Drugs

When a federal grand jury returned an indictment against the Best Friends organization, Wershe was not indicted or even mentioned in the document. The *Detroit Free Press* story indicating he was a co-founder of Best Friends was never retracted or corrected.

Separately, convicted drug gangster Johnny Curry agreed with Craft's assessment of White Boy Rick's place in the drug dealer pecking order.

"They built Rick up to be this big white boy," Curry said in a YouTube interview. "I say from a scale of 1 to 10, I'd rate Rick around about a 2 and me sittin' back as a 10. He took orders from me" In another video, Curry revised Wershe's status by saying he was "probably a 2, if that."

No evidence, no testimony, no documentation was ever produced by the police or prosecutors that Rick Wershe, Jr. was the leader of a cocaine organization—a kingpin. None. Zilch. Zip. But the herd journalists reported it, anyway.

Rick Wershe is fully aware of the role the media played in destroying his life. He has spent long hours in his cell, thinking about it. Here's what he wrote in an email to me when I asked for his view of the role the media's White Boy Rick legend played in burying him in prison:

Wershe wrote to me, "That's what stole most of my life - there (sic) lies and BS reporting! And they say not to be bitter! Let them try doing five years of this shit!"

After a thorough review of federal and local criminal court records, here are real, verifiable facts about Richard J. Wershe, Jr.:

- Wershe was never charged with drug racketeering, federally or locally.

- Wershe was never charged with operating a continuing criminal enterprise—the so-called "kingpin" criminal statute.
- Wershe was never charged with conspiracy, federally or locally.
- Wershe was never charged with leading a "gang" or "organization" or "enterprise" and no one was ever charged with being a member of a Wershe-controlled gang.
- Wershe was never charged as a conspirator or co-conspirator or unindicted co-conspirator in any of the major Detroit drug cases of that era.
- Wershe was never charged with a violent crime, participating in a violent crime or with ordering a violent crime.

A big part of the Wershe smear was timing. As noted in Chapter 11, in 1986 the nation was caught up in anxiety over a cocaine "epidemic", fueled by breathless, scare-mongering media coverage of cocaine use following the overdose death of supposedly clean-living star basketball player Len Bias. A media-fueled myth arose that the babies of crack users were being born addicted to cocaine. It was false; another example of shoddy reporting. A medical study in Philadelphia later proved the crack-baby myth was just that. But this fact-free "news" received widespread coverage by the journalism herd and it contributed to cocaine hysteria.

Reporters and editors love a frightening, ain't-it-awful story. A TV news producer I once worked with called this syndrome, "The bombers are over Lansing—Take cover—Goodnight."

Crack cocaine was a gift, in a way, to the DEA. The public panic over crack was an opportunity to push for a bigger budget—a sacred quest for all federal agencies, always.

In what turned out to be a savvy management decision, the Drug Enforcement Administration had named Robert Stutman to be the SAC—Special Agent in Charge—of the New York office. New York is the media capital of the nation. And Robert Stutman was a media showman of the first order. He correctly saw an opportunity to exploit the media over the crack cocaine scare. But first, he had to convince Washington that crack was a problem. In 1985 it was so new no one except street people had heard of the stuff.

In her book, *Making Crime Pay*, Katherine Beckett quotes Stutman as saying, "In order to convince Washington, I needed to make it a national issue and quickly. I began a lobbying effort and I used the media. The media were only too willing to cooperate, because as far as the New York media was concerned, crack was the hottest combat reporting story to come along since the end of the Vietnam war."

The DEA usually does its business covertly. Stutman changed that. He repeatedly invited reporters and TV cameras along on door-kicking drug raids. It provided the "action" footage the TV news business craves. Stutman's comparison of the battle against crack cocaine with the battles in the jungles of Vietnam made for great soundbites and newspaper quotes.

Beckett said the *New York Times* increased its drug-related stories from 43 in the last half of 1985 to 220 in the last half of 1986.

Vince Wade

In media-savvy Los Angeles, Police Chief Darryl Gates, who dreamed of becoming California's governor, knew journalistic catnip and a politically-rich photo op when he saw them.

In the spring of 1989 Gates hosted former First Lady Nancy Reagan at what amounted to a police street drug bust party and invited reporters along.

As Reagan and Gates sat in an air-conditioned motor home nibbling on fruit salad, a SWAT team kicked in the door of a crack house in South Central Los Angeles.

Mrs. Reagan freshened her makeup, put on a blue police windbreaker with her name stenciled on the front, and she and Gates went inside the crack house.

"These people in here are beyond the point of teaching and rehabilitating," Mrs. Reagan told reporters. "There's no life, and that's very discouraging." She concluded the handcuffed wretches in the house were beyond her Just Say No anti-drug mantra.

Sometimes, wild animals eat their young. Sometimes, journalists devour their own. The late Gary Webb is an example of this.

Webb was an investigative reporter for the *San Jose Mercury News*, the hometown paper of Silicon Valley.

In a stunning three-part series called "Dark Alliance", Webb reported that CIA-backed Contra rebels and associates had sold tons of cocaine to drug dealers in Los Angeles.

Webb's reporting suggested Ollie North's favorite anti-Communist rebel group was largely responsible for the crack cocaine that engulfed the black neighborhoods of Los

Angeles and that profits from Contra cocaine dealing went
to support the covert war against the Leftist Nicaraguan
Sandinistas.

"It is one of the most bizarre alliances in modern
history: the union of a U.S.-backed army attempting to
overthrow a revolutionary socialist government and the
Uzi-toting "gangstas" of Compton and South-Central Los
Angeles," Webb wrote.

Much of this had been hinted at and inferred in the
exhaustive Iran/Contra hearings led by then-Senator John
Kerry in 1988.

Those hearings received scant coverage in the *New
York Times*, the *Washington Post* and the *Los Angeles
Times*.

The Reagan Administration hated the exposure of CIA
involvement with drug smugglers and apparently the Big
Media did not want to incur the wrath of the Reagan White
House. The Big Media had already brought down one
Republican President. They may have been reluctant to go
after another one who was much more popular with many
readers and viewers.

When Webb's stories came out, the Big Papers became
aggressive—against Webb. He was criticized mercilessly.
His stories were fly-specked, but not pursued or advanced,
despite compelling evidence. It's true that Webb's
implication that the Contras were responsible for the
explosion of crack use in the Los Angeles ghetto was
dubious, and some of his reporting didn't check out, but
most of it did. He was hounded out of the news business by
pompous editors and reporters who had been scooped by
one reporter working at a medium-sized newspaper.

Unable to find work, Webb committed suicide, a victim of another media stampede. The journalism herd doesn't like to be scooped and shown for what it truly is.

The current *Washington Post* online edition features the slogan: "Democracy Dies in Darkness." Yes, it does. And so do some journalists who expose the failure of the *Post* and other major papers to pursue a big story for what appear to be craven reasons.

Chapter 15—Life without Parole

"Hang 'em first, try 'em later."
—Judge Roy Bean, 1800s Texas saloon-keeper, judge
and "the Law West of the Pecos River."

The cocaine trial of Richard J. Wershe, Jr.. was an
injustice, but not for the usual reasons. For one thing,
Wershe was guilty. Years later, when he was fighting for
parole, Wershe admitted he did the crime.

Still, his case was tainted by injustice that had three
components.

One was the political and criminal-justice intrigue that
surrounded the case and doomed the appeal that followed.

The second was the disproportionate sentence. A life-
without-parole prison sentence for a non-violent drug
offense committed when the defendant was a teen was
totally out of proportion in the world of crime and
punishment, even though it was mandated by state law.
Some laws are unjust.

The third element was the media frenzy surrounding
his case. Wershe went through trial by media before he
ever entered a courtroom and the media jury verdict was:
guilty.

Wershe had been charged with possession of cocaine
with intent to deliver in excess of 650 grams, or about a
pound and a half. In Michigan at that time, that was a life-
without-parole offense. The Michigan "650 Lifer" had
been on the books since 1978, when the Michigan
legislature mimicked New York in adopting draconian
narcotics laws.

The harsh drug penalty was eventually changed to life with the possibility of parole. Even so, Richard Wershe, Jr. remained in prison and that is part of the injustice in his story.

Before his trial began, Rick Wershe had one more secret encounter with the FBI. The feds had done nothing to help Wershe after his arrest.

Ordinarily, they would go to the local prosecutor and quietly explain the defendant was a confidential informant who had been cooperative and helpful in major case work. That usually helped get the charges reduced to what the legal trade calls a lesser included offense. It didn't happen in Wershe's case. If the Detroit FBI had stepped forward in Wershe's behalf, they would have had to admit they had been using a juvenile as an informant in a dangerous undercover capacity and falsifying their records to cover the ruse. That would stir things up at FBI headquarters and at the Justice Department, not to mention there would be sensational stories in the media.

In late November, 1987, with the drug trial approaching, Richard Wershe, Sr. reached out to Herm Groman of the FBI, seeking help for Rick. Knowing all of the upper echelon intrigue surrounding Rick Wershe's informant status, Groman arranged a meeting between the Wershes and Ken Walton, the Special Agent in Charge of the Detroit FBI. Groman wanted the big boss to handle this.

It was highly unusual for an FBI Special Agent in Charge to go in the field and meet with an informant. The fiction that Wershe Senior had been the informant in the Curry case was maintained for the meeting. It was handled as if Richard Wershe, Jr. was a new actor on the informant scene.

Young Wershe offered up information indicating the kinds of cases he could help the FBI develop. He said he had two sources of supply in Miami. He identified them as a group of Cubans and a group of Colombians and that the Colombians appeared to have access to larger quantities of cocaine. Rick said his Miami connections had fronted him a large quantity of cocaine worth close to two-hundred thousand in cash. He wanted newspaper clippings about his arrest to prove to his sources in Miami that he had been busted and had not ripped them off.

As young Wershe described the situation, he had a businessman contact in downtown Detroit who was active in the drug smuggling business and who could help him with financing. He also told Walton and Groman that he had given his attorney, William Bufalino II, ten-thousand dollars to pay as a bribe to a sergeant in the Detroit Police Narcotics Section to ensure his stash house wouldn't be raided. He concluded by claiming he knew a Michigan State Police trooper who was trafficking in military ordnance.

Walton gave the Wershes the same pitch any prospective informant would hear. According to an FBI 302 summary of the meeting, Walton told the younger Wershe that he would have to be fully debriefed, that absolute truthfulness was essential. He was told it was likely he would have to work undercover wearing a wire to record drug transaction meetings and it was probable that he would have to testify as a government witness in court.

The Wershes didn't like the scenario Walton described. Walton and Groman countered that Rick was facing a sentence of life without parole if he was convicted and it would take a significant effort on his part to make it worthwhile for the FBI to call in such a big favor from the Wayne County Prosecutor. Even at that, the Wershes were warned, Rick was likely to face some prison time, no matter what.

After the meeting, the Wershe family huddled and concluded the FBI's demands were too risky considering the kinds of people Rick would be expected to help send to prison. They decided Rick would take his chances with a jury trial. Ed Bell and Sam Gardner were offering smooth reassurances that acquittal was likely.

The Richard Wershe, Jr.. cocaine possession trial began on Monday, January 4, 1988. That same day, former Michigan State Senator Basil Brown, one of Coleman Young's longtime friends and one of his closest allies, was sentenced to six months in prison for providing marijuana and cocaine to a prostitute. Brown had been chairman of the Michigan Senate Judiciary Committee and he had led efforts to enact tougher drug laws. He died in 1997.

Rick Wershe's trial judge was Thomas Jackson, a black judge with a reputation as a straight shooter. While Sam Gardner, a former criminal court judge, had initially arranged to take over the Wershe defense, the trial was handled by Edward Bell, who also was a former county judge. Bell was suffering from prostate cancer, but he insisted on leading the defense. There were times during the Wershe trial that Bell was too ill to proceed and his inexperienced female assistant would try to continue, with mixed success.

"I think he was probably dying," Robert Healy, the case prosecutor said. Indeed, Bell passed away five months after the trial.

Healy, the assistant prosecutor who made that blunt assessment of Bell's health was a laconic man prone to occasional sarcastic observations and fond of getting out on the streets with the cops, sometimes to their dismay. He preferred working in police squad areas to toiling at his desk in the prosecutor's office. Healy liked to carry a full-sized .357 magnum pistol in a shoulder holster when he when out on raids and search warrant forays with the cops. One cop told me he was always scared to death Healy would actually draw his weapon at a raid and cause chaos, or worse.

Healy told me he was not aware of Officer Biernacki's Pinocchio nickname, but he said, "I'm not terribly surprised. That's one of the reasons I was working with these guys on the street. I had to have direct knowledge, so if someone was lying to me, I'd know it."

Healy said it is his recollection that Biernacki was "the lead copper" on the Rick Wershe, Jr. investigation.

"I knew Biernacki was a heavy drinker," Healy said. "I knew he was somewhat unstable." That was evident when it came time for Biernacki to testify in the Wershe trial. Witnesses in Detroit criminal cases usually wait on benches outside the courtrooms. When it was time to testify, Biernacki was not on a hallway bench. He was nowhere to be found. In a bit of panic, Healy said he called Biernacki's lieutenant and said it was urgent that Biernacki be found. The lieutenant found him—someplace.

Wershe's jury trial was the result of a police traffic stop that quickly plunged in to chaos. The night of his arrest, Wershe was on his way to his grandmother's house to pick up two kilos of cocaine stored there without her knowledge. His grandmother, a law-abiding elderly lady, lived across Hampshire street from Wershe's residence.

The buyer, Brian McClendon, had already paid him for the dope. Wershe had a plastic grocery store shopping bag on the floorboard of the car, stuffed with $34-thousand in cash.

On the way to get the cocaine and deliver it to McClendon, who was following in another car, Wershe and his friend Roy Grisson, who was driving, were stopped by Detroit Police officers Jeffrey Clyburn and Rodney Grandison, members of the Detroit Police Gang Squad who were working in uniform in a marked patrol car. The officers just happened, so they said, to be on a side street that intersected Wershe's street when they saw Wershe and Grisson pass in front of them, driving at high speed through the residential neighborhood. That was the stated reason for the traffic stop.

Grisson and Wershe got out of the car in front of Grandma Wershe's house as the officers approached. Trial prosecutor Robert Healy, asked Clyburn if Wershe had anything in his hands.

Clyburn: "He had one of those mobile telephones."

Healy: "Alright. So, he's got one of those fancy mobile telephones that you can call from anywhere?"

Clyburn: "That's correct."

Grandison testified he saw a plastic grocery bag of money on the floorboard of the car and alerted Clyburn, his partner. Clyburn reached in the car to grab the bag of money. "I observed money in the bag, and I reached down to retrieve the bag," Clyburn testified. "I opened it slightly. I saw what appeared to be a gun in the bag."

Grandison's testimony in cross examination by defense attorney Ed Bell did not corroborate the testimony of Clyburn.

Bell: "Did you see a gun, sir?"

Grandison: "No, I didn't."

Bell: "You did not see a gun; you saw money?"

Grandison: "Correct."

Bell had zeroed in on the first of several questionable actions of the cops that night.

Bell: "What was so unusual about seeing money? Was that a crime?

Grandison: "It seemed kind of unusual."

Bell: "Was it a crime, I'm asking you?"

Grandison: "No, it's not."

No gun was retrieved in the incident, but Clyburn *claimed* he saw "…what appeared to be a gun…" This dubious claim enhanced the confiscation of the cash under the so-called "plain view" legal doctrine. The police can examine suspicious items in a car that are in plain view. It could be argued that a plastic shopping bag stuffed with cash qualifies as a suspicious item.

A loud, profane scuffle broke out as the police tried to confiscate the money. Wershe's father came out in the street, joined the struggle and grabbed the bag of money, while the younger Wershe was exchanging blows and insults with Officer Clyburn. The elder Wershe ran to his mother's house, Rick's grandmother, with the police in pursuit. Rick's older sister Dawn grabbed the money from her father, ran in the house, and slammed the door.

On direct examination by trial prosecutor Healy, Officer Grandison lied under oath as he described the struggle.

Healy: "Now, you talk about Dawn Wershe and Wershe, Senior and Wershe, Junior. Had you seen any of those three people before this incident?

Grandison: "No, I haven't."

Healy: "Did you know who they were?"

Grandison: "No, I didn't."

This was a lie. Actually, two lies. Twice, when asked by the prosecutor, Grandison testified he didn't know any of the Wershes. It was perjury—a felony.

Grandison was well-acquainted with Richard Wershe, Jr. Wershe says Officer Grandison used to invite him on occasion to his house to, um, relax and socialize.

The falsity of Grandison's testimony was verified by the FBI several years later in a tape-recorded telephone call. Agent Herman Groman, who had been Rick Wershe's handler when he was a confidential informant in the Curry case, visited him in Marquette State Prison to persuade Wershe to help him—from prison—with another case. This time, Groman was after corrupt cops. Wershe told him about Grandison lying on the witness stand in his drug trial.

Agent Groman quickly arranged for Wershe to make a consensually-recorded phone call from prison to Officer Grandison at home. The call, which lasted fifteen or twenty minutes, wasn't about anything significant. The conversation wasn't important. What it established, beyond any doubt, is that Detroit Police Officer Rodney Grandison did, indeed, know Richard J. Wershe, Jr well enough to

have a friendly conversation and he lied under oath at
Wershe's trial when he said he didn't know him or his
family.

While his family and the police were fighting over the
cash, Rick Wershe simply walked away. He was not
carrying anything. That quickly changed. Wershe
eventually told the Michigan Parole Board he went to his
grandmother's detached garage and got a box of drugs that
had arrived that day.

Wershe's pal, the late Steve Rousell, had put the drugs
in the garage after a shipment had arrived from Miami.
Rousell was murdered later that year in what Wershe says
was a love-triangle.

Wershe took the box of drugs to the next block where
he hid it under a residential porch. Somehow, he managed
to do this without getting his fingerprints or palm prints on
the box.

"We were in a panic," Wershe said. He admits he
encountered some residents who were outdoors on a nice
spring night. But counter to witness testimony at his trial,
Wershe denied he offered to pay five-hundred dollars to a
neighborhood woman to keep the box hidden.

After he stashed the box of drugs, "I was on a porch,
trying to look inconspicuous," Wershe said. It didn't work.

Officer Grandison arrived a few minutes later on foot
and took Wershe in to custody. Wershe said another officer
joined Grandison and they put him in handcuffs and
walked him between the houses to where the traffic-stop
and scuffle occurred. There was a fence between the
houses. Wershe said Grandison pulled him over the fence
gate by a gold chain he had around his neck, then threw

him to the ground. "He pistol-whipped me," Wershe later told the Parole Board. His eye socket was shattered and Wershe wound up going to the hospital that night.

After the police left with the Wershe family in custody, the neighbors found the box of drugs and allegedly called the police. The call is alleged and in question because it wasn't recorded by the 911 system, which records all incoming calls to the police. The police claimed they were "changing the tapes" when the call about the box of dope came in to the local precinct desk. 911 systems have redundant backup systems to avoid missing calls when tapes are "changed."

Did the citizen call contain information the police didn't want revealed at Wershe's trial? The question can't be answered because the police tape of the call was never found. In any event, Gerard Biernacki and Greg Woods of the No Crack Crew went to Camden Street where the box was found and Woods took custody of the drugs about an hour after Rick Wershe was arrested.

There's one more nagging mystery related to the arrest of Rick Wershe.

At his 2017 parole hearing, Wershe was asked about the discrepancy regarding the cash he had in the car when the police stopped them. Wershe swore the grocery bag contained $34-thousand dollars. At the end of the night the police claimed the bag contained $29-thousand dollars. What happened to the rest of the money, Wershe was asked. "You'll have to ask the Detroit Police," Wershe replied.

The jury in Wershe's trial deliberated over four days before returning their verdict: guilty. But like so many things in the Rick Wershe story, there was a lot more behind the scenes and below the radar in this tale of a white teenaged drug dealer in a mostly black city.

Part of the intrigue of Rick Wershe's big drug case involved his legal help. Ed Bell, who defended Wershe in his court case, was not Wershe's initial trial attorney. That was William E. Bufalino II, who always insisted on being named just that way. He was the rotund son of William E. Bufalino, who gained some fame as the lawyer for former Teamsters President Jimmy Hoffa.

The younger Bufalino was one of Detroit's veteran criminal defense attorneys. He represented Wershe in his early court appearances, including the preliminary examination, in which the prosecution has to reveal enough evidence and testimony to persuade a judge that there is a viable case to be presented to a jury.

After reviewing the case against Wershe, one of the first things Bufalino did was file a motion to suppress the evidence. It was an important legal move. This was the 17 pounds of cocaine the police seized an hour after Wershe's arrest. The box of drugs did not have Wershe's fingerprints or palm prints on it.

There is an element of law known as constructive possession, which, in drug cases, means a defendant has knowledge of the drugs and some control of the contraband. The drugs could arguably be linked to Wershe even if he didn't have them in his direct possession. Still, the time lag between his arrest and the police gaining control of the drugs and questions about who handled the drugs during that time gap were sufficient reasons for the motion to suppress the evidence. If the judge denied the motion at trial, it still left an important basis for an appeal of the conviction. Wershe never had that option. Wershe replaced Bufalino as his trial attorney and the first thing Bell did was withdraw the motion to suppress the drug evidence. It meant if Wershe was found guilty, he had no basis to appeal his life sentence. Why would a defense attorney leave his client exposed like that? Why indeed.

In Chapter 13 it was noted that Wershe was having a hot fling with Cathy Volsan Curry, the niece of Detroit Mayor Coleman Young, at the time of his arrest. Wershe says Cathy's "family" had urged her to persuade Rick to get black legal help for his trial in Recorder's Court, Detroit's criminal court. The jury pools in Recorder's Court are mostly black citizens. The reasoning was that a black defense attorney for a white defendant would have a better chance of persuading a mostly black jury to vote for acquittal.

But there's a more sinister element to the legal representation in the Wershe case. Cathy Volsan Curry and her mother, the late Juanita Volsan, the mayor's sister, urged Wershe to hire the Bell and Gardner law firm. Ed Bell and Sam Gardner were both black attorneys and both were former judges. Perhaps more important, both men were allies of Mayor Coleman Young. They were in the orbit of Young's corrupt political machine.

When Cathy invited Rick to her bed, her uncle made it clear he never wanted to see the two of them together. In the summer of 1987 Rick and Cathy would sometimes spend the night at her mother's house in northwest Detroit. Wershe told me the mayor's security detail would call ahead if the mayor wanted to stop at his sister's house. They would ask if White Boy Rick was there. If so, they said, he would have to leave because the mayor would be there soon. Since Young demanded to know any police intelligence that might involve his family, it is certain that he knew who White Boy Rick was—and he knew his niece was sleeping with him. If White Boy Rick were to go to prison for life, it would be one less headache for the emperor-mayor of Detroit.

The change in legal representation for Wershe began with Sam Gardner. He had been the chief judge of Recorder's Court, Detroit's criminal court for many years. He resigned about a month after the FBI raided Recorder's Court in January of 1987 as part of a corruption investigation, which eventually led to the indictment and conviction of several judges. Wershe was arrested in May of that year.

After he resigned his judgeship, Gardner joined the Bell law firm. Johnny and Cathy Volsan Curry were his neighbors on Navarre Place, an upscale condo enclave less than a mile from the courthouse. When Johnny Curry was jailed in the FBI drug case and Rick Wershe moved in with Cathy, she introduced him to Gardner.

The late Enid Lawlor, the resident who kept an eye on the intrigues of the Navarre Place neighborhood, told me in a 1988 interview that Gardner, who was married, was a notable neighbor, but not because he was a judge. "He has lots of girls there," Lawlor told me in that interview. "He beats them. Some of them ran naked from his condo" after Gardner beat them.

Lawlor told me of one episode where a lieutenant from police headquarters intervened when "a semi-nude young woman showed up at a neighbor's door begging for help."

Lawlor's observations about Sam Gardner might be dismissed as nosiness by a neighborhood busybody, except for more serious accusations from the late Kae Resh, mentioned in Chapter 5 as "the conscience of Recorder's Court" for her honesty and integrity. Before she passed away at age 93, she shared with me her recollections of Gardner. During his tenure as chief judge, Resh worked for a time as a special assistant to Gardner. She suspected she was named to the position so he could keep an eye on her.

Resh told me she thought Gardner was corrupt. She was troubled by Gardner's high-living lifestyle, which she knew to be far above a local judge's pay. Recorder's Court judges are paid decently, but Gardner was buying custom-made suits from a famous tailor across the river in Windsor, Canada. The tailor, the late Lou Myles, made bespoke suits for Muhammed Ali, Michael Jordan, Frank Sinatra—and Sam Gardner.

Resh recalled that Gardner and Bell took their wives to Paris on the supersonic, and super-expensive, Concorde— twice.

She also recalled a time she was at Gardner's condo for a Sunday patio lunch. Resh had become friendly with the judge's wife. Resh and Mrs. Gardner were setting the table when a well-known Detroit defense attorney arrived. The judge was moving about the condo, chatting amiably with the attorney, who produced a stack of cash, perhaps three or four inches high as Resh remembers it, and placed it on a breakfast nook table—and departed. It was obvious to Resh this was a bribe. Shaken, she went to the patio and remained there for the rest of her visit.

Why, she was asked, did she suppose this happened in front of a court employee known for integrity? "Arrogance," Resh replied. "They were all-powerful in those days and they had the attitude, 'Who is going to stop us?'"

During Wershe's cocaine possession trial, reporters noted and wrote about a number of young men who showed up at court decked out in designer warm-up suits and lots of gold chains and pagers. They gave the appearance of being part of a Wershe "gang", or at least, buddies and pals.

Nate Craft, the admitted hitman we met in Chapter 12, told me police officers bribed the street guys to show up at court, wearing their gaudiest bling.

"We was paid to come down and protest about Rick," Craft said. "The cops had us wear bling. They wanted us to pack the court." Not everyone received cash payments, according to Craft. He said some guys were promised the narcs would go easy on them in the next raid if they came to court and made a show while Wershe was on trial.

The police effort to create a false impression about Wershe worked. Reporters wrote about the cacophony of pagers beeping in the courtroom. The implication was these suspected dopers were Wershe's friends, his posse, part of his *gang*. And the trial judge, Thomas Jackson, remarked about it from the bench. He wondered if the flashy young men were there out of concern for Wershe or out of concern over who might take his place on the street.

William Bufalino, the veteran defense lawyer who had been relegated to the second string in favor of the Bell and Gardner law firm, said he obtained affidavits from several of the young men stating they had been paid by the police to show up at the Wershe trial.

Officer Biernacki got one last ounce of revenge after Rick Wershe was convicted.

Richard Wershe, Sr., always a hot head, encountered Biernacki in a stairwell adjacent to the courtroom. The senior Wershe said he hoped Biernacki would sleep well that night. Biernacki reported it as a threat, and in the charged atmosphere, Richard Wershe, Sr was jailed for

Vince Wade

threatening a federal officer. Biernacki was a deputized
U.S. marshal, which was a designation for all the local
cops working on the anti-drug task force.

Not long after that, the Bureau of Alcohol, Tobacco
and Firearms—BATF—brought a case against the elder
Wershe for possession of gun suppressors or silencers.

The same day Wershe was being sentenced to life in
prison without parole, Detroit's narcs were out on the
streets, doing their buy-busts, kicking in the doors of crack
houses. They found Gerald Harrington, a former
anchorman for WDIV-TV, the NBC affiliate where Chris
Hansen was then working, in a crack house. Harrington,
who had left the station a few months earlier and was
working at a radio station, tried to flee but he was
apprehended and ticketed for loitering in a place of illegal
occupation.

Between the verdict and sentencing in the Rick Wershe
case, his father told Robert Ankeny of the *Detroit News*
that he and his son had been federal informers for several
years. He said it started when he tried to get the FBI to help
him with his daughter's drug addiction problems. The
senior Wershe said he and Rick were paid thousands of
dollars to gather evidence in dope deals. It was true, but
disregarded by the media when Lawrence Bunting, an
Assistant United States Attorney assigned to the Wershe
gun case, told the *News* he knew nothing about the father
and son as federal snitches.

It turns out Bunting was ignorant of the truth. As part
of discovery prior to the firearms trial, the FBI was
compelled to turn over about 75 pages showing Wershe-

related informant work. There was no media coverage of
the revealing documents.

After Rick Wershe's conviction. Officer Mick
Biernacki of the No Crack Crew had what might be called
remorse.

In one of life's ironies, Biernacki, a severe alcoholic,
used to drink at a bar called J. Edgar's, a play on the name
of legendary FBI chief J. Edgar Hoover. Rick Wershe's
Mom tended bar there.

One day Biernacki announced to Darlene, Rick's mom,
he wanted to help Rick. She contacted Patrick McQueeney,
Rick's appeals attorney. They met at J. Edgar's, where
Biernacki drank through the hour-long meeting. "I didn't
think he was lying to me but I also didn't feel he was
giving me much information that was helpful,"
McQueeney said.

Before Rick Wershe began serving his life sentence,
there was another flurry of behind-the-scenes intrigue. He
told Herm Groman, his FBI handler, about a quarterly
bribe scheme involving a Detroit police sergeant. Groman
passed the info along to the Wayne County Prosecutor's
office. This got the attention of a lot of people with badges,
and the media, of course.

In reporting the story for the *Detroit News*, Mike
Martindale, Earle Eldridge and Rob Zeiger referred to
Wershe in their lead paragraph as "eastside convicted drug
kingpin White Boy Rick", and later in the piece as a
"young *druglord* sic)." At the *Detroit Free Press*, reporters
Joe Swickard and Brian Flanigan matter-of-factly
described him as *convicted eastside drug kingpin* Richard
Wershe, Jr. The characterization was false in both
newspapers, as explained in the previous chapter. By this

271

time, however, the truth-challenged smear was routine in writing about young Rick Wershe. The drip, drip, drip of this journalistic malpractice contributed significantly to the false legend that was growing up around the prison inmate routinely described as White Boy Rick.

Wershe told Groman that he and his one-time partner, Chuckie Lewis, were the victims of a shakedown by a Detroit Police sergeant who wanted a 10-thousand-dollar bribe every three months to ensure narcs would not raid a stash house where Wershe stored money and drugs. In addition, the sergeant was to provide them with all police intelligence info about their operation.

Assistant Wayne County Prosecutor Patrick Foley, accompanied by two officers from the Detroit Police Internal Affairs unit, visited Wershe at a local prison facility. They wanted Wershe to tell them about the sergeant, who was also said to be under investigation for the disappearance of seven-thousand dollars from a raid related to the Wershe investigation.

Wershe wanted to know what was in it for him. For starters, he demanded immunity from prosecution for anything he might say about the crooked sergeant. He also wanted to know what the prosecutor was prepared to do about reducing his life prison sentence. The answer was—nothing.

Foley told Wershe he would have to fully cooperate, including testimony. Then and only then the prosecutor's office *might* consider doing something for him. Wershe told Foley, in effect, what he could do with himself and walked out of the meeting. Wershe told me he later learned Prosecutor John O'Hair was infuriated by this turn of events.

At about the same time, things were going badly for
the prosecutor in another big case. Larry Moore, a popular
high school basketball coach, had been busted in his own
home in a raid that netted 649 grams of cocaine, one-gram
short of Michigan's drug "lifer" law. The defense claimed
the drugs belonged to the coach's son. As the case against
the coach moved forward, it became evident to prosecutors
that there were problems.

Their fears were realized when the police informant in
the case said he had been bribed by Sgt. Ron Ferguson to
lie about the case. This is the same Sgt. Ferguson noted in
Chapter 13 as the supervisor in charge of the officer who
arrested Rick Wershe in his big drug case.

As explained earlier in this chapter, that officer,
Rodney Grandison, lied under oath when he said he didn't
know Rick Wershe. The FBI proved that Grandison knew
Wershe by tape recording a phone call between Wershe
and Grandison from the Marquette State Prison.

Terrance Boyle, the judge presiding over Coach
Moore's drug trial, was harshly critical of Sgt. Ferguson
and of police lying in the high-profile case. Judge Boyle
said Ferguson's crew had a "sorry record" in their sworn
affidavits in drug cases.

Larry Moore, the basketball coach, was acquitted and
Sgt. Ferguson's behavior was deemed so outrageous he
was officially charged by the prosecutor's office with
perjury. After an internal hearing, the police department
fired him. Ferguson beat the perjury charge and an
arbitrator overturned his firing. He sued the city and settled
out of court.

Police perjury in drug cases is so widespread and
common it has its own term: testilying.

In an opinion column in the *Los Angeles Times* in 1996, Joseph D. McNamara, former police chief of Kansas City and San Jose, California and a 35-year police veteran wrote: "I've come to believe that hundreds of thousands of law-enforcement officers commit felony perjury every year testifying about drug arrests." As McNamara explained it, "They don't feel lying under oath is wrong because politicians tell them they are engaged in a 'holy war' fighting evil."

Peter Keane, a former San Francisco Police commissioner, said narcs lying under oath, "...is a perversion of the American justice system that strikes directly at the rule of law. Yet it is the routine way of doing business in courtrooms everywhere in America."

Testilying isn't limited to drug cases. The Orange County, California Sheriff's Department became embroiled in a shameful scandal involving jailhouse snitches who help deputies gather incriminating admissions from other inmates facing a variety of charges, including murder. The scandal jeopardized the prosecution of one multiple-victim murder case. The sheriff's department's behavior had been so outrageous the FBI launched an investigation, only to find deputies shredding files containing potentially incriminating information.

In what has to be one of the most astounding statements in the history of law enforcement, Orange County Sheriff Sandra Hutchens said two of her veteran deputies didn't know they were supposed to tell the truth when they were testifying under oath in court.

In June of 1988, the year of Rick Wershe's cocaine trial and sentencing, *Fortune* magazine ran a piece profiling the business of cocaine. The opening sentence stated, "The illicit drug trade is probably the fastest-growing industry in the world and is unquestionably the most profitable." The business magazine's profile of the cocaine trade noted, "The American market, the world's biggest for these drugs, produces annual revenues of at least $100 billion at retail--twice what U.S. consumers spend for oil."

In August, 1988, Attorney General Edwin Meese gave a speech and said, "...the Reagan Administration has had extraordinary success in battling the scourge of drugs in America..."

In October, the *New York Times* editorialized, "Two summers ago, American discovered crack and overdosed on oratory."

Chapter 16—Another War Deployment

"Everyone has a price. The important thing is to find out what it is."
—Pablo Escobar, Co-founder of Colombia's Medellín cocaine cartel

Special Agent Mike Castro was bored. He was a new agent in the Detroit office of the FBI, having transferred from the Bureau office in the U.S. Virgin Islands. Castro had been a street cop in Milwaukee before joining the FBI. In Detroit, he was assigned to the public corruption squad but his primary case was winding down and he wanted an investigation with some meat on the bones. He expressed his frustration to Herm Groman, the agent who had been transferred to public corruption after getting in bureaucratic trouble once too often in the Curry drug case. Castro was thinking he should ask to be re-assigned to the drug squad, where there was more action.

Groman told him about the public corruption element of the killing of Damion Lucas, the 13-year old Detroit boy who died when members of the Curry drug gang shot up the boy's uncle's house over a drug debt. For Groman, the Damion Lucas killing was an injustice that nagged at him. The killing of an innocent kid was bad enough. The blatant police obstruction of justice to please Detroit's mayor was particularly galling.

Groman told Castro the story of how he had an underage informant named Rick Wershe who provided important information about the Damion Lucas homicide, yet the Detroit Police refused to pursue the leads about the real killers in order to protect the mayor's niece who was married to the drug gang leader. What's worse, Groman said, the police had worked to frame an innocent man in the case.

Groman also told him the "toothbrush" incident, where he almost went to jail to protect his juvenile informant's identity. Castro learned the crisis was defused without revealing Rick Wershe's name. The local prosecutor eventually dropped charges against the man who had been falsely arrested in the case, yet showed little interest in demanding a thorough, honest investigation of the Damion Lucas homicide. A state grand jury was empaneled to investigate, but it was a half-hearted effort, at best. The prosecutor, John O'Hair, cultivated the image of a man of probity and integrity. No one questioned those qualities in O'Hair, but his position was elected. There was incentive to rationalize ways to bow to the will of the same corrupt Detroit/Wayne County political machine that repeatedly anointed Coleman Young mayor/emperor.

Groman showed Castro the pen register tapes from the Curry case, the morning after the Damion Lucas killing, the ones that had recorded the to/from and duration data of calls from Johnny Curry's home phone to the unlisted phones of Sgt. James Harris of the Homicide Section, followed by a longer call to the private unlisted office phone of Inspector Gil Hill, then the head of the Homicide Section.

Castro found it appalling. The conversation between Groman and Castro continued. Castro was hooked. This was a public corruption case with some real substance. Groman and Castro brainstormed how they could develop the case.

Groman made a phone call to Wershe at the state prison in Marquette. Groman had been in touch with his

former informant from time to time since his conviction
and life sentence. Built in 1889, the Marquette State Prison
was a maximum-security lockup in the boondocks of
Michigan's Upper Peninsula. Groman figured Wershe
would be glad to hear a familiar voice.

Groman told Wershe he had a couple of ideas he
wanted to run past him and suggested a visit. Wershe said
that would be fine.

Following that call, the first move Groman and Castro
made was to visit Dawn Wershe, Rick Wershe's older
sister. As Groman and Castro chatted with Dawn it was
obvious she was struggling to make ends meet. She had
kids but no job. Castro had some cash in his pocket,
government cash, designated for another case.

Castro recalled how Groman shrewdly used the
moment to win Dawn Wershe's cooperation:

"We're all talking and Herm said, 'Give her the
money.'

I said, 'What money?'

Herm said, 'That money you have for the other case.'

I go, 'What money are you talking about?'

She's listening and she's watching me argue with
Herm."

Castro said he is thinking, 'this is against all the rules.'
He hadn't learned that rules weren't in Special Agent
Groman's regular vocabulary. Castro said the good cop/bad
cop back-and-forth continued a little longer. Groman
wasn't backing off. He repeated himself slowly, with
emphasis:

"He said, 'Give…her…the… money.'

I said, 'No, I'm not.'

He said it again, 'Give her the money.'

I finally said, 'OK' and I gave her the money."

As he gave Dawn Wershe the roll of cash, Castro realized what had just happened. "That had an effect on Dawn, which she related to Rick," Castro said. "We took care of her. Not so much the money, but someone championed looking out for her."

Giving Dawn Wershe cash they weren't authorized to dispense in order to win an ally was an example of why John Anthony, the agent/legal adviser for the Detroit FBI, said management knew whatever Groman was up to would develop in to a great case, but the bosses would need an ample supply of liquor to make it through Groman ignoring the rule book.

Agent Groman flew to Marquette to visit his old informant. The Marquette prison might be an apt visual depiction of hell freezing over. It is located on the southern end of Lake Superior, where frigid winds from Canada roar in unimpeded. During the winter months, the daytime high seldom gets above freezing. The average snowfall in Marquette is 119 inches.

"To me, it was a very depressing place," Groman recalled. "It was like *The Shawshank Redemption*." They brought Wershe in to a meeting room. Even the room seemed harsh. Groman recalls Wershe was happy to see him, but in truth, he was feeling down, discouraged and apprehensive. His appeals of his conviction had been exhausted. The reality of life in prison had sunk in. He told Groman he could survive on his reputation as White Boy

Rick for a while, but that wouldn't last. He asked Groman if there was anything he, Groman, could do.

"So, I sprang it on him," Groman said. He made a pitch to Wershe for an undercover sting operation intended to catch corrupt cops. Wershe didn't hesitate. He told Groman, sure, let's do it.

It probably didn't occur to Wershe, but he was being recruited once again to go to battle in the War on Drugs. It was six years later, he was in prison this time, but he was being recruited a second time as a combatant in a futile war that had put him behind bars for life.

Groman returned to Detroit and briefed Mike Castro. They decided to go to see Wershe together. A plan was taking shape.

During their visit, Wershe had a big surprise for them. Cathy Volsan Curry was living in Marquette, too; the City of Marquette.

Wershe told them she was a student at a local college. In truth, she was there in a rehab center in yet another attempt to kick her drug habit. The agents were stunned at the coincidence and amazed that an opportunity like this had dropped in their laps. They learned Rick and Cathy were still in touch, despite their stormy relationship and despite the fact he was serving a life prison term.

Groman told Wershe he couldn't make promises, but if Wershe helped them pull off a sting operation against corrupt police officers, he would work hard to get Wershe transferred to WitSec—Witness Security—the government protection program for prison inmates who provide information and help in important cases. It is a prisoner version of the Witness Protection program for people

Vince Wade

whose lives are at risk for having helped the government prosecute major criminals. All of the federal WitSec prisons are a vast improvement over Marquette State Prison in terms of a prisoner's quality of life. They are not quite the fabled country-club prisons, but they are close.

Groman and Castro later flew to Marquette for a third visit with Wershe, but this one was different. They brought Dawn Wershe and her children with them. The occasion was Rick Wershe's 21st birthday in mid-July of 1990. The story was that Castro, posing as international drug dealer Mike Diaz, was taking care of Dawn Wershe out of gratitude to Rick for not ratting him out when Rick was arrested. Diaz' story was he had paid for Dawn and her kids to fly to Marquette with him to visit Rick for his birthday.

Castro went to the prison as a visitor. That is, he presented himself as a visitor with a fake but authentic-looking Virgin Islands driver's license. He said he was there to see inmate 190234—Richard Wershe, Jr. No one at the prison remembered him from the previous visit. With Rick Wershe's 21st birthday at hand, Groman "opened" Rick Wershe, Jr., at long last, as an on-the-books FBI informant.

Castro, who is Hispanic, must have been persuasive in his undercover role. After his visit, officials at the prison contacted the Detroit office of the FBI to notify them that a guy they suspected was a "big" drug dealer had come to Marquette to visit Richard Wershe, Jr.

Rick Wershe arranged a get-acquainted dinner meeting for his new old pal, Mike Diaz, his sister Dawn and Cathy Volsan Curry. Dawn knew Cathy from the days when her brother was living with the mayor's niece prior to his trial and conviction. She pretended she knew Mike Diaz as one

282

of her brother's "connects" from Florida. Dawn was there to add credibility for the undercover agent.

Agent Groman "opened" Dawn Wershe in the FBI files as a cooperating witness/informer. Thus, in the summer of 1990, a third member of the Wershe family went on the FBI books as an informer. Richard Wershe, Senior and Junior were already listed. Snitching had become a family sideline business.

Agent Castro brought a Nagra body-recorder with him to Marquette, even though they were not authorized to use it. He and Groman decided they should record the meeting, anyway. Groman would be his back-up for the restaurant meeting, sitting nearby to observe the discussion.

Over dinner, Cathy Volsan Curry was remarkably candid and unguarded. "She laid it all out," Castro said. With Dawn Wershe at the table listening, Cathy Volsan Curry told "Mike Diaz" about her connections in Detroit's drug underworld. She told him about her police contacts. She told the undercover FBI agent her informants in the Detroit Police Department had "people in the FBI" who give them information. She explained that's how she knew to move a car the FBI was about to seize under a sealed court order.

Agent Castro recorded all of this, but there was that one little problem. They didn't have permission to make the secret recording. Agent Groman, the maverick, came to the rescue with yet another audacious scheme.

When they returned to Detroit, Groman ignored protocol and directly called U.S. Attorney Stephen Markman and asked for a meeting. Markman agreed. Without notifying the Detroit FBI chain of command,

Groman and Castro took the recording of Cathy Volsan Curry to Markman and played it for him.

Castro remembers Markman had a big smile after listening to the tape. This had the potential to be a big public corruption case. The agents expressed concern to Markman that they had breached protocol as well as the rules by meeting with him directly and by making the recording in the first place. Markman told them to proceed with the investigation and not to worry about it.

All hell would have broken loose, except for Markman. Groman hadn't told FBI managers about the clandestine taping of Cathy Volsan Curry. The first that Special Agent in Charge Hal Helterhoff knew of the tape was when Markman told him about it. His two assistant agents in charge didn't know about it, either. Neither did the public corruption squad supervisor. They all learned about it from the U.S. Attorney.

Markman had called Helterhoff and said Groman and Castro were on to a big case and to make sure it happened. Furthermore, Markman told Helterhoff not to punish the agents for making the unauthorized audio recording. Markman was becoming a hero among local FBI agents. None of it was in keeping with the Established Order of Things in the FBI bureaucratic universe.

"What are you guys doing to me?" Mike Castro recalls Dave Ries the Detroit FBI's public corruption squad supervisor, plaintively asking after the Markman meeting and the revelation of the unauthorized tape. Ries looked like he was going to have a heart attack, Castro said.

Castro and Groman—the rules-averse agent—had given a convict's sister nearly a thousand-dollars of FBI cash they weren't authorized to spend, they had flown out of town and made a covert audio recording they weren't authorized to make and they took it to the U.S. Attorney and played it for him without permission and without telling any of their superiors about the tape, in violation of, well, just about everything.

While their supervisor sat in his office and probably contemplated the end of his career and pension, Groman and Castro were ordered to get cracking on what is known as a Group 1 UCO proposal. That's bureaucratic jargon for a high-powered, high-priority top-level undercover operation (UCO) to investigate public corruption. The firing squad for Groman and Castro would have to wait. The proposal for what came to be known as Operation Backbone was written, polished and given to John Anthony, the Detroit office legal advisor. Anthony flew it to Washington and personally walked it through the Group One review committee. The investigation was approved.

These cases are so sensitive that a special committee at the Department of Justice must review all major moves in the investigation. That kind of cumbersome oversight makes perfect sense to a bureaucrat but it is likely one of the reasons for repeated failure in the War on Drugs.

"When criminals are ready, you have to go," Castro explained. "A lot of times they test informants or undercover agents by saying, 'Be at this place at this time with this amount of money.'" Savvy criminals know the government can't move fast. They've learned that stalling in money transactions is often a sign they are dealing with narcs. In Operation Backbone, bureaucratic dithering allowed the biggest fish of the case to get away.

Castro and Groman got the impression Cathy Volsan Curry was going to try to be the orchestra leader for the

Vince Wade

police protection "Mike Diaz" said he needed for his money laundering and drug dealing. They believe she saw a revenue opportunity for herself as the protection broker.

The first cop Cathy Volsan Curry brought to meet Mike Diaz (Castro) was Sylvester Chapman, a supposedly deep undercover cop noted in Chapter 8, who was working exclusively for Police Chief William Hart on phantom super-secret cases no one knew about. The government later portrayed Chapman as the bagman for Chief Hart's looting of the police department's "secret service" fund for the War on Drugs.

Chapman, Cathy Volsan Curry and undercover agent Castro met in a suite of a Detroit-area hotel and had room-service dinner. Castro/Diaz was wired, of course.

The undercover agent bluntly explained what he wanted. Chapman said, "You know, I could arrest you for that." Castro told him to do what he had to do. He recalls Chapman laughed and said no, he would go along with the scheme.

The arrangement didn't last long. Chapman screwed it up by shooting a man in the arm with an Uzi during a neighborhood disturbance near Chapman's home. Chapman was suddenly under departmental scrutiny. He was "hot" and out of the picture.

Cathy Volsan Curry was under pressure to come up with another police officer willing to be bribed to help a guy claiming to be a drug money launderer. Alas, her "contacts" in the police department weren't that deep. Getting police narcotics intelligence from cops looking to curry favor with the mayor was one thing. Asking them to participate in a drug conspiracy was another matter. She turned to her father, Willie Clyde Volsan, for help.

Prisoner of War:
The Story of White Boy Rick and The War on Drugs

Arrangements were made for Castro to meet Cathy
Volsan Curry at the Detroit airport for his first money-
laundering operation. He supposedly had a million dollars
in a briefcase. She was to bring a willing police officer who
would provide protection from robbery as the undercover
agent took the cash to a local bank supposedly participating
in the money-laundering scheme.

They were to meet at noon. Cathy was a no-show. In a
real drug operation, the money man would not stick
around. Only cops, eager to do a deal, hang around when
arrangements aren't followed. Only criminals who are
greedy for cash ignore this warning sign and go forward
with a guy who has violated his own ground rules.

Cathy Volsan Curry eventually showed up,
accompanied by an older man who implied he was a police
officer. It was her father, Willie Volsan, described in FBI
files as a career criminal. They went to a waiting Cadillac
and Castro got in the back seat with Cathy. A black man,
who turned out to be a police officer from Highland Park, a
Detroit suburb, suddenly appeared and got in the front
passenger seat. Castro asked him who he was. He wouldn't
answer. He finally told the undercover agent to look behind
him. Castro saw another car occupied by some black men.
Castro realized this was a robbery in the making. They
intended to drive him someplace, take his briefcase, and
kill him. He jumped out of the car and made eye contact
with a uniformed sheriff's deputy, who took a hard look at
the two Cadillacs. The second Cadillac departed and Castro
bolted for the terminal. An FBI surveillance team
apparently thought Castro was in the second car and they
followed it to the freeway. Castro, unarmed, no longer had
any backup.

Willie Volsan followed Castro in to the terminal and
demanded his money. Castro said he would call his partner
in Miami and see if he could give Volsan a portion of the

Vince Wade

money. Castro was actually calling an FBI command post at the airport. The FBI backup team suddenly realized Castro was alone and unprotected. Agent Groman sprinted to the terminal and made eye contact with Castro, who walked away from the briefcase and in to the terminal crowd as Groman moved in and took the briefcase.

Castro and Groman later concluded this major screw-up worked to their advantage. If Castro was an undercover Fed, back-up agents with guns drawn would have swarmed the scene when trouble started. In a twisted way, this failure of law enforcement back-up to come to Castro's rescue gave him street credibility.

Castro later called Willie Volsan and said he knew Volsan had tried to rob him. Castro, posing as Diaz, said if you want to make some serious money meet me in the morning for breakfast. Thus, began a series of undercover encounters purportedly involving drugs and lots of money to be laundered.

Willie Volsan took over arranging police protection for the drug and cash shipments and pushed his daughter aside, much to her displeasure. Her opportunity to act as a broker was greatly diminished. Willie brought in Detroit Police Sgt. Jimmy Harris, the homicide cop who doubled as the fixer of police problems for Mayor Young's family.

Harris said he had been Volsan's paper-boy when he was a kid. "I might have known, maybe, that he was in numbers," Harris said slyly when I asked what he knew about Volsan's life of crime.

Volsan and Harris met the FBI undercover agent for dinner at the luxurious Ritz-Carleton hotel. Castro remembers Harris was well-dressed. "He came across to me as a very savvy street police officer," Castro said. "One you couldn't fool. He was smart, articulate. I had a hard time believing he was a criminal. I knew I had to be watchful of him because he's a seasoned investigator. If I was going to get foiled in this FBI undercover sting, I thought it would be him. I was worried about him."

Castro believes greed overcame Harris's considerable street smarts. Castro tried to keep contact to a minimum, but Harris showed up at the U.S. Attorney's office one day, asking them what they knew about a doper named Mike Diaz. He met with an Assistant U.S. Attorney who knew about the undercover operation and played dumb about Diaz.

As part of a plan to solidify Castro's undercover image as a high-flying drug dealer, Harris and Volsan were invited to Miami to discuss drug business. Volsan wanted "Mike Diaz" to arrange large-quantity cocaine shipments to him. They went for an inland waterway cruise aboard the same "yacht" the FBI used in the so-called Abscam investigation of corrupt Washington politicians some years earlier.

Castro said the Abscam "yacht" was an embarrassment. It was fully wired for audio and video but it was old, dirty and hadn't been kept up. It wasn't much of a yacht, and it was hardly the kind of watercraft a high-flying drug dealer would use.

This highlights an enduring mystery of the War on Drugs. The U.S. government has seized tens of billions of dollars in cash and belongings from drug dealers under asset forfeiture laws. The confiscations include yachts (newer and more luxurious than the Abscam boat), private jets and too many luxury cars to count. They've seized jewelry and designer clothes. Enough to fill a warehouse or two. Yet, Castro had to jump through bureaucratic hoops to take a Rolex watch from the inventory of seized assets to use as a prop in his undercover role.

Why is it so difficult to use seized assets to allow undercover agents to play the role of a successful criminal? Why doesn't the Justice Department have its own wardrobe and prop department for undercover operations? They seize so much property from so many people that finding correct sizes in the inventory should be simple. Planes, boats, jewelry and "toys" are in abundant supply. Yet it's a bureaucratic struggle to put these things to use in a taxpayer-funded investigation.

The bad guys are keenly aware of the trappings of success in the drug underworld. Designer clothes and expensive jewelry are part of the culture. An undercover federal agent wearing a Rolex watch and a cheap agent's suit is a strobe-light warning to any street-savvy bad guy who doesn't let greed blind his criminal intuition.

Some agents will argue the bad guys let greed blind them to warning signals. But how many cases quietly fall apart because of half-assed, penny-wise and pound-foolish police role playing?

Roy Grisson, Rick Wershe's street-savvy sidekick, told me he used to laugh at federal agents trying to pass themselves off as major dopers. "They'd wear the same one or two cheap suits over and over and think we were fooled as to who they were," Grisson said.

It's not likely to change. Federal bureaucratic minds can come up with endless "yes, but" reasons for not using seized assets to blend in with the animals they are pursuing in the drug jungle.

When Operation Backbone came up for a six-month Group 1 renewal review, the contours of the case were clearly established. In the section "Criminal Activity of Suspects" the first name on the list was Detroit City

Councilman Gil Hill. His was the biggest, highest profile name under investigation.

"Hill was a personal friend of Sgt. James R. Harris, DPD, and Willie Volsan," the report states. "Volsan has a reputation as a large-scale drug trafficker...(and)...Volsan has stated on several occasions to UCA (Undercover Agent) Michael Castro that Hill is in a position to help Castro's money laundering operation."

The fake money laundering and drug shipments continued and additional police officers, about a dozen in all, were lured in to the undercover sting. There was a dinner meeting at a hotel aimed at ensnaring Gil Hill. Three FBI agents were there. So was Willie Volsan. Councilman Hill brought a man identified as a producer for a popular music group. The music man didn't say much, but he watched everyone in the meeting. He took note of glances between Castro and another agent when something potentially incriminating was said. He later warned Hill that he got "weird vibes" at dinner. Hill ignored the warning.

The undercover team hatched a plan to have City Councilman Hill help find businesses willing to help launder drug profits and to help them re-zone some property to be used in the scheme.

At a weekend breakfast meeting, Agent Castro, and another undercover agent from Miami, laid it all out for Hill in blunt terms—we're seeking your help with large-scale drug money laundering.

After breakfast, Hill sat in Willie Volsan's Cadillac and discussed the proposition. Volsan's car was bugged and the FBI was listening. "I didn't want to say anything to them, but ah, but ah, I got to get some money from those guys," Hill told Volsan. "I'm gonna take a couple of people to lunch."

Hill told Volsan he was concerned that the two men posing as drug dealers had been so plainspoken about their business.

"Listen, you know what?" Volsan said to Hill. "We got it in the open. It might be the beginning of something good." "Hopefully," Councilman Hill replied.

Hill's indication he wanted money to "take some people to lunch" was a solicitation of a bribe. Giving a Detroit city councilman federal bribe money would take the investigation to a higher level.

There was another urgent meeting later that Saturday. This one at the Detroit FBI office. Should they bribe Gil Hill? The agents were for it. Steve Markman, the U.S. Attorney was in favor of going forward. But Hal Helterhoff, the Special Agent in Charge, had cold feet. "He didn't want to do it," Castro said. "We didn't have permission from FBI headquarters and the Department of Justice to bribe a public official. Well, that's not consistent with the way we operated this case."

Plus, it was a weekend. Criminality is a 24/7/365 business but Washington bureaucrats operate by normal business hours, Monday through Friday.

The bribe wasn't paid to Gil Hill and he slipped out of their grasp.

I asked Mike Castro, now retired, for his view of the late Gil Hill, the movie star cop who became Detroit's city council president.

"He's a criminal that never got busted," Castro said flatly. "There's no other way to describe the guy. He's a criminal."

Indictments were returned in May of 1991. Sgt. Harris and Willie Volsan were the "lead" defendants. Councilman Hill was not named. The first indictment included Cathy Volsan Curry, too. Defense attorneys quickly objected it was unfair to name a drug addict in the indictment. The government agreed and she was quickly dropped from the case.

Harris emphasizes he was never involved with drugs, but he admits greed got the best of him. "I had no dealings with the Curry Brothers at all," Harris said. As for that FBI sting, Harris says, "I fell for it. Willie Volsan fell for it. Gil Hill fell for it. It was only for greed."

The arrests were front-page news. The *Detroit Free Press*, never missing an opportunity to smear Wershe's name, had a lead story by William J. Mitchell, David McHugh and Jim Schaefer which stated: "Authorities said imprisoned Detroit *drug lord* (italics added) Richard (White Boy Rick) Wershe was instrumental..." in setting up the FBI sting. As noted earlier, there was no evidence to support calling Wershe a "drug lord" by any legal standard, but they did it anyway. It had become part of the journalistic boilerplate when writing a story about Richard J. Wershe, Jr

In the sting trial, Sgt. Harris mounted the most aggressive defense. His position was the FBI sting was a thinly-disguised effort to try to nail Mayor Coleman Young by prosecuting Cathy and Willie Volsan. Through his defense attorney, Harris argued he suspected the sting

Vince Wade

operation from the start and had informed Detroit Police Chief William Hart who, Harris claimed, told him to conduct a secret counter-investigation and report directly to him in meetings in the garage at Detroit Police headquarters.

After federal prosecutors rested their case they knew they would have to rebut the Harris story of a secret counter-investigation. But how? The trial was in recess for a long weekend. At a Saturday brainstorming session, it was suggested that ex-Chief Hart could easily knock down the Harris defense. Would he do it? The case agents thought it was worth a try.

One of the FBI agents working on Operation Backbone was Martin "Marty" Torgler. On a Sunday morning, Torgler caught a plane to San Francisco to meet with ex-Chief Hart who was serving his prison term at a federal "country club" corrections facility known as FCI Dublin in San Francisco. At the Detroit airport as he waited to board his flight, Torgler spotted a Detroit newspaper with a splashy story about the anticipated Harris defense. Torgler figured the newspaper article might help in his meeting with Bill Hart.

When Torgler, now retired, met Hart in the prison he showed him that day's newspaper story in one of the Detroit papers. "He's a bald-faced liar," Torgler remembers Hart saying after he read the story about the Harris defense planning to say Harris was doing a secret counter-investigation on orders from the Chief.

Torgler knew Hart hated having his family dragged into the spotlight of his misdeeds. The agent says he told Hart if Harris gets away with using this defense, every Detroit cop arrested for corruption in the future would use the same defense, causing more pain for Hart's family.

Hart immediately agreed to testify for the prosecution. There was still some honest cop left in him. "If I was still in Detroit I would like to be able to go out with you and put the handcuffs on him," Hart told Torgler. The agent felt sorry for Bill Hart. "He was a broken man," Torgler said.

When the trial resumed Agent Torgler brought ex-Chief Hart into the courtroom. "You could see the wind come out of his (Harris) sails," Torgler remembers.

Harris was found guilty and was sentenced to thirty years in prison. Willie Volsan was convicted, too, and sentenced to nineteen years. Volsan died in 2006. In 2008 Harris received a commutation of his sentence by President George W. Bush. It was one of eleven commutations and pardons Bush granted during his presidency. Harris had cooperated with the FBI regarding the Damion Lucas murder cited in Chapter 8 and he was featured in an FBI training video in which he beseeches rookie cops and agents not to follow in his footsteps.

After Operation Backbone played out in court, there was no doubt Rick Wershe was an informant for the FBI, even while doing time. Wershe was at risk. There are lots of ways to kill a man in prison and plenty of inmates willing to do it for a price or just to gain a "rep."

Agent Groman and Assistant United States Attorney Lynn Helland worked quickly to get Wershe in to the federal Witness Security (WitSec) system. Wershe was transferred from the cold and bleak Marquette State Prison to a federal WitSec lockup in sunny Phoenix, Arizona. Wershe would be safe, but he would be doing time with some very notorious criminals who had turned informant in some very high-profile cases.

Chapter 17—Snitching on a Mafia Snitch

"Don't let your tongue be your worst enemy."
—John "Sonny" Franzeze – former underboss,
Colombo Crime Family

Richard Wershe, Jr. went from pine trees to palm trees after the convictions of a dozen or so police officers and Detroit Mayor Coleman Young's brother-in-law in Operation Backbone.

He was transferred from the old Marquette maximum security state prison in the boondocks of Michigan's upper peninsula to a WitSec or Witness Security unit at sun-drenched FCI Phoenix. The Marquette prison was built in 1889. The Phoenix prison was built in 1985. Federal Correctional Institution (FCI) Phoenix is one of a handful of federal penitentiaries with special units designed to protect the lives of criminal informants who have helped the federal government make cases against important, high-profile defendants.

Wershe had helped the FBI get the Operation Backbone sting going by vouching for Mike Castro, the undercover agent who was posing as an international drug dealer and money launderer. Wershe said before he went to prison, Castro, who called himself Mike Diaz, was one of his Miami "connects."

In the crime underworld, there's a saying that 'snitches get stitches.'

Bad guys claim to loathe and despise informants, but it's a big farce. Sooner or later nearly all criminals become rats, finks, stool pigeons, stoolies, or snitches. Turning informant is the key to plea agreements, the key to getting a long sentence reduced. The criminal justice system would be crippled without criminals rolling over against other criminals in exchange for reduced prison time. Inmates rant about rats but almost every one of them will testify in a heartbeat against associates, friends and even family members if it gets them a time reduction. Hypocrisy is not exclusive to people on the outside.

In a WitSec unit, doing time is not as bleak as living in a general population prison. The food is better, the accommodations are better, the overall vibe is better. There's a wary comfort in knowing the other inmates are there for the same reason; they informed on or testified against someone the government wanted to prosecute in the worst way. Communication with the outside world is sometimes harder because the federal Bureau of Prisons wants to minimize the people who know where a valued informant is serving time.

When Rick Wershe was sent to the WitSec unit in Phoenix, several of his fellow inmates were internationally notorious. One was Carlos Enrique Lehder Rivas, known simply as Carlos Lehder. His father was German, his mother Colombian. Lehder was one of the co-founders of the infamous Medellín Cartel, a Colombian cocaine empire that had transformed smuggling to the United States from a trickle to a flood. Other founders included Jorge Ochoa and Pablo Escobar.

Lehder was born in Colombia but eventually moved to New York City and began a life of crime with stolen cars. He was arrested by the U.S. Border Patrol in Detroit in 1973 as he drove through the tunnel between Detroit and Windsor, Ontario, Canada. The arrest was based on a warrant issued in an FBI investigation of a car theft ring in Hartford, Connecticut. Investigators noticed Lehder was

298

making frequent trips to Canada. He was prosecuted and did time in prison in Danbury, Connecticut. In addition to the car theft prosecution, Lehder caught a marijuana case in Miami and was eventually deported to Colombia. During his time in the U.S. Lehder observed a potentially vast market for cocaine. When he returned to Colombia he joined forces with the nation's other emerging cocaine kings to form the Medellín Cartel. At one point the Cartel was alleged to be supplying over three-quarters of the U.S. cocaine market and by one estimate it was raking in 60-million-dollars per day in drug profits.

Lehder, a self-proclaimed neo-Nazi, was a drug smuggling innovator. He bought Norman's Cay in the Bahamas and pioneered the concept of moving large loads of cocaine to the Caribbean island, then flying the drugs to the U.S. in small aircraft. Previously, cocaine had been smuggled by individual travelers known as mules. Lehder innovated smuggling on a massive scale. On Norman's Cay, Lehder claims he teamed up with Robert Vesco, often identified as a "fugitive financier" from Detroit. Vesco was under investigation by the Securities and Exchange Commission when he fled the country, living in various Caribbean nations, including Cuba. Lehder called him "one of my partners in the Bahamas."

How did Lehder, an important figure in international cocaine smuggling, end up in the Witness Security program? The answer is politics. In Ronald Reagan's era, there was no higher calling than fighting Communism anywhere and everywhere.

Panama's military leader, Manuel Noriega, was a player in the Medellín Cartel smuggling organization, an underling of sorts to Carlos Lehder, but the CIA, the State Department and the White House overlooked Noriega's drug trafficking for a time because he also provided intelligence about the Communist government of Fidel Castro in Cuba.

At some point Noriega and the U.S. government had a falling out and a decision was made to prosecute Noriega for drug crimes. The government needed witnesses who could testify about Noriega's drug dealing. Carlos Lehder was one such witness.

Lehder's federal prosecutor disagreed with Lehder's plea deal. The late Robert "Mad Dog" Merkle, the former U.S. Attorney in Tampa, was quoted in the *Pittsburgh Post Gazette* as saying, "...Lehder's testimony was entirely gratuitous and unnecessary for a conviction of Noriega."

Merkle, often criticized as the epitome of an over-zealous prosecutor, was appalled at the deal Washington gave Lehder. "I never contemplated any kind of deal with Carlos Lehder," Merkle said.

Lehder was extradited to the U.S. after a falling out with cartel leader Pablo Escobar. It is believed that Escobar tipped authorities on where to find Lehder. He was captured after a gun battle and flown to Florida to face charges, where Merkle called him "the embodiment of narco-terrorism."

Lehder was described by a former cellmate as a man who hated the United States and saw cocaine as a way to destroy it from within. George Jung, Lehder's former cellmate in the Connecticut prison, testified that Lehder used to pore over maps of the United States in the prison library, studying potential smuggling routes. When Lehder and Jung were released from prison they went in to the smuggling business together and Jung became, for a time, one of America's largest cocaine dealers. The movie *Blow*, starring Johnny Depp, was a film version of the George Jung story.

Lehder was convicted on charges he smuggled over
three tons of cocaine into the United States. He was
sentenced to life plus 135 years. After he testified against
Noriega, the government had his sentenced reduced to 55
years and placed him in the Witness Security program. He
wound up in FCI-Phoenix.

Rick Wershe says he had conversations with Lehder
and he recalls the infamous Medellín Cartel leader was
always interested in discussing the money to be made in
the cocaine business. Lehder could always be engaged in
conversations about the price-per-kilo, what kind of mark-
up the market would bear and similar money-making
issues. Wershe also recalled that Lehder didn't seem to
bathe much.

Rick Wershe also did time in Phoenix with another
government witness in the trial of Panama's military
leader, Manuel Noriega. Steven Kalish, profiled in Chapter
10, was one of the defendants in the massive smuggling
case the FBI developed in Detroit, Miami and other
locations. Kalish was partners with Leigh Ritch and
Michael Vogel. The three of them smuggled tons of
marijuana and cocaine into the United States with help of
Michael Palmer, the CIA Contra pilot also noted in Chapter
10. Because of his CIA and White House connections and
his skill at manipulating federal law enforcement, Palmer
walked away with all charges dropped, no guilty plea, no
time in prison. Steve Kalish wasn't that lucky. Kalish was
in business with Noriega for a time, moving massive
quantities of marijuana and acquiring massive quantities of
cash, which he stashed in banks in Panama. Kalish bought
a home in Panama and he was so tight with Noriega he had
a Panamanian diplomatic passport.

Kalish was far more important to the prosecution of Manuel Noriega than Carlos Lehder. He had much more interaction with the Panamanian leader. If anyone thought about the irony of two of the government's witnesses against the Panamanian leader being locked up in the same protected prison unit, no one mentioned it.

Like many of the government's star inmate/witnesses, Kalish had special privileges. Wershe remembers Kalish spent a lot of time working on his business investments with the aid of a special satellite-linked device in his cell. In exchange for testifying against Noriega, Kalish had been allowed to keep a significant portion of the millions he made smuggling drugs. Apparently, he used that money to make even more through legit investments. From his prison cell, Kalish disproved the old adage that crime doesn't pay.

Kalish, who is from Texas, was defended for a time by Dick DeGuerin, one of the top criminal defense attorneys in Houston. "He applied himself to the business end of smuggling," DeGuerin told the *Sun-Sentinel*, a South Florida newspaper. "He could have been a top executive. It just happened that he went into marijuana instead."

Kalish has been out of prison for some time. To no one's surprise, he prospered in business. He has been living in Hawaii in recent years.

One of Rick Wershe's closest friends in the WitSec unit in Phoenix was one of the most vicious gangsters in the annals of crime. Salvatore "Sammy the Bull" Gravano had been the underboss to John Gotti, Sr., the head of New York's powerful Gambino Mafia crime family.

Gravano stunned the organized crime underworld by turning informant against Gotti, perhaps the most notorious of Mafia bosses. Gravano had murdered 19 individuals, that he admitted to, but the FBI and Justice Department were so eager to get John Gotti that Gravano got a five-year prison sentence in Witness Security in exchange for his testimony against the gangster known as the "Teflon Don. Gravano's testimony also put three dozen others in prison.

Sammy the Bull quickly became the government's star informant—first among all witnesses. He was the golden goose and he was treated accordingly. "He was very cocky and he was a true tough guy," Wershe told me.

For whatever reason, Sammy the Bull took White Boy Rick under his wing. "We had a tight crew," Wershe said. "Meaning we all ate together and hung out together, played racquetball together and lived like kings, for being in prison."

Retired FBI special agent Herman Groman confirms that Wershe and Gravano were tight. Groman, who had been Wershe's "handler" in the FBI, stayed in touch with him after he helped get Wershe transferred to WitSec. They would talk by phone once a week, sometimes more.

"Wershe would put him (Gravano) on the phone with me, so we would talk occasionally," Groman said. "We developed a kind of weird relationship." Groman recalls Gravano saying something to him that echoed Groman's own thinking about Rick Wershe.

"He said, 'Let me understand this. I whacked 19 guys on behalf of John Gotti's organization, and I'm getting' out in April. This kid here, never pulled the trigger on anybody. All he did was sell dope. And he didn't do it for very long. And he's got to stay here for the rest of his life? That don't make no sense.'"

Groman remembers his reply to Gravano. "I said, 'Sammy, it doesn't make sense to me, either.'"

"Our clique ran the WitSec unit in Phoenix," Wershe said. He was impressed that Sammy the Bull had his own Vitamix in his cell. He had cigars flown in when his supply ran low.

"The Mob guys were the best cooks and we had free reign of the kitchen," Wershe said. "We ate what we wanted, when we wanted. At Thanksgiving, we took over the whole visiting room and put the tables together and ate like a real family. We had whole turkeys and all the trimmings. We were as close as a bunch of cons could be."

Wershe said Gravano's fearsome reputation warded off most trouble, except for the time a Mexican gangster in the WitSec unit got drunk and came to Gravano's cell and started insulting Sammy the Bull's cell mate, calling him a rat. It was an odd insult since everyone in the WitSec unit was a rat—an informer—including the Mexican gangster. Gravano told him to take it somewhere else. The Mexican foolishly told Gravano, "I'll fuck you up." With that, Sammy the Bull hauled the drunken macho man to the prison laundry and gave him the beating of his life. The drubbing was so severe the Mexican's head was swollen out of shape. The guards knew who did it, but when the Mexican gangster sobered up he knew better than to tell who worked him over.

❖

Wershe was amazed at how the FBI and Justice Department went to extraordinary lengths to turn a blind eye to their star informer. Wershe said Gravano wasn't the least bit discreet about his plans to form a new "crew." The Feds knew it, Wershe said, but they ignored it.

"They also knew all this guy talked about was drugs," Wershe said. "Me and him and Carlos Lehder would sit

around for hours and talk about the profits in drugs.
Sammy wanted Lehder to 'plug him in.' Carlos wasn't
buying in to him or his B.S."

Wershe was fully aware of the importance of these two
men in the criminal underworld. "Vince, I used to think to
myself: how the hell did I end up sitting at a table with
Sammy the Bull Gravano and Carlos Lehder? Carlos could
not believe I was serving life for three keys of coke."

One of Wershe's prison phone calls to Special Agent
Groman caused a crisis within the FBI and the Justice
Department.

"I have to share this with somebody," Wershe said to
Groman. "I need to stop this." What, Groman wanted to
know, was Wershe talking about. Stop what?

"Sammy is very upset about John Gotti, Jr. going
around New York talking smack about him," Wershe told
Groman. "A lot of disparaging things and Sammy is
furious."

Then, Wershe dropped a bombshell. Sammy the Bull
Gravano was plotting the murder of John Gotti, Jr.—from
prison. Gravano knew from his conversations with Wershe
that Wershe's father was a licensed gun dealer in
Michigan. Gravano said he wanted Wershe to help him get
guns and weapons his mob pals could use to rub out Gotti,
Jr., guns that wouldn't be from New York.

Groman said Wershe told him 'I don't know what to
do with this thing.' Groman added: "I didn't know what to
do with this thing!"

Groman notes there was a self-serving element in
Wershe's tip. If things worked out, it could be a bargaining

chip for a reduced sentence. But still. "For White Boy Rick to report on Sammy the Bull Gravano put him in great danger," Groman said. "He's in the same cell block with him. He can't get away."

Gravano was one of the government's most important criminal witnesses. The *New York Daily News* had called him "the Mob rat of all rats." A lot of criminal convictions were riding on his credibility. "Here he was, implicating himself in yet another hit and at the same time he was a government witness," Groman said. "When Wershe opened that Pandora's box with me, I had to report it. I knew there'd be some resistance on this thing." That was an understatement.

Faster than you can say Botta Bing Botta Boom the New York office of the FBI, the U.S. Attorney's office in New York, FBI Headquarters and the Criminal Division of the Department of Justice were all weighing in on the information from one snitch about another snitch—their Golden Goose snitch.

In his report through channels, Agent Groman suggested temporarily removing Wershe from WitSec Phoenix, fully debriefing him, then devising a plan for Wershe to somehow secretly bug the prison yard with sensitive listening devices that could capture Gravano making incriminating statements. Groman says a top-ranking Justice Department official—he claims he can't remember the name—nixed the plan and said, 'We're not going to do this.'

Groman, never one to be cowed by the federal law enforcement bureaucracy, decided to press the issue. "I'm thinking, you've got a bona fide murder conspiracy going on involving a national organized crime figure, and you just can't walk away from it," Groman said.

Groman wrote a follow-up communication "and I cited by name the Justice Dept. attorney who had rendered this decision." Groman wanted someone to get the credit or the blame. Groman wrote, "All efforts to thwart the assassination of John Gotti, Jr. will be terminated. We won't pursue it."

Groman's memo ensured if John Gotti, Jr. was murdered, there would be a paper trail, through channels, indicating the federal government knew about it and could have taken steps to stop it, but chose not to do so. The buck would stop at just one desk. In the Department of Justice.

A decision was quickly made to pursue the information, but only after Wershe had taken a polygraph test. Groman thought this was sensible. He advocated sending word to the prison that Wershe was going to return to Detroit to appear before a federal grand jury. Gravano wouldn't give it a second thought because he was taken out of the WitSec unit from time to time for the same reason.

The next thing Groman knew he was making an abrupt trip to the Phoenix office of the FBI. When Groman arrived, he found a badly shaken and puzzled Richard Wershe, Jr. in manacles, chained to a chair in a small room. There was an FBI SWAT team agent in a black commando-like outfit standing behind and over Wershe with a Heckler & Koch MP 5 submachine gun, ready for action.

Instead of quietly and matter-of-factly removing Wershe in a routine manner, an FBI SWAT Team from the Phoenix office barged in to the prison in the middle of the night and yanked Wershe out of his cell and whisked him away in a SWAT van.

Thoroughly stressed, Wershe took the polygraph exam. The results came back: inconclusive.

FBI-Phoenix lamely told Groman they had to take "precautions" because Wershe was serving a life sentence. It was ludicrous. Wershe had never attempted an escape and he was never listed as a flight risk in any prison paperwork, anywhere. "It was purely mishandled, I mean grossly mishandled," Groman said.

Was all of this done to deliberately botch the polygraph exam? With the advancement of so many careers riding on the credibility of Sammy the Bull, would the FBI and Department of Justice sabotage possible charges of murder conspiracy against their prized witness?

Groman doesn't say so, but the SWAT team stunt seemed to be a deliberate attempt to undermine the polygraph exam. It worked. The Justice Department, FBI headquarters and the FBI's New York office now had cover for dropping the investigation of a possible murder plot by their star, Sammy the Bull Gravano.

Gravano finished his five-year sentence and he was released, still under the Witness Protection program. He remained in the Phoenix area and quickly became enmeshed in selling drugs. Federal investigators were either clueless or ignored the information. It was left to the Phoenix Police to make a case against Gravano for peddling Ecstasy, a euphoric "club" drug. He was sentenced in federal court in New York and state court in Arizona to 20-years in a state prison, to run concurrently. In New York Gravano was charged with violating the terms of his original, sweet, five-year plea deal.

After the Sammy the Bull murder plot fiasco, Rick Wershe was too hot to remain in the Phoenix WitSec unit. He was transferred to another witness protection unit in northern Florida, where he was destined to find more trouble.

Chapter 18—Rick's Kangaroo Court

"Sentence first! Verdict afterwards."
—The Queen of Hearts, *Alice in Wonderland* by
Lewis Carroll

Richard Wershe, Jr. spent most of the Nineties in
relative obscurity in the federal Witness Security program.
But the decade didn't start out that way.

When Operation Backbone, the FBI sting operation
targeting corrupt Detroit cops ended in indictments,
Wershe was in the news again as the jailhouse informant
who got it all started by vouching for Mike Castro, the
undercover agent. Police officers who distrusted Wershe
now had solid evidence he was a snitch willing to tell on
corrupt cops.

No one understood this better than Gil Hill, the former
head of Detroit Police Homicide who had become a
member of the Detroit City Council. Hill had political
ambitions, but the *Detroit News* published several lengthy
reports by Norman Sinclair and Allan Lengel citing the
FBI's pursuit of Hill for possible criminality in the Damion
Lucas case and the bribe paid to him by Johnny Curry. The
paper reported how close Hill came to getting caught in
Operation Backbone. Hill denied all.

Hill was never charged with a crime. The story faded
from the headlines and Wershe faded from view. But the
Drug Enforcement Administration in Detroit, apparently
noting Wershe's repeated assistance to the FBI, decided the
imprisoned informant could help them make a case against
the Best Friends murder-for-hire drug gang. They already
had the cooperation of Nate "Boone" Craft, one of the key

members of the killer group. Craft turned against the Best Friends when they killed his brother. Craft knew specifics, but Wershe had criminal star power.

Detroit DEA agents Anthony Pratapas and Fernando Cerroni flew to Phoenix to plead with Wershe to return to Detroit to testify before a federal grand jury investigating the Best Friends. There were vague promises of help with his case. Wershe agreed.

Back in Detroit, Wershe was taken to a conference room where he described a chaotic free-for-all with cops from various agencies competing to ask questions about suspected dopers.

For his part, Wershe wanted to know what *he* was going to get out of all of this. According to Wershe, Assistant United States Attorneys William Soisson and James King gave him broad assurances they would help him with his life sentence in the state case if he would help them prosecute the Best Friends. "I'll never forget King said he would go 'balls to the wall' to help me," Wershe recalled.

Wershe said it was made clear to him the DEA wanted to prosecute local defense attorney Paul Curtis. Two witnesses against the Best Friends were murdered and prosecutors suspected Curtis had identified them to the gang.

Wershe said he didn't know much about the Best Friends or Paul Curtis. This did not please the feds. As hitman Nate Craft explained in Chapter 12, the Best Friends didn't trust Wershe. They suspected he might be an informant and at one point they tried to kill him.

That didn't stop *Detroit Free Press* reporters Margaret Trimer and Joe Swickard from making a big splash with a sensational front-page story about the Best Friends gang.

Headlined "The New Big Boys" it featured an organizational chart and photos depicting Wershe and Richard "Maserati Rick" Carter as the founders of the Best Friends.

Nate Craft said when he was in the DEA office being debriefed after agreeing to cooperate, he saw an organizational chart similar to the one in the *Free Press*. Craft said he told Special Agent Pratapas the chart was completely wrong in featuring Rick Wershe. "He shouldn't have been on the chart, period," Craft told me. "He wasn't no big-time drug dealer. He wasn't no big-time anything. He was movin' some, but we believed he was settin' people up," Craft said.

Wershe believes the only reason for bringing him back to Detroit was for the marquee value of his name, to impress the grand jurors this was a big-time case. "Ladies and gentlemen, this is Richard J. Wershe, Jr, also known as White Boy Rick," Wershe remembers the assistant U.S. attorney saying as he entered the grand jury room. It was like a circus ringmaster introducing an animal act.

Wershe's testimony was inconsequential. The grand jury returned an indictment against the Best Friends, but it wasn't based on anything Wershe said. Wershe was not named in the indictment as a defendant or unindicted co-conspirator. He wasn't called as a trial witness. The *Free Press* did not print a retraction or correction after smearing Wershe as the founder of a drug trafficking murder group. Wershe was returned to the WitSec unit in Phoenix and Assistant United States Attorneys Soisson and King did nothing to help Wershe with his life sentence.

In the mid-90s, the American public was still angry and fed up with street crime and unimpeded drug trafficking. Voters wanted to kick ass. President Bill Clinton and Congress responded with the Violent Crime and Law Enforcement Act of 1994. That law has been often cited as the catalyst for mass incarceration in America. The legislation came out of the Senate Judiciary Committee, chaired by Sen. Joe Biden. In truth, the 1994 crime bill accelerated an imprisonment trend that was already underway.

Clinton apologists like to note the increase in the nation's prison population was mostly at the state level. This ignores the fact the 1994 crime law provided $9.7 billion in federal grants for prison construction for states that adopted so-called truth-in-sentencing laws. This was financial incentive to ensure longer prison sentences, and it worked. Twenty-nine states passed truth-in-sentencing (TIS) laws. State and local politicians like to rail against the federal government, yet they seldom pass up an opportunity to get their state's share at the federal grant money trough.

Many states couldn't build new prisons fast enough to satisfy America's desire for punishment above all else.

By 2001 Gil Hill was a proven vote-getter. He had become the City Council President. Hill decided the time was right to run for mayor, but he was trounced in the primary and general election by Kwame Kilpatrick, the flamboyant black Democratic leader of the Michigan House of Representatives. After serving seven years as mayor, Kilpatrick was tried, convicted and sentenced to 28 years in prison for extortion, bribery and racketeering.

Some said Hill blamed the election loss partly on White Boy Rick and his informant tips to the FBI. In 1991, during the FBI undercover sting operation aimed at prosecuting corrupt cops, Gil Hill was secretly recorded during a meeting with undercover federal agents and Willie Volsan saying he was unsure about running for mayor because "I got skeletons in my closet."

Only Gil Hill, who is deceased, knows if he was referring to Damion Lucas. But Hill knew Rick Wershe had snitched on him, and he was not the kind of man to forget it.

Rick Wershe's vital informant role in the 1985 killing of Damion Lucas re-surfaced in 2001. Mike Cox, an Assistant Wayne County Prosecutor with ambition to become the next Michigan Attorney General, took a second look at the Damion Lucas killing. Cox says he thinks it was part of a cold-case review.

Rick Wershe claims Cox reached out to him for help with the case, a claim Cox strongly disputes. The two have sharply differing recollections of what happened.

Wershe, who had lost his appeal of his drug conviction, decided to tell Cox what he knew about the Damion Lucas matter.

Wershe claims Cox, like other prosecutors, promised to help with his life sentence if he helped solve the Damion Lucas killing. For Cox, it was the kind of case he could ballyhoo in an election year and ride in to office as the Attorney General of Michigan. Wershe admits he had nothing in writing from Cox. They talked by phone several times and, Wershe says, it became apparent to him that Cox was concerned about the case implicating Gil Hill and Sam Gardner.

At that time Gardner was the chief assistant in the Wayne County Prosecutor's Office. He had returned to public life. Cox answered to him. "Will Sam Gardner's name come up?" Wershe recalls Cox asking him.

It seemed to Wershe that the politically ambitious Cox wanted to have a headline-grabbing prosecution, but not if it meant exposing the dirty dealings of two politically powerful men who might influence his chances to become Michigan Attorney General.

"That's just bullshit," Cox said. "That's ludicrous. He never gave up any names." Cox says Wershe called him out of the blue.

"He was pitching me a bunch of bullshit," Cox recalled. "He didn't really tell me anything. He wanted the world (in terms of a deal on his life sentence). You get these (let's-do-a-deal calls) all the time. He never gave up Gil Hill or Sam Gardner. He was just trying to worm his way out. From my experience, he's a fucking liar."

Even so, Cox says Wershe shouldn't be in prison as long as he has been there. Cox told me the mandatory minimums in state drug cases were way too high.

Leon Lucas, the uncle of Damion Lucas, confirmed the Wayne County Prosecutor's Office seemed interested—briefly—in re-visiting the killing at about the time Wershe says he was engaged in phone calls with Mike Cox.

Lucas says he was told he would have to deal with Augustus "Augie" Hutting, the assistant prosecutor, now deceased, who had spent so much time trying to falsely convict LeKeas Davis in the case.

The FBI investigation presented Hutting with powerful circumstantial evidence indicating Gil Hill was guilty of obstruction of justice in the Damion Lucas homicide.

Hutting ignored it. In an internal prosecutor's office memo Hutting acknowledged it was likely that Curry henchmen Wyman Jenkins and Sidney Dwayne Goodwin were the likely shooters but he concluded the chances of a conviction were low, so he declined to prosecute.

Leon Lucas got no justice at the time of his nephew's killing and he got none when Mike Cox decided to take another look at the case. "I wanted justice for the child," Lucas said. Lucas told me he called the prosecutor's office repeatedly, sometimes talking with Hutting, other times talking with Cox. Eventually, Lucas said, Cox told him they were not going to pursue the case. "They treated me bad," Lucas said.

Mike Cox went on to win the state Attorney General election without pursuing the Damion Lucas case.

It took a quarter of a century, but in 1998 Michigan finally modified its harsh "650-life" drug law, the one Rick Wershe was sentenced under in 1988. Over the years Wershe grew up and became a man. The former cocky punk taught himself manners and concern for others. He was regarded as a model inmate.

Wershe became eligible for parole in early 2003. When the Parole Board notified the Wayne County Prosecutor's Office that Wershe was scheduled for a parole hearing, battle station klaxons went off. There was a mad scramble to oppose parole for White Boy Rick. One of those scrambling was Gil Hill.

The Prosecutor's office fired off a letter of opposition to the Parole Board purportedly written by Michael Duggan, then the Wayne County Prosecutor, who went on to be elected mayor. The true author of the letter is not certain. Duggan claimed he doesn't remember it. The letter was full of vitriol and errors. But coming from the prosecutor in Michigan's most populous county, it carried weight. It is an example of reckless disregard for the truth.

The purported Duggan letter blatantly misstated and mischaracterized the testimony and facts presented in Wershe's drug trial.

For example, the prosecutor's letter states: "From the records, it appears that Wershe's gang and the police were contemporaneously looking for the cocaine up and down the street, both trying to find it first." There is nothing in the testimony in the Wershe case or in court documents to substantiate the statement that Wershe had a "gang" as the term is commonly used in law enforcement. No one was ever charged as an associate or member of a Wershe "gang." The "records" contain nothing to suggest a search "up and down the street."

The letter to the Michigan Parole Board falsely claimed, "Several of Wershe's gang members were found dead."

William Rice, who followed Gil Hill as the Inspector of Detroit Police Homicide, testified that Wershe's name "never came up" in any homicide investigations in the years he was in charge of the unit. If any drug-related homicide had been associated with Wershe, Rice would have known it. Steve Rousell, one of Wershe's friends, was murdered, but that case involved a romantic triangle, not drugs.

The prosecutor's letter stated "Wershe's violent collateral crimes and the sheer volume of controlled substances that were introduced to the City of Detroit confirm that Wershe is a serious danger to the People of the City of Detroit and all of Southeastern Michigan, in particular."

Richard Wershe, Jr. was never charged with committing, ordering or participating in any violent crime. Regarding "the sheer volume of controlled substances" Wershe was never charged, federally or locally, with drug racketeering, narcotics conspiracy or operating a continuing criminal enterprise. Those are the "kingpin" laws.

This kind of blatant dishonesty is the prosecutorial equivalent of "testilying" by police officers. It is a fact that when prosecutors lie and mislead, they are seldom—if ever—held accountable.

In the weeks leading up to Wershe's parole hearing, there was a feverish effort to ensure the board would vote against releasing him.

Retired FBI agent John Anthony recalled an urgent phone call from Commander Dennis Richardson of the Detroit Police Major Crimes Unit. Richardson wanted dirt on Rick Wershe. Anthony said he wasn't about to give him any FBI investigative files. Anthony told him all he could offer was a stack of newspaper clippings about White Boy Rick. "He was in a panic to get the newspaper clippings," Anthony said. He found the request odd. "Denny never worked drugs," Anthony noted.

One member of federal law enforcement seemed only too happy to help the Wershe opponents. Jeffrey Collins, the U.S. Attorney for Detroit at that time, had started his legal career in the Bell and Gardner law firm. Ed Bell had defended Wershe in his drug trial.

Bell apparently encouraged Collins to become politically active, which is how he was named the U.S. Attorney for Detroit. U.S. Attorneys are presidential appointees.

❖

Assistant U.S. Attorney Lynn Helland, who prosecuted the Operation Backbone police corruption case, was well aware of Wershe's value as an FBI informant. Helland wrote a letter to the Parole Board recommending that Wershe be released.

His boss, Collins, took the highly unusual step of sending his own letter to the Michigan Parole Board rescinding Helland's letter. "The United States Attorney's Office does not support the release into the community of Richard Wershe, Jr.," Collins wrote.

FBI agents familiar with Wershe's informant work sent letters supporting Wershe's release. Kevin Brock, an assistant special agent in charge in the Detroit office, sent a two-page letter to the Parole Board citing instances where Wershe was instrumental in helping the FBI make cases. Brock later became an Assistant FBI Director and later the deputy director of the National Terrorism Center.

Brock's letter and the letters of the other agents were undercut by a letter from Willie Hulon, the Special Agent in Charge of the Detroit Division at that time. It's not known if Hulon had a conversation with Jeffrey Collins regarding Wershe, but Hulon had his own problems with FBI informants.

During Wershe's parole hearing, Hulon was under a secret FBI internal investigation for charges originating with Bureau informants. Several drug snitches claimed Hulon provided them with drug intelligence. It was a lie that was part of a scam in which three informants conned the FBI out of $150-thousand in informant fees. Hulon was removed from his post for a time but eventually he was exonerated and returned to duty.

In a March 24, 2003 letter to the Michigan Parole
Board, amid his under-the-radar battle with informants,
Hulon noted the letters from the other agents, but he wrote,
"the FBI takes no position on whether Richard Wershe, Jr.
should or should not be paroled."

Special Agent Groman, who had been Wershe's FBI
handler, asked for permission to return to Detroit to testify
in Wershe's behalf. Groman had been re-assigned to the
Las Vegas office by choice. Groman's request for the FBI
to fly him back to testify for Wershe was denied. Always
resourceful, Groman had Wershe's defense attorney
subpoena him to testify at the hearing. The FBI didn't fight
the subpoena, but the Bureau refused to pay Groman's
expenses. He paid his own way back to Detroit.

Wershe's 2003 parole hearing was like a court trial
without the usual rules and rights. The testimony
sometimes bordered on the bizarre, such as the statement
by Bob Ritchie, known to some pop music fans as Kid
Rock.

"I first just want to start by saying that I know who I
am and being a celebrity and what not," Ritchie began
immodestly, "...and that's absolutely not my reason for
being here..."

John Rubitschun, the Parole Board chairman,
interrupted and quickly deflated Ritchie's introduction of
himself. "Who are you?" Rubitschun asked. He had never
heard of Kid Rock.

Ritchie stated he was a singer who knew from his own
teen years how difficult the drug scene can be. "I'm not a
fan of anyone in here and...and...and...I sometimes ask
myself, what am I doing here?" Ritchie testified. Many in
the courtroom probably wondered the same thing. Ritchie

had recorded a track called *Back from The Dead*, an ode to himself as a rising bad-ass rap star. It included a line which didn't do Rick Wershe any favors. Kid Rock rapped that he had "more fucking cash" than White Boy Rick.

The Parole Board didn't ask many questions of the witnesses and neither did Charles Schettler, an Assistant State Attorney General who functioned as legal counsel for the Board.

In his sworn testimony, William E. Bufalino II, Wershe's original defense attorney, made several startling claims.

"I was personally told by Coleman Young that this...stay out of this," Bufalino testified. He said Young added: "This is bigger than you think it is."

Why was the mayor of the City of Detroit sticking his nose in a criminal case? What did he mean when he told Bufalino, "this is bigger than you think it is"? The Parole Board didn't ask.

The veteran defense attorney went on to essentially accuse Ed Bell and Sam Gardner of legal malpractice in the Wershe case. "It was Bell and Gardner," Bufalino said. "They guaranteed him that he would walk. They pulled a motion, a dispositive motion on a search and seizure issue regarding this case. They hung this boy out to dry." This was a serious accusation for one lawyer to make against others. The Parole Board remained silent.

Bufalino offered plenty of allegations to consider—if the panel was truly interested in getting a complete picture.

"… the mayor's office was bad, the prosecutor's office was bad," Bufalino told the panel. What did Bufalino

mean? Were they corrupt? The Parole Board didn't ask
him to explain.

One oddity about Rick Wershe's 2003 parole hearing
was none of the Detroit cops who arrested him in the drug
case testified. The roster of prosecution witnesses opposing
Wershe's parole seemed chosen for the marquee value of
their job titles. Commanders and inspectors are more
impressive than lowly sergeants and police officers.

Thus, one of the witnesses was Commander Dennis
Richardson of the Major Crimes Division.

"I don't know Richard Wershe," Richardson admitted
in his testimony. "I never arrested him, uh, I was never
involved in any of his cases."

So, why was he there opposing parole for an inmate he
didn't know?

Bill Rice the Homicide Inspector who was one of the
other witnesses, worked for Richardson. In Rice's opinion,
there wasn't a secret motive behind Richardson testifying
against someone he knew nothing about. "He was what you
would call a brown-noser," Rice said. "He would do
anything that would get him favor."

Like Commander Richardson, Inspector Rice's
testimony at the parole hearing was vague. Rice spoke of
the devastating effect of drugs and said "the drug war was
real." Nevertheless, when it came to the prison inmate who
was the focus of the hearing, Rice testified, "I did not know
Mr. Wershe." Rice later said he was ordered by
Commander Richardson to testify against Wershe.

Eventually Rice became a prison inmate himself. He and his girlfriend were convicted in a mortgage fraud case and they were charged with dealing in prescription pills and marijuana. Ironically, Rice wound up in the same prison as Rick Wershe.

Wershe said years later when he and Rice were in the same prison, he confronted the former cop one day about his parole hearing testimony. Wershe sat down across from Rice at lunch and stared until the ex-cop noticed. As Wershe recounts it, Rice said, "Do I know you?" Wershe replied, "You are part of the reason I'm in here." Rice was stunned. They talked. Rice told Wershe he testified under orders and that Commander Richardson told him he had been "selected" to testify. Rice said he didn't understand why. In a written statement Rice told Ralph Musilli, Wershe's attorney, "In my thirty years at Homicide, I had no contact with him (Wershe) nor had he been a suspect in any case."

Rice later signed a sworn affidavit that revealed more. Rice stated, "I spoke with former homicide Inspector Gilbert Hill, who told me that he believed I was recommended by Jeffrey Collins, who was, at the time, a United States Attorney for the area."

In his affidavit, Rice stated that prior to testifying he was ordered to visit the office of Assistant Wayne County Prosecutor Karen Woodside.

Rice said he was given a stack of documents to review. There were police reports, intelligence files—and Wershe's federal grand jury testimony in the Best Friends case. Grand jury testimony is secret unless a judge formally unseals it. Wershe's grand jury testimony was never unsealed.

How did Assistant Prosecutor Woodside obtain a copy of secret federal grand jury testimony? If she had a copy it had to come from someone within the federal courts—or the United States Attorney's Office.

The "substance" of the case against Richard Wershe fell to two DEA agents who were poorly prepared.

Their sworn testimony was riddled with errors and distortions. They were soldiers in the War on Drugs sent on another dubious mission. The truth took a back seat to perpetuating the law enforcement lie that White Boy Rick Wershe was a menace to society.

DEA squad supervisor Greg Anderson held himself out as an authority on the drug trade in Detroit. "I am a Detroit native, so I have extensive knowledge of the City of Detroit," Anderson testified. He proceeded to show how much he didn't know.

Anderson told the Parole Board large scale dope dealing in Detroit began in the 1970s with YBI—Young Boys Incorporated. The gang hired juveniles whose police records would start anew when they turned 18.

Special Agent Anderson described Young Boys Incorporated as an *east* side gang. "YBI basically controlled the east side of Detroit," Anderson testified. He was either abysmally ignorant about one of the biggest drug conspiracies the Detroit DEA ever took down, or he was "testilying" as so many narcs have done in the War on Drugs. This was a way to insinuate White Boy Rick was from the same neighborhood as Young Boys Incorporated. Except it wasn't true. YBI was a *west* side drug gang.

Agent Anderson's ignorance or mendacity continued when he testified that Rick's father introduced him to the

Curry Brothers. As we saw in Chapter 5, the elder Wershe had no idea who the men were in the FBI surveillance photos until his son identified them as the Currys.

What purpose was served in lying under oath about the senior Wershe's familiarity with the Curry gang? One possible motive was to show the Parole Board Rick Wershe came from a no-good, crime-prone family. In parole cases the inmate's family is an important consideration regarding release.

The DEA supervisor tried to portray White Boy Rick Wershe as a major supplier to the major Detroit cocaine pushers of the 80s. Wershe had indeed sold drugs occasionally to big dealers who were running low, but he was not their major supplier.

Anderson overreached by claiming Wershe was responsible for 200-300 kilos of cocaine flooding the streets of Detroit every month. It was an astounding amount, beyond the importing capabilities of many major Colombian cocaine suppliers in Miami. This hyperbole was too much even for the Assistant State Attorney General who acted as the Parole Board's lawyer in the hearing.

"Can you tell us what is the basis for this information? Charles Schettler asked.

"Uh, that would be, intelligence briefings, uh, uh, getting intelligence debriefings," Anderson stammered. He seemed unprepared to answer questions. "Talking to, uh, informants, basically, and other law enforcement personnel," Anderson said. In other words, the accusation that Wershe was distributing over 660 pounds of cocaine in Detroit every month wasn't based on any actual evidence. It was criminal gossip, street talk—"intelligence"—from deal-seeking DEA snitches and from other cops who relied on *their* deal-seeking snitches for "intelligence."

Anderson was claiming an out-of-nowhere white teenager was smuggling and selling up to 3,600 pounds of cocaine in Detroit annually. It was preposterous, but Anderson was there to somehow justify law enforcement's unsupported—and unsupportable—claim that Wershe was a kingpin, a drug lord.

Anderson was followed by DEA Special Agent Richard Crock, the nominal leader of the Federal Task Force No Crack Crew. Crock submitted a letter to the Board and gave live testimony that essentially covered similar ground.

Crock told the Parole Board he participated in a raid in April, 1987 where "a quantity of cocaine" was seized from Wershe and his pal, Steve Rousell, along with some guns, bullet-proof vests and a money counting machine. In truth, the "quantity" of cocaine seized in that raid was 2.1 grams, which would fill about half a teaspoon. Crock didn't mention Wershe was acquitted by a jury in this case.

Crock said he personally participated in another arrest of Wershe in October of 1987 for five kilos of cocaine. The DEA agent testified Wershe was never prosecuted on this case because he was already facing a life sentence for the May arrest. This was totally false testimony from a DEA agent who worked closely with Detroit Police narc Gerard Biernacki, known as Pinocchio for his habitual lying under oath in court.

Wershe was indeed arrested in October of 1987 in a case involving five kilos that the cops claimed belonged to him. Crock forgot to mention to the Parole Board that this case was dismissed by the same judge who presided over Wershe's main trial.

Judge Thomas Jackson ruled the drugs were seized illegally. That is, Officer Gerard "Mick" Biernacki of the No Crack Crew—aka Pinocchio—"phoned in" a search warrant request. Biernacki called Recorder's Court Judge Michael Talbot, a diminutive man known for throwing his weight around in criminal cases just because he could. He's now on the Michigan Court of Appeals. Talbot once bragged to one of his neighbors about how he "stuck it" to some criminal defendant in court. The neighbor was Herman Groman, the FBI agent who was Rick Wershe's handler.

Judge Talbot granted Biernacki's search warrant request—by phone—which was a blatant violation of court procedure. Biernacki says he assured the judge he had a "reliable informant" in the case. Biernacki later said the judge told him to execute the search warrant—conduct a raid—and bring him the search warrant paperwork later.

Wershe claims the drugs were planted by the police. He told me Robert Healy, the prosecutor on his case, showed up at the raid scene and asked, "Is that your car?" Wershe said yes, but he told Healy there were no drugs in the car. Wershe claims Healy told him, "there are now." That suggests the police planted the drugs. In an interview Healy denied Wershe's recollection of the events and suggests the aspiring young dope dealer misinterpreted what he said about the drugs.

It all became moot when Judge Jackson tossed the case after ruling the drug seizure by the No Crack Crew was illegal due to the phoned-in search warrant request. Crock told the Parole Board the case wasn't prosecuted because Wershe was facing life in the bigger case. The case *was* prosecuted, but it was tossed out for police and judicial misconduct.

Agent Crock's misleading testimony and documentation didn't stop with Rick Wershe's arrests.

Crock tried to show the Parole Board a connection between Wershe and Detroit's infamous Chambers Brothers drug gang. But Crock's information was apparently supplied by Terry Colbert, an informant who was such an outrageous and prodigious liar that the federal government indicted, tried and convicted him and sent him to prison for lying; lying to a federal grand jury and lying on the witness stand at trial.

Colbert told William Adler, author of *Land of Opportunity*, the book about the rise and fall of the Chambers Brothers drug operation, that he was smoking substantial amounts of crack cocaine when he became a police informant. Colbert used his informant payments to buy more crack, stating, "…whatever bullshit the cops asked me, I said yes this, no that. Whatever they wanted," Colbert told Adler.

Crock's presentation included a DEA report of information from the convicted liar Terry Colbert.

In an August 1, 1991 report that Crock wrote for the DEA's Chambers Brothers investigative file, he stated: "On July 31, 1991 Terry Colbert was sentenced by U.S. District Judge Paul Gadolla (sic) (Gadola), Eastern District of Michigan, subsequent to his conviction on eight counts of perjury."

Colbert's sentence for perjury was in 1991. The Wershe parole hearing was in 2003. Crock knew he was providing the Parole Board with "evidence" from a convicted liar, but he did it anyway.

Special Agent Crock tried to link Wershe, "the menace to society" to drug violence with a dubious DEA report. But the parole hearing was not about fact-finding.

329

Crock presented a DEA 6 report on a "debriefing" of Wershe's longtime friend Roy Grisson, who was shot by a man named Mike Riley in the summer of 1987. The DEA report said Grisson was in Detroit Receiving Hospital and was taken in to "protective custody." The report made it appear the shooting was an attempted hit.

When I located Grisson he told me a very different story. He said the shooting was an attempted robbery, plain and simple. Grisson said Riley thought he, Grisson, had drugs. He did not.

Grisson said the DEA and Detroit Police narcs kidnapped him from the hospital where he was recovering from his wounds. They wheeled him to a plain van and drove him to a suburban motel where Grisson said they "sweated" him all night, attempting to coerce him in to claiming Riley was trying to kill him on orders from White Boy Rick. They also demanded info about Rick Wershe's drug dealing. Grisson said he wouldn't cooperate and early in the morning the narcs drove him to downtown Detroit and dumped him in front of a clothing store. Grisson said he went in to hiding—from the narcs. Grisson said any "signed" statement from him in the DEA files is a forgery and he would sign a sworn affidavit that the DEA version of events was a total fabrication.

Assistant Wayne County Prosecutor Karen Woodside summed up the case against parole for Rick Wershe in a disjointed presentation which relied heavily on newspaper clippings about White Boy Rick, as opposed to investigative files to support the claim that he was a menace to society.

"Um, we gave you a clipping file of all the things that had appeared in the *Detroit News* and that's in that, um, large document pack I gave you that has the black binder on it," Woodside testified.

The hearing transcript shows Woodside told the Board Wershe, "still presents a clear and present danger to the community." She cited a magazine comment from William Coonce, then Special Agent in Charge of the DEA in Detroit:

Woodside quoted Coonce as saying "'Detroit is our Vietnam.' She went on: "If that is true, then White Boy Rick could be considered a teenage Ho Chi Minh."

She plagiarized the Ho Chi Minh line from a March, 1988 edition of a *Detroit Monthly* magazine profile on White Boy Rick.

The prosecution's case against White Boy Rick was so weak Woodside had to recite a quote from a magazine article in an attempt to persuade the Parole Board that he was a danger to community.

Woodside also quoted more articles from the *Detroit News*. She cited police domestic abuse complaints about fights between Dawn Wershe and her father to show Rick came from a bad family.

Even though three FBI agents testified under oath at the hearing about Rick Wershe's help in various criminal cases, Woodside doubted the FBI agents were telling the truth—because a newspaper article quoted Assistant U.S. Attorney Lawrence Bunting as saying if Wershe had been an informant, he was sure he would know about it. Rick Wershe was indeed an FBI paid snitch and AUSA Bunting was ignorant of that fact.

When I tried to interview Woodside for this book, she gave me the time-honored dodge of memory-challenged witnesses appearing before various committees in Washington.

"I don't have any independent recollection of any of that," she said.

Her memory lapses call to mind those of Attorney General Jeff Sessions about Russian interference in the 2016 Donald Trump campaign and Al Gore's repeated memory lapses about Chinese fundraising for the 1996 election, which was allegedly a Chinese intelligence mission to influence the U.S. vote to allow China to join the WTO—World Trade Organization

Through all of this, the Parole Board and the Assistant State Attorney General were curiously incurious. No one asked why federal law enforcement couldn't agree on what to do about Rick Wershe.

The Board never asked attorney William Bufalino about his testimony that Detroit Mayor Coleman Young warned him to stay out of this case because it was bigger than Bufalino thought it was.

The Board never wondered why the prosecution called two police executives to testify who admitted they had not had any law enforcement contact with Wershe.

The hearing seemed to be a stacked deck.

The Michigan Parole Board voted against releasing White Boy Rick Wershe on parole.

Chapter 19— Retribution, a Bit of Justice and No Justice at All

"You know, Mr. Wade, out here on the streets ain't nuthin' ever changes but the names."
—Sage interview observation by a Detroit junkie-hooker

After his Michigan parole hearing, Rick Wershe was returned to the Witness Security program at a federal prison in northern Florida. His days in WitSec were numbered.

Rick Wershe has made bad choices from time to time throughout his life. One of his worst was to get involved in a scheme in Florida to sell used cars from prison. Wershe has always been a car buff. He kept up with *Auto Trader* and read car auction reports sent to him by friends on the outside. Wershe says he learned of a Florida used car operation called Renny Auto Sales and he told his sister Dawn about it. His idea, he said, was to help her sell some used cars to make money to support the family, including Wershe's daughter. Wershe had had kids out of wedlock during his freewheeling teen years.

Wershe's thinking was, used cars were cheaper in Florida and his sister could sell them at a mark-up in Michigan. On the first car, he figured she could make as much as fifteen hundred dollars. Wershe says his sister bought several cars through this arrangement.

Wershe was in prison with Lorenzo "Fat Cat" Nichols, who had a son living in Virginia. The younger Nichols wanted in on the used-car action, too, so Lorenzo Nichols,

Jr. visited Renny Auto Sales. The Renny-to-prison link was established. It wasn't long before the buying and selling involved stolen cars that had been "re-tagged." This is a reference to changing the Vehicle Identification Number or VIN of a car.

Wershe eventually learned from his fellow inmate, Nichols, that some of the cars they were moving were stolen. Wershe made a fateful decision to keep selling the cars through his sister regardless of whether they were stolen or legit.

He made some other stupid decisions. He persuaded his Michigan defense attorney, Patrick McQueeney, to obtain a cell phone so they could maintain better contact. Wershe, who habitually talks to many people, wanted to be able to reach McQueeney after business hours.

McQueeney obtained the cell phone, which the Wershe family paid for, and listed the number with the feds. In other words, it was a phone number listed as part of the attorney-client relationship.

Unknown to McQueeney, his former secretary (fired over this episode) took the phone home and she would accept calls from Wershe in prison and forward them to Wershe's family and others, using the attorney-client cell phone. Knowingly or unknowingly, she was helping Rick Wershe move stolen cars and he was abusing the phone privileges afforded inmates when they are talking with their attorneys. The prison thought he was calling his lawyer, when in fact, he was sometimes discussing used car business with the phone.

Eventually, the scheme came crashing down. A Florida auto theft task force charged Wershe and ten others. Authorities said 250 stolen vehicles were sold with altered vehicle identification numbers and paperwork. Wershe said he and his sister were involved with selling three or four cars. Carlos Ponce, "the King of Cars," was identified by prosecutors as the ringleader.

Wershe and Nichols had used their prison phone privileges to participate in the scheme but they were not the major players. "They're just a small part of the overall case," William Shepherd, the Florida Attorney General special prosecutor assigned to the case told the *Palm Beach Post* in 2006. "But we couldn't do this without closing the loop on them, too."

Shepard's comment to a newspaper reporter, "*They're just a small part of the overall case,*" is significant when evaluating the proposition that officials in Michigan engaged in a vendetta against an FBI informer who had told on powerful criminals who were friends with, or allied with, the Detroit and Wayne County political machine.

Most of the defendants in the car case pleaded guilty and were given sentences of probation and restitution. Wershe and Nichols were singled out for harsher treatment.

The prosecutor told Wershe if he didn't plead guilty as charged to racketeering and racketeering conspiracy, they would bring charges against Wershe's sister and mother. It was a pure bluff, but Wershe bought it. To spare his mother and sister, he pleaded guilty as charged and received a five-year sentence to run *consecutive* to his life sentence.

Ordinarily, a defense attorney would object to a consecutive sentence and argue for a concurrent sentence. That didn't happen. Wershe was represented at his sentencing by a court-appointed attorney he had never met who did not object to the consecutive term. This meant if Wershe ever did get parole from his life sentence in Michigan, he would have to do additional time in Florida.

Wershe claims the Florida prosecutor was surprised by demands from Michigan that they come down hard on him. "What did you do to piss off those people in Michigan?" Wershe says Shepard asked him. According to Wershe, Shepard told him if he had been a cooperating witness in Florida and did as much as he did in Michigan to help prosecute public corruption, that he, Shepard, would do what he had to do to personally walk him out of prison. Shepard claims he does not recall having this conversation with Wershe.

If Wershe's recollections of his conversations with his case prosecutor are correct, it means someone in Michigan went to the trouble to ensure the Detroit/Wayne County law enforcement vendetta against Wershe continued in another state. Was it Mike Cox, then the Michigan Attorney General, leaning on the Attorney General of Florida to come down hard on Wershe because the FBI informant posed a threat to politically powerful people in Detroit who could impact Cox's career? Or was it Wayne County Prosecutor Kym Worthy, continuing her office's long-running hostility toward Wershe for refusing to help them after he helped the FBI, and for exposing corruption in the criminal justice system in which she worked?

In response to a Freedom of Information Act request, the Florida Attorney General's office claims it has no memos or emails urging harsh treatment of Wershe. Such a request could have been handled by telephone, of course. William Shepard, the Florida prosecutor in the car case, now in private practice, is tight-lipped about the case.

Wershe's conviction for committing a crime while in Witness Security was grounds to be kicked out of the program. After he pled guilty and was sentenced, he was quickly returned to the custody of the Michigan

Department of Corrections. He was placed in Oaks
Correctional facility, which has a unit designated for
inmates whose lives may be at risk for one reason or
another.

After the Florida fiasco, Wershe needed a new
attorney. He turned to Ralph Musilli, who had represented
his father for a time. Musilli, sometimes prone to verbosity,
might be likened to a legal profession marathon runner.
That was what Wershe needed. The inmate known as
White Boy Rick was in prison for life and he had a few
more years to serve on top of that. He had lost his appeal.
He had lost his relatively comfortable spot in the Witness
Security program. He had alienated FBI agent Herm
Groman by getting in serious trouble after Groman had
risked internal FBI wrath for testifying at Wershe's parole
hearing. He alienated Lynn Helland in the U.S. Attorney's
office by getting involved in the car theft scam after
Helland had arranged to have him placed in the WitSec
program. Wershe was a man with few friends and fewer
legal options.

One possibility was to seek a pardon or commutation
from Jennifer Granholm, Michigan's then-Governor.
Patrick McQueeney tried this option in 1999 to no avail.

Musilli gave it another go. Veteran Detroit criminal
trial attorney Steve Fishman joined the effort. He wrote a
letter in support of commutation or a pardon which stated:
"To our knowledge, Mr. Wershe is the only person
sentenced under the original 'over 650' statute who
remains in prison today." Fishman added, "As far as we
can see, the only possible reason for this anomaly is the
extraordinary amount of media attention that was paid to
the case when it was tried twenty-three years ago."

Governor Granholm rejected Wershe's petition.

Fishman had been a defense attorney in almost all of the major Detroit drug trafficking trials of the 1980s. Fishman said he had never heard of White Boy Rick until the media publicity describing him as a kingpin of Detroit narcotics: "The notion that a 16, 17-year old kid, white black, purple with yellow stripes, was bossing around the guys that I represented and was the kingpin, particularly on the east side of all places, in this town, in those days, is so absurd that it deserves no further comment. It's that ridiculous." Fishman represented some of the baddest asses in Detroit in that era. "The time I saw him, he looked like a 12-year old!" Fishman recalled. "And this is the one bossing my (clients) guys? I don't think so."

Detroit's "street" agrees. As Nate Craft, the admitted hitman of the Best Friends murder-for-hire gang said of Wershe, "He wasn't no top dog. He didn't run us. He ain't never run us."

Fishman is not surprised that Governor Granholm turned down Wershe's petition for a pardon or commutation. He notes she's a former assistant United States attorney—a prosecutor. "She or others around her probably said, 'Why take this chance? He's a dope dealer and while he was locked up he got himself involved in some other stupid stuff down in Florida and God forbid, I let him out and he kills somebody.' This is how politicians think."

Fishman believes Wershe's involvement in the Florida stolen car ring, however peripheral, is largely responsible for some of the years he has served, even though the Michigan Parole Board claimed it didn't consider the Florida matter in repeatedly denying him parole.

But the bigger, intertwined reasons for Wershe's extraordinarily long time behind bars, in Fishman's view, is the media smear that turned him in to an urban legend and the fact he is white.

"Had he not been white he'd never be in this position today, there's no doubt," Fishman said. "You know it's that White Boy Rick nickname. If Wershe would have been black he'd be just another kid. But the media loved it. 'White Boy Rick.' 'White Boy Rick.' 'White Boy Rick.'"

For a long time, it appeared as if Rick Wershe would spend his entire life in prison. He had run out of options. He had been forgotten, just as his enemies in the criminal justice system had hoped. There were some bleak years.

At one point, the only interest in his case came from obscure Internet news sites focused on prison inmate rights. It wasn't much, but it attracted the attention of a few Hollywood-types who are always on the prowl for intriguing stories. Once word got out that Hollywood was sniffing around the White Boy Rick story, the general news media became interested again.

Wershe's legal battle was a slow slog until the U.S. Supreme Court and Michigan Supreme Court issued opinions stating lower courts should take a second look at cases where a juvenile was sentenced to life in prison for a non-violent drug crime. Wershe fit that description.

Ralph Musilli, Wershe's attorney, filed a federal lawsuit against the Michigan Department of Corrections, alleging a violation of Wershe's civil rights because they refused to give him meaningful consideration for parole. Judges don't like prisoner-rights lawsuits and U.S. District Judge Gordon Quist of Grand Rapids was no exception. He tossed the case.

Musilli appealed to the U.S. Sixth Circuit Court of Appeals. The federal appellate court basically told Judge Quist, not so fast. The issue of a fair parole hearing for Wershe was worthy of further exploration. They sent the case back to Quist for re-consideration. Judges don't like to be corrected by appeals courts. Judge Quist let Wershe's case languish on the docket.

Nationally, there was a growing recognition that maybe, just perhaps, the harsh drug laws needed to be reviewed. In 2010 the U.S. Supreme Court ruled in *Graham v. Florida* that juveniles cannot be sentenced to life without parole in cases that don't involve homicides. This was followed in 2012 by a ruling in *Miller v. Alabama* that mandatory sentences of life without parole for juveniles is cruel and unusual punishment under the Eighth Amendment of the Constitution. Together, these rulings put pressure on the states to revise their harsh sentencing laws regarding juveniles. Wershe was a juvenile when he was arrested, tried and convicted.

In the summer of 2015, the Michigan Supreme Court in *People v. Lockridge* struck down the mandatory element of criminal sentencing guidelines, giving trial judges greater discretion.

After the Graham and Miller rulings came down, defense attorney Musilli had argued, to no avail, that Wershe should be re-sentenced. After the Lockridge ruling, Musilli immediately filed a motion to re-sentence Wershe.

Thomas Jackson, Wershe's trial judge, had retired and Jackson's docket was assumed by Judge Dana Hathaway. She was a young jurist from a family with a long history as judges and prosecutors in Wayne County.

Judge Hathaway immediately accepted Musilli's motion and scheduled it for a hearing. It was the first significant legal movement in the Wershe case in years. Suddenly, White Boy Rick was back in the news. Judge Hathaway took an active interest in the Wershe case. She stunned many in the criminal justice system by researching the case law and issuing her own 18-page opinion granting Wershe a re-sentencing. "Defendant has already served 27 years of an indeterminate sentence...the Defendant's non-violent, non-assaultive crime which he committed as a juvenile would appear to fail the test of proportionality," Judge Hathaway wrote.

Kym Worthy, the Wayne County Prosecutor, maintained the tradition of her office of going off the deep end about anything related to Richard Wershe, Jr.

From the time of his arrest, the Wayne County Prosecutor's Office, through three successive prosecutors, had insisted loudly and publicly that White Boy Rick was a dangerous criminal. Worthy immediately announced an appeal of Hathaway's decision.

Worthy was a rookie assistant prosecutor when Wershe was put on trial. But she watched her predecessors in the top job stubbornly cling to the fiction that White Boy Rick, a white kid, was somehow the boss of prison-hardened adult black men and the Chief Executive Officer of Detroit's illegal drug trade.

I filed a Freedom of Information Act request with her office, demanding copies of all files and reports in her possession supporting the contention of her predecessor, Mike Duggan, that Wershe was a violent gangster and a menace to society.

The response from her office to my FOIA request stated, in part, "After a diligent search for the requested records, we have determined and certify the records do not exist."

Some have speculated this was a poorly written way of saying the records had been purged due to age. This written response, from an office of lawyers, does not say that. Nor does it say the records are missing or misplaced. They "certify" the records "do not exist."

In any event, the Wayne County Prosecutor's office was admitting it had no evidence, no records of any kind, to support the wild police/prosecution charges against a defendant in one of the highest profile Detroit drug cases of modern times.

Like many prosecutors who stand for election and re-election, Kym Worthy believes she must appear "tough on crime." The word "justice" apparently isn't a vote-getter.

In 2016, the Harvard Law School Fair Sentencing Project singled out Kym Worthy among 2,400 prosecutors in the nation as "an extreme outlier" on sentencing juveniles to life without parole. It is easy to see why Wershe's youth and immaturity at the time of his arrest and conviction meant nothing to Prosecutor Worthy.

In near-record time, a three-judge panel of the Michigan Court of Appeals overruled Judge Hathaway on the re-sentencing of Richard Wershe. The chief judge of the Court of Appeals was Michael Talbot, the judge who allowed Police Officer Gerard Biernacki to "phone in" a request for a search warrant against Rick Wershe, in violation of proper procedure. Talbot, who had seen the evidence against Wershe thrown out by another judge due to Talbot's careless administration of justice in the matter of a search warrant, was among the three judges who voted to reverse Hathaway regarding Wershe.

The case went to the Michigan Supreme Court, which refused to hear the case without explanation. In a blatant example of judicial cowardice, none of the judges of the Michigan Supreme Court signed the order.

Justice Stephen Markman had recused himself from the case because he had benefited considerably from Wershe's undercover work when Markman was the United States Attorney in Detroit during Operation Backbone, the FBI sting operation. That case was a career highlight for Markman and it happened because of Wershe's cooperation with the government. Markman's colleagues on the Michigan Supreme Court did not have the moral courage or legal integrity to put their names behind the refusal to consider Wershe's re-sentencing, even though they had issued the Lockridge ruling which was a key factor in favor of re-visiting the Wershe sentence. It's pure conjecture, but the Michigan Supreme Court seems to have known that Wershe should be re-sentenced under their own Lockridge ruling, but they cravenly ducked the case because they knew White Boy Rick was a hot crime legend.

Wershe's hopes were dashed. His sentence of life in prison continued.

All of the renewed news coverage about White Boy Rick had an upside. Hollywood's fascination with his story grew stronger. Rival White Boy Rick movie projects emerged. Studios were competing to tell his story. His tale made Hollywood's "Black List" for 2015, a survey of undeveloped screenplays 250 Hollywood executives believe should be produced as motion pictures. Eventually a deal was developed and Matthew McConaughey was signed to play Rick Wershe's father in the movie. A previously unknown teen was cast to play the part of White Boy Rick.

The Hollywood buzz created more media interest in the Rick Wershe story. His life in prison was no longer in the shadows. He was not a prisoner to be forgotten until he died.

Wershe's struggle to be free of his life sentence changed suddenly just before Christmas, 2016. Ralph Musilli and his law firm associates decided to file a habeas corpus motion against the State of Michigan in Detroit federal court. Habeas Corpus means "you have the body." In law, it is a demand for an explanation for why someone is being held in custody. It was a long shot. U.S. Supreme Court rulings had made habeas corpus motions tougher to win.

Thus, it was a bit astonishing when U.S. District Judge George Steeh agreed to hear the case. He was willing to order the State of Michigan to come to court and explain why they had denied parole for Wershe half a dozen times when they were releasing others similarly sentenced under the Lockridge and Graham rulings.

Wershe's odds may have been helped by Paul Louisell, the attorney chosen to prepare the habeas corpus motion. Paul Louisell's father was a legend in Detroit legal circles. Joe Louisell was hailed as Detroit's Perry Mason of the 1950s and 60s for his ability to get clients acquitted in seemingly hopeless cases. The name Louisell has long had marquee value in Michigan legal circles.

Within a week of the filing of the habeas corpus motion, and the judge's agreement to hear it, the State of Michigan attitude toward Rick Wershe suddenly and dramatically changed.

He was due for another routine parole review in the fall and winter of 2017. Suddenly, that was bumped up to

February. Michael Eagen, the chair of the 10-member
Michigan Parole Board, took control of the parole review
process in the Wershe case. He interviewed Wershe
personally, which was followed by a public hearing,
Wershe's first since 2003.

Some in the media like to pat themselves on the back
and take credit for the change in attitude by the State of
Michigan toward prison inmate Richard J. Wershe, Jr.
They like to think their pressure changed the system's
attitude toward White Boy Rick. That's nonsense.
Wershe's fate changed when a federal judge agreed (the
habeas corpus motion) that that State of Michigan should
come to court and explain why Wershe was still behind
bars when so many others similarly charged had been
released. Suddenly, the wheels were in motion for a parole
for Inmate 192034.

On June 8, 2017, Wershe had his second parole
hearing. The hearing room in Jackson, Michigan was
packed with reporters and supporters. The hearing lasted
over four hours. Wershe essentially reviewed his life of
crime. He knew truthfulness was vital. The assistant state
attorney general leading the questioning made it clear he
had done a lot of homework on Wershe's misdeeds.

Wershe repeatedly expressed regret for his drug
crimes. "I was stupid," Wershe told the Parole Board. "I
know that the drugs I sold destroyed people's lives. I can't
take it back. My life has been destroyed, my sister's life.
It's ruined my kids' lives. It's ruined my niece and
nephews' lives. I know what it does."

Wershe ended by pleading with the Parole Board. "I've
lost 30 years of my life," Wershe said. "All I can give you
is my word. I'll never commit another crime."

The month after Wershe's hearing, the Michigan Parole board voted unanimously to grant Richard J. Wershe, Jr parole.

In August, 2017, The Florida Department of Corrections brought Wershe back to serve the remainder of his five-year sentence in the car theft case. With time served during his arraignment and plea and with good behavior "gain time," Wershe was scheduled for release in the spring of 2021, with the possibility of early release if the state clemency board decided it was warranted.

It took nearly 30 years, but Richard J. Wershe, Jr finally got a measure of justice. He was out from under his life sentence. Others who had done far worse served much less time. But others had not snitched on the powers-that-be in big-city politics. While individual agents did what they could, the federal government, which benefited greatly from Wershe's informant work after they recruited him at age 14 to immerse himself in a life of crime, was shameful in its refusal to come to his aid after he got in trouble doing what they had taught him to do. They are the ones who lured him in to the drug underworld. To later claim he shouldn't have chosen to dabble in drugs after they dropped him as an informant and left him to fend for himself is self-serving ass-covering at a federal level.

It would be encouraging to say justice prevailed in the end in the White Boy Rick saga. But it would be untrue.

Richard J. Wershe, Jr deserved some jail time for his decision to try to become a cocaine wholesaler. But he should have served five years, perhaps, not twenty-nine-and-a-half years of a life term. In Florida, Wershe earned a second felony conviction, but arguably the sentence should have been probation and restitution like his co-defendants, not a five-year *consecutive* sentence for racketeering and racketeering conspiracy.

Gil Hill and others in the command ranks of the Detroit Police Department should have been seriously evaluated for indictment for an array of obstruction of justice-related crimes in the death of 13-year old Damion Lucas and the attempted railroading of an innocent man, LeKeas Davis. As explained in Chapter 8, Homicide Inspector Gil Hill was bribed by drug dealer Johnny Curry to keep the Damion Lucas investigation away from the Curry drug gang. The FBI confronted several top command officers in the police department, including the chief, with information pointing at the true killers and nothing was done.

Likewise, Assistant Prosecuting Attorney Augustus Hutting (deceased) was fully briefed on the FBI's information and repeated attempts to move the homicide investigation in the right direction. Yet, he did nothing to stop the injustice until forced to do so. Why didn't Hutting recommend to Prosecutor John O'Hair that the Michigan State Police be called in to investigate possible police corruption in the Damion Lucas case? The top command personnel of the Prosecutor's office had to know something was amiss in this case where the FBI was insisting they were prosecuting an innocent man. Where was Prosecutor John O'Hair? Why didn't he demand an investigation? Did O'Hair shirk his duty for fear of political repercussions if he pursued an investigation that would necessarily involve Mayor Young's niece?

Where was his chief assistant, Elliott Hall, one of the power figures of Detroit's black political establishment? Hall had been corporation counsel—city attorney—for a time under Coleman Young. Hall, who went on to be named vice president of governmental affairs for the Ford Motor Company, is a smart lawyer and an experienced player in politics. Did Hall dodge his responsibility in the Damion Lucas/LeKeas Davis matter to avoid the ire of Coleman Young, the most powerful politician in southeast Michigan?

The Feds took action but they could have done more with the travesty of justice that surrounded the Damion Lucas killing. In the spring of 1985 the FBI had informant and wiretap information indicating potential corruption and investigative interference regarding Homicide Inspector Gil Hill.

When FBI agents took solid leads and information in the Damion Lucas/LeKeas Davis case to the top brass of the Detroit Police Department and nothing was done, why didn't Special Agent in Charge Kenneth Walton, the "Caped Crusader", open a police corruption investigation, independent of the Curry drug case? Why wasn't there an investigation of a conspiracy to obstruct justice by several top executives of the Detroit Police Department? This is the same FBI boss who staged a made-for-media raid of Detroit's Recorder's Court in an investigation of judicial corruption.

The U.S. Attorney's office was fully aware of the FBI's wiretap recordings pointing to possible corruption regarding Gil Hill.

Yet, the late Roy "Call me Joe" Hayes, the Detroit United States Attorney for Detroit from 1985 through 1989 apparently did nothing and demanded nothing regarding the evidence and informant tips suggesting Hill was corrupt and other command officers may have been in on thwarting the homicide investigation. The federal statute of limitations on obstruction of justice is five years. The Hill corruption information and evidence surfaced in 1985. Hayes did nothing for four of the five years of potential prosecution of Gil Hill and other command personnel.

Hayes' successor, Stephen Markman, was aggressive on public corruption. Yet, he, too, apparently did nothing in terms of an independent investigation of the corruption of Gil Hill and the possible collusion of the top leadership of the Detroit Police Department. Why?

Some argue there simply wasn't sufficient evidence to bring charges against Hill or anyone else in the Detroit Police Department in the Damion Lucas/LeKeas Davis matter.

In any conspiracy or complex case, there is seldom "sufficient" evidence at the outset. That is what investigations are for and about. There are many legal tools available to force the disclosure of facts in criminal investigations. But there must be a will to use them. Controversial trials can't be won without such will.

As often as not, the Justice Department lacks balls in politically charged investigations. Author Jesse Eisinger calls the Justice Department the Chickenshit Club in his book of the same name. The absence of gonads and backbones in the Justice Department is why Special Agent Groman slyly named the police corruption sting investigation Operation Backbone.

Some of the key figures in this failure of justice are dead. Most of those still living are lawyers hiding behind "ethical" concerns. That's a convenient and craven dodge, particularly among current and former federal prosecutors. "No comment" is sometimes a spineless way to avoid explaining a failure to do one's duty.

Hollywood is partly responsible for the lack of justice in the bribery of Gil Hill. He had become a Detroit celebrity and hero for his role as the foul-mouthed police boss of comedian Eddie Murphy in the *Beverly Hills Cop* movies. Hill parlayed his brief roles in those films in to local popularity and rode that fame to political power.

John Anthony, the special agent legal advisor to the Detroit FBI during this era puts the issue of prosecuting Gil Hill this way: "He's in movies. He's connected with the Police Department. He's connected with the Mayor. You better have a signed confession from Gil Hill if you're going to go after him."

In his book *The Star Chamber: How Celebrities Go Free and Their Lawyers Become Famous*, Eric Dunson argues American juries seldom convict celebrities. They ask for autographs. The celebrities cash in "their lifetime of accumulated fame to walk free." Convicting a celebrity would be like convicting someone who has provided memories and entertainment. Dunson cites the child molesting case against Michael Jackson as one example.

Comedian Dave Chappelle also noted the Jackson case in a TV comedy sketch about jury selection in celebrity trials. Chappelle plays a prospective juror being questioned for possible duty in the Jackson case.

Actor playing lawyer: "So do you think Michael Jackson is guilty of the charges against him?"

Chappelle as prospective juror: "No, man. He made Thriller."

Detroit is a grim city starved for heroes and celebrities, particularly black ones. In Detroit, Gil Hill was a hero and celebrity. Fear of his fame appears to be a driving force behind the failure of the Wayne County Prosecutor, the FBI, the U.S. Attorney and the Justice Department to pursue Gil Hill and other police command officers for corruption and obstruction of justice in the Damion Lucas homicide and the attempted railroading of LeKeas Davis as the shooter.

That fear was driven by concern that prosecutors couldn't find a jury that would convict this popular black public figure. A more likely reason is there might be political consequences. Furthermore, bureaucrats of all stripes live in fear of being accused of racism. Scoundrels like Gil Hill know this. They understand the political power of whining that "they're picking on me because I'm black." Gil Hill and Damion Lucas were both black. Gil Hill had power. Damion Lucas had none. Gil Hill escaped justice. Damion Lucas got none.

Chapter 20—Exit ramps off the Road to Futility

"One definition of insanity is doing the same thing over and over again and expecting a different result."
—Alcoholics Anonymous Pamphlet

One afternoon in late summer of 1989 I received a phone call from Paul Phillip, one of the Assistant Special Agents in Charge of the Detroit FBI.

"Can you come down to the office after you finish work?" Phillip asked me. "Sure," I said. "What's up?"

"Just bring the biggest gym bag you can find," he said. He had my attention.

Phillip is a tall black man with law enforcement street experience. When I arrived, he had some black and white surveillance photos spread on his desk. He got right to the point.

"We have reliable informant information that these three guys have been hired by the Kalasho-Akrawi drug gang to kill you and/or Lou Palombella of DEA, whichever of you they can find first," Phillip said. The three black mopes in the FBI surveillance photos looked as dumb as a box of rocks, but it doesn't take much IQ to pull a trigger.

Palombella had been leading an in-your-face investigation of the Kalasho-Akrawi drug gang after a series of murders as the gang fought with rivals for control of drug sales in the predominately Chaldean 7 Mile and Woodward area of Detroit. Chaldeans are Christian Iraqis, persecuted over the years by Saddam Hussein. The young, usually hot-headed and undisciplined Chaldean dopers had watched Al Pacino's *Scarface* too many times.

I had started working for WJBK-TV Ch. 2, earlier that year. The Chaldean dopers got my attention after they began lobbing lighted sticks of dynamite on the front porches of rivals and gunning each other down in the streets. My reporting irritated the Kalasho-Akrawi gang. They wanted to kill me.

Paul Phillip reached behind his desk and pulled up a large, heavy, bullet-stopping raid vest.

"I'm not worried about Palombella," Phillip said." DEA has his back. But I don't want a TV celebrity murdered on my watch," Phillip said as he handed me the bulky, heavy body armor. "We want you to wear this to and from work every day for the next few days until we can get these jokers off the street." He handed me several sets of the surveillance photos. "You should probably tell your boss about it and your local police department because these guys may try to catch you at home."

When I returned to the TV station, the bosses were in a crisis meeting. While I was at the FBI office, one of the Chaldean hotheads called the station and threatened to blow up the transmission tower.

What followed were several weeks of anxious chaos, round-the-clock armed security guards at the station and my house and experienced executive protection armed body guards for me. I continued to report on the Chaldean gangster wannabes, their leader was arrested, the TV tower was still standing, and no one was hurt. The threat—and the FBI raid vest—went away.

Prisoner of War:
The Story of White Boy Rick and The War on Drugs

The tale of the Chaldean Al Capone wannabes shows some of the combatants in the War on Drugs deserve to be in jail—for a long time. They've earned it. But far too many people, non-violent people, have been locked up for drugs with absolutely no impact on the tsunami of illegal narcotics flooding America's streets. America has had the same battle plan in the War on Drugs for over 40 years. The nation has spent more than a trillion dollars and the cost of cocaine declines periodically because there's more supply than demand.

All the king's narcs and all the king's prosecutors haven't made a dent in the market for illegal drugs after nearly half a century of trying. At least in the Prohibition Era the nation came to its senses and admitted the 18th Amendment was a big mistake. That hasn't happened yet with the War on Drugs.

In recent times crack cocaine has been overshadowed by the widespread use and abuse of opioids—an opioid "epidemic", to use a favorite cliché of politicians and the media. In 2015, "more than 33,000 Americans died as a result of an opioid overdose, including prescription opioids, heroin, and illicitly manufactured fentanyl, a powerful synthetic opioid," according to the National Institute on Drug Abuse. The government agency estimated the "economic burden" of opioid misuse and abuse at $78.5 billion.

As of 2015 about one in every ten Americans was an illegal drug user, according to government statistics. Does the lock-em-up crowd really believe we can solve, or afford to solve, the drug problem by imprisoning 27 million Americans? It's insanity.

The whack-a-mole nature of drug interdiction and enforcement is a national embarrassment. The United States keeps pleading with other nations to do what we clearly cannot do—stop the flood of illegal drugs.

In recent years dozens of tunnels have been discovered between the border with the United States and Mexico. They have facilitated the smuggling of tons of marijuana, the equivalent of beer in the Prohibition era.

The drug cartels, with pockets as deep as some nations, have started building drug smuggling min-submarines at about $1-million apiece. These narco subs can carry four to eight tons of cocaine. Even if most of them are caught, it only takes a few getting through to make the investment worthwhile for the cartels.

The latest technology in drug smuggling involves unmanned aerial vehicles, or drones. Drone smuggling is certain to increase as the aircraft feature better lift capability. Researchers are developing drone swarm technology, meaning these little aircraft will fly in squadrons with the ability to avoid mid-air collisions and to evade counter-measures.

By the end of the first decade of the new century, a major portion of an entire generation of young black men had been imprisoned under the nation's harsh-but-impotent federal and state drug laws. Then, things began to change. Slowly, there was a recognition that all the arrests, all the long sentences, all the new prisons, hadn't change a thing.

Prison reform under President Barack Obama was in fits and starts. Obama signed the Fair Sentencing Act. It addressed the 100-to-1 disparity between the penalties for crack and powder cocaine in the Anti-Drug Abuse Act of 1986. The law was based on the erroneous belief that crack was more dangerous than powered cocaine. In 2013, Attorney General Eric Holder launched what was called a Smart on Crime Initiative. It instructed the nation's U.S. attorneys to focus on serious, violent criminals and make non-violent drug offenders a low priority. It did nothing, however, to empty the prisons from the lock-em-up binge that had been underway since the cocaine death of basketball star Len Bias.

A 2017 study published in the journal *Demography* found about a third of all black men in America have been convicted of a felony.

The nation was reaping the bitter harvest of the brutal, tough-on-crime laws of the post-Len Bias scandal in the mid-1980s and the presidential and congressional pandering of the mid-1990s. By 2008, a study found that one in 100 Americans was behind bars. Harsh sentencing for drug crimes was behind a large percentage of the prison population. The explosive increase in people behind bars did not have any relationship to fluctuations in the crime rate.

Eventually Obama started granting Presidential clemency and issued commutations for non-violent drug offenders, some 1,715 in all. It was far short of the ten thousand grants of clemency Attorney General Eric Holder had predicted.

Law and Order Republicans got in on the act, too. In 2014, former House Speaker Newt Gingrich launched a campaign for prison reform, arguing it made economic sense to do so. The Republican politician who championed the Taking Back Our Streets Act of the 1990s, was now arguing mass incarceration was a costly mistake.

"In state after state, we have overused imprisonment, even for low-risk offenders. Incarceration has become the norm despite clear evidence that many nonviolent offenders can be held accountable and supervised more effectively through alternatives such as drug courts and job reporting centers," Gingrich wrote in a 2014 Op-Ed piece in the *Detroit Free Press*. Gingrich noted in Michigan one out of every five tax dollars in the state general fund was being spent on prisons and corrections. Gingrich wrote similar opinion articles for other newspapers, including the *Washington Post*.

Some corrections researchers have argued the quarter-century expansion of the prison population has more to do with media coverage than crime rates. As noted in Chapter 14, news coverage in the U.S. is often herd journalism. After more than two decades as a crime beat reporter I can say crime sells; in ratings, readership and advertising revenue. More than one news boss told me, "Big J" journalism—thoughtful, detailed, balanced reporting on major socio-economic issues, is a ratings loser.

H. Rap Brown, the 60s black militant who re-named himself Jamil Abdula Al-Amin, was right: violence is as American as cherry pie. The American public, while claiming to be horrified by violence, is transfixed by it.

There is a terrible distortion of reality that goes with media coverage of crime news. It takes on far more importance than it merits because it sells. A murder with crying relatives is likely to get several minutes of "live" coverage, even though thousands, perhaps hundreds of thousands of people, depending on the market size, had non-violent, uneventful lives that day. A dead body didn't impact their world, not even a little bit, but the TV stations act as if it did, because crime news is a ratings-getter.

This bottomless appetite for "If it bleeds, it leads"
makes viewers think crime is more widespread than it truly
is. This leads to voter demands for throw-the-book-at- 'em
laws. Pandering politicians are happy to oblige. The surge
in America's prison population should surprise no one,
least of all reporters and editors.

There's another mostly overlooked element in the mass
incarceration issue. It is class discrimination, a bias toward
people in the lower classes.

Among the taboo subjects in American discourse, class
struggle has to rank near the top. It's just not discussed.
Untold forests have been devoured for the paper devoted to
books and articles on racism, discrimination and bigotry in
the United States. These are durable moral viruses. But
much of the injustice labeled as racism is actually classism.
Some discrimination is driven by socio-economic class, not
skin color. Yet, Americans shun any suggestion that class
bias is part of the social fabric of the United States. We
fought the British ruling class, created a new nation and
proclaimed all men are created equal, didn't we?

Upper-class whites shun what they call poor white
trash almost as much as they avoid ghetto blacks or
Latinos. It's about revulsion toward the uneducated and
poor.

One element of class struggle that is not discussed,
particularly in racially mixed company, is the attitude of
middle and upper-middle class blacks toward ghetto
blacks.

The Jeffersons, a popular black family TV sitcom of
the 70s and 80s featured a theme song which proclaimed,
they were *Movin on up.* The theme song celebrated the fact
they—the Jeffersons—finally got a piece of the pie.

Vince Wade

Movin' up and movin' out was part of the post-Civil Rights experience of many American blacks with jobs and careers. They moved away from the inner cities for the same reasons whites did; safer neighborhoods, better schools, lower taxes, a better quality of life. Much has been made in the Detroit media over the years about "white flight." Less attention has been paid to black flight to suburbs like Oak Park, Southfield, Redford, Clinton Township and others.

Southfield, a major Detroit suburb, is a good example. The 1980 census showed Southfield had 6,976 black residents. By 2002, Southfield's black population was 42,259. Blacks who could escape the ghetto did, often paying top dollar for a home in Southfield. Along came the Great Recession of 2008, and in the years that followed, a lot of homes went in to foreclosure, allowing an influx of lower-income Detroiters who bought Southfield homes at distressed prices.

In 2011, the Associated Press carried a story about Southfield blacks resenting an influx of ghetto blacks who were "movin on up" due to foreclosure property bargains.

"I've got people of color who don't want people of color to move into the city," the AP quoted Southfield Police Chief Joseph Thomas stating, "It's not a black-white thing. This is a black-black thing. My six-figure blacks are very concerned about multiple-family, economically depressed people moving into rental homes and apartments, bringing in their bad behaviors." Thomas is black.

Middle class black disdain for ghetto-dwellers is different from well-documented white racism. But class struggle—middle and upper-middle class whites and blacks resisting the perceived lawlessness and depravities of the lower classes—is an important, yet mostly unspoken part of the mass incarceration debate. As noted in Chapters 4 and 11, blacks have been strong voices in the citizen chorus demanding ever-tougher prosecution of crimes, particularly drug crimes.

All of this had importance for Richard J. Wershe, Jr. He had grown up lower-class white. But as a teen, Rick Wershe ran with blacks. He hung with blacks. The ghetto dialect was his dialect.

Wershe recalls an encounter he had not long before his drug trial. It was with Bill Jasper, the Detroit Police narc who had used him so extensively to make drug buys in crack houses when Rick was working as an informant for the FBI and the Task Force. They met at another raid. This one targeted Wershe's father over gun silencer parts. The younger Wershe says he and Officer Jasper had a conversation on the front lawn during that raid. Wershe says he will never forget it.

Wershe claims Jasper told him he was worse than a black ghetto drug dealer.

Wershe had risked his neck time and again to make drug buys for Bill Jasper and now, Wershe recalls, the narc was telling him he was lower than a ghetto black.

Rick Wershe walked, talked, and acted black, which astonished many people. FBI agents, black and white, mentioned it to me in interviews. It would not be surprising to learn some Detroit police officers viewed Wershe as a traitor to his race.

Wershe fared no better among blacks. He started raising suspicions because he was making drug buys here, there and everywhere in his undercover work. His attempt to "act black" raised suspicions—among blacks.

As admitted hitman Nate Craft explained in Chapter 12, the murder-for-hire hitmen of the Best Friends gang, disliked and distrusted Wershe and wanted to kill him.

Wershe had no friends among Detroit's black power elite, either. He had the audacity to shack up with the favorite niece of Coleman Young, the mayor and de facto emperor of the City of Detroit. Cathy Volsan Curry had a history of sleeping with major drug dealers, but now she was sleeping with a white doper with aspirations for the big time. Later, when it was revealed that Wershe had been secretly snitching for the FBI against blacks, he became a young white man to be loathed and punished with lifelong revenge. He was a white guy who insinuated himself to a degree in to Detroit's black culture, only to be exposed as a snitch for the hated FBI. Wershe managed to make enemies among powerful blacks and whites in the political and law enforcement establishments. Rick Wershe, Jr. has the dubious distinction of being an outcast from two races.

My longtime friendship and working relationship with Bill Dwyer of the Detroit Police Department began in earnest in the fall of 1975. My work as a cop beat reporter put me in the middle of an unusual drug story. Through a strange turn of events, I wound up on a red-eye flight from Detroit to McAllen, Texas, accompanied by my camera crew, Mike Kalush and Bill Hevron, and three Detroit police command officers carrying a briefcase stuffed with city cash. One of them was Bill Dwyer. Another was Bill Hart, then a Deputy Chief. We were on a bizarre and dangerous adventure and the cash came in handy in the days ahead.

Prisoner of War:
The Story of White Boy Rick and The War on Drugs

An enterprising narc of Italian heritage had conned a Detroit Mexican drug gang with family drug ties in Mexico in to believing he was the son of a Detroit Mafia leader. He said he was trying to arrange a major drug buy to make his "bones" with the "family." He had insisted on meeting the patrón, the Big Guy, of the Mexican drug family. The Mexican dopers went for it. The Detroit Police contacted DEA in Mexico and major arrests were made in Reynosa, Mexico, just across the Rio Grande from McAllen, Texas. The Detroit Police had never made a case of this magnitude.

The cooperation between the Detroit Police and the Drug Enforcement Administration stopped, however, when the DPD asked the DEA to let them cross the border and help them establish intelligence liaison with the Mexican federales. DEA didn't want the Detroit police or Detroit reporters in Mexico. I needed to shoot film (we used film in those days) on the Mexican side of the border to tell that side of the story. Desperation inspired me to contact the Associated Press bureau chief in Mexico City and explain our dilemma. A few hours later he called back and told me to call the publisher of the main newspaper in Monterrey, Mexico. Alejandro Junco de la Vega was a powerful University of Texas-educated journalist who published the *El Norte* newspaper. He now publishes the *Reforma* newspaper, one of the most popular in Mexico City.

De la Vega arranged for the Detroit narcs, my camera crew and me to make a middle-of-the-night drive from Reynosa to Monterrey, where he set up a meeting for us with the Attorney General for the state of Nuevo León in northern Mexico, where the case had developed. The Detroit police established direct liaison with the Attorney General's staff and we had a major "perp walk" for our cameras and film of the crude heroin labs in Durango, Mexico. We never encountered DEA in Mexico.

As I mentioned, Lt. Bill Dwyer was one of the
Detroit Police officers on that 1975 trip. He is currently the
Chief of Police in Warren, Michigan, the state's third-
largest city. I went on many drug raids in Detroit with
Dwyer and his narcs, dutifully reporting each night on the
"progress" being made in the War on Drugs. Years later,
Dwyer and I agreed. We were fooling ourselves. There was
no progress.

"I remember our trip to Mexico. As a young narcotics
commander, I really believed when we were making 10
raids a day that we really were going to significantly
decrease the use and sale of drugs," Dwyer said. "We
haven't done that. We're not winning the war on drugs.
We're losing the war on drugs."

Rudy Thomas, who eventually followed Dwyer as the
boss of Detroit Police Narcotics, and retired as a Deputy
Chief of the Detroit Police Department, is similarly glum
about the drug war.

"We really didn't accomplish anything," Thomas said.
"The impetus was on locking up all drug dealers. "The
ones we arrested were the minorities, the blacks. Those
numbers were large. The mules who were carrying the
(large amounts) of cocaine were getting life terms and they
were just making money to survive."

The illegal drug market is the ultimate example of
supply and demand. Thomas notes U.S. law enforcement
has ignored the demand side of the drug business. "What
about those that were using cocaine?" Thomas wonders.
"I'm thinking white males and white females, blacks and
whites. They were given little to no time in jail at all."

Prisoner of War:
The Story of White Boy Rick and The War on Drugs

Michael Levine also wonders why the nation has done
so little to reduce the demand side of the War on Drugs.
Levine was a top undercover narc for the DEA for 25
years. The CBS newsmagazine *60 Minutes* once called him
"America's top undercover cop." He is the author of
several books—*Deep Cover, The Big White Lie*—that are
sharply critical of the "drug war bureaucrats" and the
"suits" of the Drug Enforcement Administration.

Levine says there are 53 government agencies with
some claim to participation in the War on Drugs. "None of
these bureaucracies even consider the possibility of
successfully completing their goals (to win the War on
Drugs)," Levine said in a seminar. "On the contrary, they
all vie with each other for bigger cases, headlines and
media exposure which translate down to a bigger cut of the
budget, more money, more authority and more power." The
War on Drugs is a bureaucratic jobs creator, providing
career employment for thousands.

Levine says there is no question the U.S. government,
through the CIA, has for years secretly condoned the drug
smuggling racket when it benefited our "allies" in
Southeast Asia and the Southern Hemisphere in the never-
ending struggle against Communism. He calls the Central
Intelligence Agency "out of control" and claims they
impede drug cases if the investigation involves CIA
"assets," as we saw in the story of Michael Palmer, the
drug pilot, in Chapter 10.

Levine says he upset the established order of the War
on Drugs in New York in the spring of 1989. He got
permission to try an experiment. Backed by a team of
about 15 agents, Levine targeted the *buyers* in a drug-
infested block in New York City. The drug pushers were
not targeted. Levine's DEA agents stopped the drug buyers
a few blocks away, after they had made a purchase. Cars
were searched. Arrests were made. Many of the customers

were white. Frightened out of their minds, most were released with a warning that if they returned to that neighborhood they faced certain arrest. Business for the drug dealers slowed to a trickle. Yet, the DEA bureaucracy and the New York Police seemed indifferent to Levine's experiment. It's not how they had been fighting the War on Drugs since 1971. Levine called his experiment "Fight Back." He believes it can work everywhere, if given a real chance. Levine's approach was similar to the tactic used by vice squads around the nation in keeping street prostitution under control. Vice cops target the "Johns' in red light districts often with excellent results. The customers are threatened with arrest and confiscation of their vehicles.

Demand reduction, serious and widespread demand reduction, has never been tried in the War on Drugs. Law and order conservatives like to loudly—and falsely— equate demand reduction with drug legalization. A sustained national campaign to target drug users would wipe out the customer base for illegal drugs. Perhaps we should consider an alcoholism and drunk driving strategy for the drug problem. Instead of automatic felony convictions, such an approach would require new, revised laws that impose high misdemeanor charges and levy severe fines on drug buyers. Repeat offenders could face vehicle forfeiture and the loss of their driver's license. Court-ordered *mandatory* and intense drug rehabilitation would add teeth to the demand reduction initiative.

The Drug Policy Alliance estimates the United States spends $51 billion annually on the War on Drugs. A fraction of that money could buy a powerful mass media campaign against drug use, similar to the anti-smoking campaigns targeted at teens and young people.

Prisoner of War:
The Story of White Boy Rick and The War on Drugs

There's a tendency to pursue drug dealers operating up to a certain level, but federal investigators seem to avoid the truly big smugglers operating nationally and internationally. Bankers and money men are seldom prosecuted.

To catch the truly big fish, law enforcement must change the way it does business.

Retired FBI agent Gregg Schwarz who concluded the Curry Brothers investigation where Rick Wershe was the undercover informant, contends the FBI needs to abandon what is known as the Career Development Program. It's how FBI bosses move up the ladder. It's about tours of duty and managerial posts, not case productivity. Other federal law enforcement agencies have similar programs.

Schwarz advocates the establishment of a true crime czar with authority over all of federal law enforcement, including the Justice Department with the ability to put an end to jurisdictional and inter-agency squabbles through negative career development. That is, downward career mobility for law enforcement bosses and Justice Department attorneys who don't cooperate in big, multi-jurisdictional cases. The "not-my-office-so-it's-not-my job" attitude is an impediment to making bigger cases, he believes.

There's a saying among federal agents and prosecutors. Big case, big problems. Small case, small problems. No case, no problems. Little wonder the location-hopping large-scale smugglers are seldom prosecuted.

Schwarz is convinced the constant rotation of Special Agents in Charge (SACs) and Assistant Special Agents in Charge (ASACs) in FBI field offices is one reason no one followed through on helping Rick Wershe when he got in trouble. "The career development program changed people over again and again and again," Schwarz said. "Every 18 months a new SAC, a new ASAC. It just keeps rolling, rolling, rolling." The result is no continuity. No one in management is invested in long-term case and informant development and management.

In FBI management, SACs—Special Agents in Charge—are seldom in one office long enough to become vested in the on-going case work, the agents doing the work and the quality of the informants who make it happen. FBI managers focus on "punching the ticket" of career advancement, rather than managing complex investigations.

This jurisdictional stove piping of criminal case work is exacerbated by jealousies and rivalries between United States Attorneys. It's all about who gets to have the high-profile trial, and who gets the credit. U.S. attorneys are political appointees and usually have political ambitions. A big case is a political gold star.

Douglas McCullough was an assistant U.S. Attorney in the Eastern District of North Carolina when the massive Kalish, Ritch, Vogel smuggling case was busted, as detailed in Chapter 10.

McCullough wrote a book about the case called *Sea of Greed*, in which he describes the tug-of-war between his office and the office of the late Robert "Mad Dog" Merkle, the U.S. attorney in Tampa, over which office would try the case. McCullough described a meeting in Tampa led by Special Agent Ned Timmons, who developed the key informant who helped break the case. Attending were FBI agents and assistant United States attorneys from North Carolina, Texas and Florida. As Timmons detailed the scope of the investigation, McCullough recounts how he whispered to FBI Agent Terry Peters, who was working the North Carolina angle of the investigation. "The fight over jurisdiction on this one will rival Vietnam," McCullough recalls saying. He was right.

It seemed no one in that prosecution strategy session remembered the famous line from President Harry Truman: "It is amazing what you can accomplish if you do not care who gets the credit."

Robert Stutman was the showman-like DEA Special Agent in Charge of the New York office during the crack-crazed 1980s. Stutman relished whipping the news media in to a frenzy about the battles of the War on Drugs. He convinced numerous reporters that this was the hottest combat story since Vietnam.

Today, Stutman is among the seasoned narcotics veterans who say the "war" has been a total failure. In the spring of 2017, Stutman wrote an open memorandum to U.S. Attorney General Jeff Sessions telling him a return to harsh penalties and lengthy prison terms is the wrong approach to the nation's drug problems.

Among Stutman's key points:

- Incarceration doesn't work. Been there. Done that.

"There is now a considerable burden of evidence indicating that incarcerating drug offenders doesn't rehabilitate or deter crime, and has minimal effects on the reduction of crime," Stutman wrote.

- We were dead wrong.

"At best, I have seen incarceration increase the prison population of non-violent offenders while doing nothing to reduce drug use or increase public safety," Stutman argues.

- People are doping and dropping like flies.

"To add salt to the wound, increased spending on prisons has been shown to correlate with a reduction in spending on education, education being one of the most effective investments a country can make in preventing drug use," Stutman wrote.

- Let's bark up the right tree. Treatment.

"I have come to realize that drug abuse is a mental health issue. Treatment is less expensive than imprisonment and more effectively uses valuable resources for the prevention and treatment of drug use disorders," Stutman wrote.

Stutman and others experienced in the drug war trenches emphasize treatment and with good reason. There's no evidence prison motivates drug users to kick their habit. Other countries treat drug addiction as a public health problem, not a law enforcement problem. But "we've-always-done-it-this-way" dies hard, particularly in a country that enjoys punishment.

Stutman, Levine, Dwyer and Thomas are just four of many experienced voices in law enforcement who say the War on Drugs is a costly failure and we need to fundamentally change our approach.

The problem is, America has a heritage of punishment. Many Americans *like* sending people to prison, hanging them, strapping them in electric chairs.

Prisons are part of a" corrections" system, which is an oxymoron. Prison is about punishment, not corrections. After 40-plus years and a trillion dollars wasted, it ought to be obvious to all that the nation cannot punish its way out of the illegal drug problem.

But the punishers are a hardy lot. Many advocates of long prison sentences are the same people who howl about taxes. It never occurs to them that they are required under numerous court rulings to provide health care for aging inmates. Their tax dollars are providing "free" health care to those they insist on keeping locked up. This is in addition to providing room and board to several million people behind bars.

Punishment needs to be re-thought. A felony conviction is a life sentence, economically. A scarlet "F" dooms most paroled offenders to jobs on the margins, if they find jobs at all.

Perhaps we need to think in terms of productive punishment. Perhaps crime convictions should require mandatory skilled trade training with jail time as an alternative. The training should be aimed at making criminals add to the nation's productivity.

There's a middle ground between legalizing all drugs and pursuing oppressive and costly mandatory minimums for drug crimes. One essential is to quit treating the drug problem as a crime problem. Crime is a by-product. Drugs are a public health problem like alcoholism or smoking. If the nation would treat drugs the way it treats alcohol, we would still have a substance abuse problem, but it wouldn't generate billions in profit for smugglers, racketeers and cartels. Drug abuse could and should be treated like drunk driving, which often requires mandatory treatment programs and the loss of driving privileges.

What if the nation legalized drug use but maintained penalties for misuse the way it has done with alcohol? The offspring of the abstinence zealots of the Prohibition era could console themselves the same way their grandparents and great-grandparents did with alcohol. The drugs might be available legally, which would undercut drug smuggling and illegal sales, but the Just Say No crowd could support hefty taxes on abuse-type drugs. With a new source of sin revenue rivaling alcohol taxes, the nation could declare victory in the War on Drugs and maybe even have a parade.

About the Author

Vince Wade is a veteran award-winning television investigative reporter and documentary and special projects producer.

He worked for WXYZ-TV, the ABC affiliate, and WJBK-TV, the Fox affiliate, both in Detroit, Michigan.

His 20-some journalism awards include three Emmys and 1st Place for Best Local TV News Documentary in the New York and San Francisco International Film festivals.

Vince Wade began his career in radio where he won a 1st Place Associated Press award for reporting under deadline for coverage of a 1969 shoot-out between the Detroit Police and the Black Panthers.

Wade's written reporting includes two articles about White Boy Rick Wershe for *The Daily Beast* online news magazine.

He also has worked as a freelance news field producer for NBC News

Detroit is one helluva news town and Wade reported on some of its big stories. He broke the news that former Teamsters boss Jimmy Hoffa was missing. His film festival awards were for a documentary on the rise and fall of auto industry maverick John DeLorean. Wade exposed a Libyan terrorist who was secretly stalking anti-Qaddafi dissidents in North America. And he was the first to report a federal investigation of the looting of a Detroit multi-million-dollar fund for the War on Drugs—by the Chief of Police.

He lives in the Los Angeles, California area.

Index

Vince Wade

9 780692 995709

3 1333 04904 3738